Andrew Riemer is a well known critic, academic and writer. He was born in Budapest in 1936. In 1947 his parents settled in Sydney, where he now lives with his wife and two sons. The experiences of his early years in Australia form the basis of his award-winning memoir *Inside Outside*. He has also written several books on Shakespeare and is a regular contributor of book reviews to the *Sydney Morning Herald* and the *Age* in Melbourne.

ALSO BY ANDREW RIEMER

Inside Outside

THE
HABSBURG
CAFÉ

ANDREW RIEMER

 Angus&Robertson
An imprint of HarperCollins*Publishers*

AUTHOR'S NOTE

My editor, Fiona Inglis, and I put the finishing touches to the manuscript of this book on 26 November 1992, one day before several monuments in Vienna described in these pages were severely damaged by fire.

An Angus & Robertson Publication

Angus&Robertson, an imprint of
HarperCollins*Publishers*
25 Ryde Road, Pymble, Sydney, NSW 2073, Australia
31 View Road, Glenfield, Auckland 10, New Zealand

First published in Australia in 1993
Reprinted in 1993 (twice)

National Library of Australia
Cataloguing-in-Publication data:

Riemer, A. P. (Andrew P.).
   The Habsburg cafe.

   ISBN 0 207 17414 8.

   1. Riemer, A. P. (Andrew P.) — Journeys — Hungary.
   2. Riemer, A. P. (Andrew P.) — Journeys — Austria.
   3. Hungary — Description and travel — 1981 –   .
   4. Austria — Description and travel — 1981 –   .
   I. Title. (Series: Imprint travel).

914.3

Cover illustration by Julian Roberts
Typeset in 11/12pt Berner by Midland Typesetters, Maryborough, Victoria
Printed in Australia by Griffin Paperbacks, Adelaide

7 6 5 4 3
96 95 94 93

And in the good old days when there was still such a place as Imperial Austria, one could leave the train of events, get into an ordinary train on an ordinary railway-line, and travel back home.

All in all, how many remarkable things might be said about that vanished Kakania!

Robert Musil *The Man Without Qualities*

HUNGARY AND ITS NEIGHBOURS IN 1991

SQ24

Riverrun

SQ24 is scheduled to land at Vienna International Airport at 06.55 Central European Summer Time. This morning it has been delayed because of a late departure from Singapore and by head winds over India. The pilot apologises for the delay and announces that we will be in the terminal by 07.23. Below us an unremarkable landscape glows in the September haze—neat rectangular fields, clusters of houses and, near the horizon, a sizable town with plumes of smoke snaking out of thin chimneystacks. A network of roads binds together fields, villages and town; they converge on a broader stripe, obviously an important motorway.

This could be almost anywhere in the world, except that a shimmering band cutting across the toylike symmetry and neatness must be the Danube, my destination. Yet nothing other than an uneasy trust in the miracle of aeronautical navigation and in the relaxed, confident sound of the pilot's voice as he assures us that we will reach our objective within the next three quarters of an hour makes me believe that that band of water is the Danube. From this height all great rivers look the same: the shimmering band below us could just as easily be the Moldau, the Rhine or even the Volga. I believe, nevertheless, in the way that a religious person believes in God or a crank in extraterrestrial beings, that we are floating above the Danube basin—above Austria and Hungary, a world filled for me with the emblems of a powerful mythology.

The Palindrome

I left the world unfolding below us in the morning sunshine almost forty-five years ago. It was a day of bone-numbing frost.

The bright disc of the sun shining in a pale blue sky set sparks in snow-covered fields and hills. Thirty or forty of us were shivering in a wheezing bus, heavily guarded by two GIs with their fingers poised on the triggers of their submachine guns. The scratched and crazed windows of the old bus were opaque, fogged up by the heat of our shivering bodies—but if you rubbed your sleeve against the glass you could observe (until the film of mist obscured the view once more) a white world, spotted here and there by a ruined farmhouse or a gutted church. What we saw was the Central Europe of 1946, torn apart again during the previous six or seven years by war, hatred and brutality. We in that shuddering bus were the fortunate ones, those on whom the gods had smiled, for we were on our way to Vienna airport (in all probability the same airport to which this humming machine is now hurrying) where a gleaming Pan American plane was waiting to convey us to New York and freedom—provided, of course, that we reached the airfield and received permission from the Russians, who controlled that part of Austria, to take off into the icy sky.

My father had been quite friendly with some of our fellow passengers for several weeks. They were remnants (like us) of a polyglot world—citizens of Hungary, Austria, Czechoslovakia and the despised Balkan States—countries which had, not so many years before, been the domain of the pompously styled 'Imperial and Royal Austro-Hungarian Empire'. He had got to know them during the weeks he had patiently waited in the queue that formed each morning outside the hastily established Pan American office in the bomb-pitted and soot-blackened heart of the old city. Each day, from a grey dusk to the early dark of a winter afternoon, forty or fifty cold, anxious and disconsolate people stood about, stamping their feet on the hard-packed yellowing snow on what remained of the footpath, pulling the collars of their topcoats about their ears, and discussed, endlessly and circuitously, their terrible plight.

All these people had purchased, in Vienna, or in Budapest (as was the case with us), or in some other city or town, obscenely expensive tickets for the weekly flight to New York—for us the first stage of a long journey to a new life in Australia. Their hopes and expectations were quickly shattered, or at least severely discouraged, once they discovered that possessing those tickets counted almost for nothing. Before they could board the gleaming bird of their dreams, they had to obtain elusive and mysterious cards, precious reservations slips and boarding passes that alone could ensure flight and freedom. So they waited and stamped their feet, trying to keep out the biting winds and flurries of snow, and discussed from one day to the next how best to bribe the mean-faced and rapacious officials behind the makeshift counter. No doubt they kept their best ideas to themselves, for inevitably their plight produced rivalry as well as comradeship. My father returned each evening to our ill-lit hotel room, shaking his head to indicate his lack of success—until inspiration struck him one day when he discovered the magic key to unlock that intransigence in the shape of half-a-dozen bottles of Hungarian apricot brandy.

The other occupants of the bus had obviously found their own means of securing those magical cards. The rivalries and suspicions of earlier weeks vanished in our anxious happiness. A murmur rose as we caught sight of the outskirts of the airfield and, a moment or two later, the squat, shiny machine standing on the tarmac. We were comforted by the sight of a group of American soldiers, each of them reassuringly armed to the teeth. Half an hour later we were strapped into our seats; the smiling airhostess distributed boiled sweets to protect our eardrums against the stresses of take-off. Then the engines started with a roar, the plane lumbered forward to the runway and began trundling along its length, apparently earthbound. After what seemed an eternity, it finally began to rise with much clattering and shuddering. We watched the fields and hills, the ruined buildings, the thin grey stripe of a road sink away below us, as we prepared for our long winter flight. Elated that we had at last managed to escape from this world, we were also terrified because none of us had ever flown before, and all entertained, therefore, dark suspicions concerning wings and God's intentions.

I have returned to this world several times since then: one furtive, distressing visit to Budapest, my birthplace, and several much more relaxed short trips to Vienna, the city of glitz and schmaltz. Each time, however, I have approached this world of memories and phantoms from the west, by the overnight train from Paris or along Western Europe's great network of roads and motorways. It now seems appropriate that in this palindromic year of 1991, I should be describing a spiritual palindrome by coming back to this world by a reversal of the way I left it more than half a lifetime ago.

The purpose of this visit itself has a poignant though potentially hilarious symmetry about it—another instance of life's turning back on itself, retracing its apparently aimless path. I have been invited to spend some six or seven weeks in Hungary—that country of bad memories—to give a course of lectures on Australian literature and culture in various colleges and universities to young people who have, it seems likely, only the haziest notions of that distant, exotic and, for them, probably outlandish place. The enterprise itself is slightly odd, even eccentric; that I should be participating in the inception of a scheme supported by weighty governmental and academic instrumentalities is just as odd, though no doubt appropriate. For me the coming weeks are, nevertheless, filled with dangers with which I am becoming more and more preoccupied as this contraption glides lazily above the morning landscape, following the path of the winding river below us.

My greatest fear is that down there, in Hungary, my identity will be tested in an unwelcome and possibly embarrassing way. That fear is greatly increased as I become aware that my last ties with Australia are about to be broken. Boarding the plane in Singapore, I noticed a couple of faces familiar from the flight from Sydney. They also had loitered for five hours in the brightly lit antiseptic wilderness of Terminal 2, inspecting the depressing abundance of watches, cameras and calculators displayed in the glass cases of duty-free shops, and commenting on these insignia of end-of-the-century consumerism in their flat, laconic voices. A tenuous link still exists, therefore, with the place where I know, more or less, who I am, for I have lived in Australia long enough to make it possible to call myself an Australian. It is true that this identity may have been assumed or invented, yet it is an identity of sorts.

The closer Hungary approaches, the less secure am I in that identity. In Vienna, where I plan to spend some days before setting out for the disturbing country of my birth, I shall be safe enough. There a measure of ambiguity will preserve my otherness, largely because my command of German is so poor that no-one could possibly imagine that I was once intimately tied to that world too. In Hungary it will be otherwise. Even though I speak a version of Hungarian that was in currency half a century ago, and even though my command of its idioms and vocabulary is restricted to the horizons of a child, it is a language I speak with some fluency at a commonplace and everyday level. Will that competence be sufficient warrant for Hungarians to claim me as their own? In that resides perhaps the deepest of my fears and misgivings.

I do not want to be claimed by Hungary. My antipathy towards it far outweighs any residual fondness for a half-forgotten country. It is true that I know next to nothing about the place, not having seen it for almost fifty years apart from a few feverish days nine months ago filled with the anguish of the past, a time of raw nerves and gloomy introspection. For people like me, though, places are capable of possessing implications of limitless evil. We often invest the ordinary and the commonplace with diabolic intent; we see in the most mundane activities the seeds of cruelty and barbarity. For us some places have been irreversibly poisoned, like those tracts of land where radioactive material was buried long ago. We suspect that dangerous influences may still lurk under a pleasant and welcoming surface. And because we have spent our lives far away from such places, we have elaborated a mythology about them—both nostalgic and infernal—that colours all our attitudes and prejudices.

God knows what experiences will swallow me once I take that dangerous and perhaps irrevocable step across the frontier into that contaminated world. Will I fall into a void, becoming neither one thing nor another, but remain suspended between possibilities, as I am now in this marvel of modern technology, which is descending towards its destination?

ABOVE KAKANIA

My fears and alarms are balanced by other, much more pleasant and exhilarating expectations. These weeks of anxiety and apprehension are to be spent in what is for me the centre and the focus of that fabled realm—three parts fantasy, one of experience—which I call by the familiar name of Europe, the land of heart's desire I often find myself longing for in Australia, that place at the other end of the world I now know as my home. I realise only too well that for many people that mythic word 'Europe' implies worlds and experiences very different from those that have sustained my memories and fantasies during the years of my life in Australia. My Europe is that part of the continent which stretches from the Alps to the Carpathian mountains. We, the children of those towns and cities, hills and mountains, plains and rivers, believe with a passionate intensity that this world represents the essence of all that is contained within that magic word 'Europe'.

There is at heart no inconsistency, I believe, between my addiction to this world and my fears and alarms about Hungary. Hungary is real and substantial, it was the site for hardships and experiences of the sort that have been chronicled countless times by the survivors of the great conflagration that swallowed this part of the earth in the 1940s. 'Europe', though its images are lodged in an experienced past and are inevitably connected to the lives of those whom I still remember, is largely a country of the mind, fashioned out of nostalgia and fantasy. It is, nonetheless, just as real and substantial as the towns, villages and fields below us which are now becoming visible in much more detail as we continue to lose altitude, approaching our destination.

I have only confused and discontinuous memories of that world, for by the time of my earliest recollections it had all but vanished. I remember it perhaps more vividly than if I had lived in it, or enjoyed its blandishments and experienced its pressures and its texture, through the myth world my parents lovingly elaborated in the course of their life in Australia. Those beguiling myths found their characteristic emblems in a strangely muddled collection of images which have persisted in my imagination—the sights, sounds, smells, social rituals and music of the Austro-Hungarian world.

That world was certainly not Hungary with its passionate introspection, its need constantly to reassure itself of its greatness and excellence, and its obsession with those lands to the east of the river Tisza, extending as far as Transylvania, the site of the true Hungary according to nationalist rhetoric, which was shamefully lost to Romania after the Great War. Nor was it the Austria my family knew, with its fierce Catholicism, its hidebound preoccupation with caste and rank, or an Austria of Tyrolean fantasies of lederhosen and schrammel music. It was an entirely different existence, a fantasy realm, superimposed on the physical and political realities of those nations, which found its true location in a kind of extraterritoriality reflected by the characteristic images of Vienna and of the many cities and towns built in imitation of its imperial pomp and grandeur.

The inhabitants of those cities and towns—for that world which I know to be my true heritage was an essentially urban phenomenon—may have been Austrians or Hungarians, Bohemians or Slovakians through domicile and by virtue of various legal and legislative definitions. They may even have felt some pride in, or patriotism about those nations or regions. Yet they were essentially cosmopolitan people, discovering their identity in that supranational concept of the Austro-Hungarian spirit so assiduously promoted by their political masters, the ministers and advisors of the Emperor Franz Josef, the monarch whose long reign coincided almost exactly with the florescence of that strange world.

This world was given the nickname 'Kakania' in the closing decades of the Empire, as its pomp and its fantasies crumbled away into the disaster of the Great War. The name blended scatology and nostalgia. Kakania sounds romantic, an ancient duchy or quaint principality, one of those long-vanished territories or fiefdoms that came at length to be absorbed into the Austro-Hungarian Empire, yet was still remembered fondly. It was, however, cobbled out of a familiar bureaucratic abbreviation, 'k.k.', standing for the phrase '*kaiserlich und königlich*' (imperial and royal), which was used to denote the dual nature of this world—the Austro-Hungarian Empire and the Kingdom of Hungary, the fiction of the dual monarchy which, by virtue of those two 'k's, sounds like *kaka*, that is to say, ordure, faeces or manure.

The inhabitants of this realm, those people who moved easily among its various linguistic and ethnic divisions—as did my family, who had roots in Austria and Bohemia as well as in Hungary—would have been shocked by such a scatologically insulting term. Indeed, until the shadows of the disaster that was eventually to engulf them began to darken their orderly and predictable lives, they did not feel threatened by its prejudices, exclusions and hatreds. In the time of my grandparents' young adult life—in the years before the gunshot at Sarajevo that was to spread its poison through this world—these people felt safe and comfortable: safer and more comfortable than their families had felt throughout the turbulent events of the nineteenth century.

Suspended high above the fields, villages and towns of this essentially mythic realm I can only wonder, knowing what became of this world and of the people who lived so confidently within it, at the naïve trust they placed in its stability and benevolence. That trust, like Kakania itself, was based on sentiment and folly. It was touchingly fragile, only too easily blown away by that gunshot, the echoes of which are still reverberating in Croatia and Slovenia on this sunny autumn morning. (None of us knows at this time that in less than a year Sarajevo itself will once again stand as a symbol of the hatred and enmities which have always disfigured this part of the world.) Nothing could quell the fundamental and endemic violence of this world—not Kakania, nor the idealistic fable of universal brotherhood promoted by the grim-faced comrades, nor yet the very recently arisen dream of an American-inspired consumers' paradise.

My grandparents, and millions of their kind, believed fervently in that benevolent fiction. It was in turn bequeathed to my parents' generation, and to their children. For us the myth of Kakania grew weaker and weaker with the passing of the years. Two wars and appalling cruelty, not merely of Auschwitz and Treblinka but of countless other atrocities against almost every nation or race living in this troubled world, tarnished but did not corrode the conviction that it contained the essence of civility, of the good life at its best, despite the pain, despite its inhumanity. These were all fantasies, humanity's sad readiness to put its faith in illusions. Yet even for me, for whom that world is only a dim echo remembered from family stories, myths and anecdotes, and preserved in books and in music, its allure remains irresistible. In an hour or so, I tell myself, I shall (if all goes well) be setting foot once more on the cobblestones of Vienna, that city commemorated in countless cloyingly sentimental songs and ballads, which provided for many members of my family a sort of nostalgic hymnal—'My Mother was a Viennese', 'The Fiacre Song' and 'Vienna City of my Dreams'.

I know only too well of course that modern Vienna, in this palindromic year, which also marks the two hundredth anniversary of Mozart's death, is a very different place from that nostalgic fantasy-city. Yet, as this great aeroplane begins to lurch towards the earth, the images of that Vienna are superimposed on my recollections of the actual and, therefore, inevitably disappointing city I have visited fleetingly on several occasions. These images are discontinuous and quite vague. They are probably indistinguishable from images of European bourgeois life at the beginning of the twentieth century—the decades in which my family flourished despite the nightmare of a war that, they were convinced, was to be the last. That life attempted to preserve the manners and social rituals that distinguished the bourgeoisie from those below and also from those above during the closing years of the nineteenth century. Their life was, in all probability, governed by the same aspirations, goals and conventions as the life of their counterparts in Brussels and Paris, Amsterdam and Stockholm, Milan and Belgrade. For people like me, the detritus of Kakania, those commonplace experiences, dreams and prejudices are unique— they are flavoured by the creaminess of Viennese cakes, by the tang of Hungarian spices, by the fragrant ham and frothy beer of Prague.

At the distance of many years, thinking about that vanished world—to the site of which the plane is alarmingly hurrying— such images of food and its associated rituals seem to sum up its intrinsic nature. Perhaps my family, and the social phenomenon it represented, elevated food to an almost sacerdotal level because of the restrictions placed on their lives in that caste-bound world, where social mobility and indeed the expression of individuality were severely circumscribed. In that rigidly stratified society upward movement was impossible; becoming déclassé, sinking down through the strata until you were indistinguishable from your maid or the milkman, was feared with religious awe. You were confined in your niche as surely as the peasants on feudal estates, some of which persisted even into my lifetime. For that reason you had to make do with what you had, and enjoy the benefits of nature's bounty.

What scope these restrictions allowed those people seems to have satisfied them on the whole—or so it would appear from the perspective of the present restless and dissatisfied world. They accepted, often without question, arbitrary and apparently unjust restrictions. The professions open to them, the resorts where they could take their vacations, the parts of a city where they might live were all governed by rigid codes of conduct that they did not question. They always travelled in

12

second-class carriages, even though many of them could afford to be conveyed in the plush comfort of first-class, and even though some could scarcely afford a second-class fare. They saw it as their birthright: a mid-point between plebeian third and patrician first class. When they went to the theatre they would congregate in those parts of the house appropriate to their station in society. The restaurants they frequented were not those to which the great nobility or even the minor gentry of the Austro-Hungarian world flocked for its pleasures.

Yet for all this they considered themselves an essential part of that world. My Viennese relatives lived in a comfortable but undistinguished flat in a grey block in a grey street on the far side of the Danube canal, remote from the Vienna of legend and of tourist brochures. On their walks, when they went shopping or to the theatre, or to conduct a piece of business, they would often enter the magic realm of the inner city, that small section of a large and often dreary metropolis that provided material for many myths and fantasies. They would pass through the handsomely planted gardens of the Hofburg, the stronghold of Habsburg grandeur, and walk across the great courtyard into a network of streets where I too hope to be walking in a few hours' time.

In those streets they would walk past outward and visible signs of the world from which they had been excluded—aristocratic palais after palais, a roll-call of the great and powerful families of the two realms, especially that of the Esterházys, the proud lords of those borderlands where German-speakers (like my mother's family) came into often troubled contact with Hungarians speaking their barbaric tongue. Around these structures—chastely rococo or elaborately baroque—clustered purveyors of goods and services essential to the maintenance of aristocratic and patrician life, each with its imposing emblem bearing the double-headed eagle of the Habsburgs to signify the patent of imperial patronage. Even those of my relatives who lived in a somewhat provincial and decidedly raffish Budapest would have moved through a similar, though perhaps less clearly defined, world of restrictions and exclusions that nevertheless—and paradoxically—ensured their well-being and safety.

Once they had lost the hotheadedness of youth they settled into a life of responsibility and probity, feeling at one with this world, drawing sustenance from its very rigidity and stratification. The searing critics of Kakanian corruption usually came from the ranks of the powerful and privileged—Musil lacerated this world with unflagging energy; Wittgenstein's detestation of Austria proved one of his most enduring obsessions. By contrast my great-grandfather, a minor cog in the great machinery of the Austro-Hungarian state, who might well have felt exploited by that régime, which dispensed privileges in a blatantly partisan fashion, always spoke of the Emperor Franz Josef as 'that good man', and remembered the grief with which everyone greeted the news of his Empress's assassination when she boarded a pleasure boat on faraway Lake Geneva.

Remembering the experience of a terrible century, and knowing what happened to that world, it is only too easy to be aware of the hypocrisy and, indeed, the evil that must have lain at the heart of that society. Yet, I too accede willingly to the fiction and fantasy that must have governed the lives of my relatives in those two cities and in the other capitals and provincial towns of the realm. I also find the allure of those images of the Kakanian good life irresistible. For me too they provide emblems of an existence that seems in many ways ideal, even though I know that their reality is quite the contrary. I anticipate with some pleasure, therefore, this opportunity that a quirk of history—the sudden flowering in Hungary of an interest in things Australian—will give me to explore this world, the wonderful cloud-cuckoo-land of Kakania.

A VISION OF DELIGHT

The cabin screen flickers into life. With the washed-out colours and fuzzy images characteristic of in-flight movies, a succession of enticing visions floats across the screen. Here are the famous sights of Vienna—the great imperial palaces, the handsome townhouses of the inner city, the churches, theatres and parks that make it one of the most photogenic of cities. Towards the end of this short sequence, true to the spirit that had placed food at the centre of my family's way of life in those distant years when Kakania flourished, the producers of this promotional documentary had decided to display emblems of what obviously remain the most haunting insignia of this world. The screen oozes with images of rich pastries, towering gâteaux, mounds of chestnut purée surrounded by snowy peaks of whipped cream, sandwiches shimmering under films of aspic— all the fabled delicacies Vienna's cafés serve in almost indecent abundance in a world where not too far to the east there is hardship and the none-too-remote threat of famine. As in the Kakania where my family first experienced the blessings of civilised urban life, modern Austria obviously seeks to display its individuality, its charm and appeal in terms of the richest yet most delicate of foods.

The social rituals of old Kakania were certainly concentrated in the ceremonies of food. Wherever you went in that world, whatever you did, food was the focus of communal life. It accompanied, and also defined, a way of life and a trust in the essentially wholesome nature of that life in much the same way that the consecrated wafer is both the actuality and the symbol of the mystery of the redemption. The reasons for that adulation of food were complex and intimately connected with the elaborate social structures—filled with barriers and exclusions—of Kakania. More forcefully than elsewhere in bourgeois Europe, such pressures threw emphasis on the family, the group and the caste. Whatever cultural pursuits members of this world might have followed, the focus of their lives was provided by the family circle, with all its networks and ramifications. Within that network, moreover, the quality as much as the quantity of the food offered and consumed served as powerful social and spiritual emblems.

Five-o'clock-tea, a curious and copious meal, usually consisted of goose-liver paté sandwiches, quivering custard slices and that confection known as *Indianer*, made of two chocolate-glazed hemispheres of sponge held together with stiffly whipped cream—the magnified images of which are floating across the screen in front of me. These were the ritual trappings of a ceremony fundamentally important to the maintenance and preservation of a cherished way of life. People would gather at those groaning tables where the great topics of the day would be discussed to the accompaniment of solicitous urgings that Aunt Gizi or Uncle Sandor should partake of this or that delicacy, with passionate reminders that they must eat to keep up their strength, to remember poor Cousin Piroska who wasted away with TB because she would never, but never, eat enough cream and always refused to drink chocolate.

They talked about the great and disturbing events of the time: royal suicides, political assassinations—on Lake Geneva, in Sarajevo, in Vienna itself; and the ominous insurrections, pogroms, witch-hunts that disturbed the even tenor of their lives. Yet the persistent topic of conversation would have been the more immediate and perhaps more important verities— the marriages of their children and relatives, how one had foolishly strayed beyond the self-imposed limits of this society by marrying a penniless baron, while another had, wisely, married his well-to-do second cousin; the business acumen of an uncle or a friend; the death agony of somebody's grand-mother. Custard slices, paté shimmering with aspic, richly fragrant ham from Prague and spicy salami from the Hungarian plains slid from dish to plate and from plate to mouth, propelled by elaborately shaped silver implements, and throughout these ceremonies the talk or gossip that defined the ethical limits of that little world would pass from person to person with grace, ease and agility.

The rituals of the dining-room were transported beyond the heavily furnished, thickly carpeted flats where these people conducted such mystic rites. They looked for food when walking in the Vienna Woods or in the hills outside Budapest. Their mental map of the paths that wound through the bosks of these charming places was well marked with inns where you could refresh yourself with boiled sausages and horseradish sauce, washed down with beer, so that you would have enough energy to continue on your constitutional—that communication with nature which these people had learnt from the despised Germans, among whom many of them had spent years studying to become engineers or drawing-room pianists. At the theatre, the long intervals provided opportunities for visiting one of the many buffets groaning with food. There rich cakes, baroque sandwiches with their slices of meat, eggs, caviar and cheese trapped under a film of aspic, sustained them for another act of *The Countess Maritza*, *The Merry Widow* or *The Gypsy Princess*. The buffet was even more elaborate at the opera, but of course you needed sustenance for the intellectual demands of *Carmen* and *Madame Butterfly*—many could not understand how their younger relatives (like my father) could endure all those hours of that terrible antisemite, Wagner.

When the womenfolk visited the dressmaker they were offered simple refreshments (the cost of which was added, naturally, to the seamstress's bill). No shopping expedition would have been complete without a visit to a gilded café. In the lives of the men, even for those confined to the routines of an office, cafés played an intrinsic role, not merely in their leisure life but in their professions as well—for they were all 'Doctor' or 'Engineer', the two great classifications and distinguishing marks of the Kakanian bourgeoisie. Children's lives were also surrounded by the ceremonies of food. Beribboned and sailor-suited they (or we, for I was born into the tail-end of that world) would gather for polite and seemly games supervised by grown-up relatives and governesses. In one corner of the room a table overladen with 'healthy' (that is to say carbohydrate-rich) food awaited the signal summoning the young ladies and gentlemen to help themselves to its strawberry ices and *Kugelhopf*. Eating was an integral part of visits to the skating-rink in winter (for you had to keep out the cold); it replenished exhausted muscles at the swimming baths in summer, where every hour on the hour a whistle would announce that the wave-machine was about to be turned on.

It is as a legacy, no doubt, of such an obsession with food among members of my family and the society they had inhabitated that for many years I have been visited without warning by a sensation that must have had its origin in the rituals of this world. It is a potently visual and olfactory sensation, and it has remained remarkably consistent even though months or years sometimes separate its sudden and inexplicable visitations. It always comes in the same form: I am looking at the junction of two narrow cobbled streets on a wintry afternoon. There is still some light in a leaden sky but a gaslight attached to the corner building by a sturdy bracket is already alight. The conjunction of the two streets forms an acute angle, so that my gaze travels down each, allowing the buildings on either side of both streets to be seen. They are low structures with steeply pitched roofs. The large arched gates are secured by heavy wooden doors. Many of the windows are barred. A light snowfall leaves a thin layer of greyish-white ice on the cobblestones, which extend to the walls of the buildings, for there are no footpaths in these narrow streets. A little way up one of the streets, a warm orange-yellow light filters through the curtained window of a shop.

It is a banal image, culled perhaps from a painting, an illustration or even from one of those realistic stage settings that I saw as a child on outings to the theatre in one of these towns or cities. Yet its effect on me is very peculiar. I experience a sensation of great peace and contentment, mixed with an acute sense of loss, whenever the image pops into my consciousness from a recess of my personality where it has been dormant. It is accompanied, moreover, by its most curious attribute, a powerful scent, bringing to the nostrils of my imagination the characteristic odour of an Austro-Hungarian café, a heady amalgam of aromas, among which vanilla and coffee are dominant.

I can attach no precise source to this sensation, nor am I

able to find any explanation for its unheralded appearances. But I have felt, as the years pass and as it insists on returning, that it represents something fundamentally important—whatever it might be. It speaks to me of something that demands to be recovered but is perhaps no longer recoverable: innocence, the clarity of childhood, a world that has been compromised by experience and lost in time.

I have often thought that this image, sensation, or visitation is merely a trick provoked by the literary disposition, a consequence, perhaps, of reading too much Proust. Yet as it returns with its haunting insistence, sometimes in broad daylight, sometimes in a vividly remembered dream, I realise that it first struck me during my early adolescence, in the first years of my life in Australia, long before I had heard Proust's name, or read even a page of *Remembrance of Things Past*. Rather, I am convinced, it must emerge from a private vocabulary of images and memories. It is a visual and olfactory emblem of the lost fantasy-world of Kakania: the characteristic appearance of its streets in some city or town, mixed with a whiff of its equally characteristic and perhaps most significant institution—a café where the sweet odour of vanilla mingles with the pungent scent of highly roasted coffee. In my imagination, this café of the Habsburg world—in some unknown city or town of my early childhood when that Empire and realm, though no longer a political reality, still exerted an influence throughout its former territories—has assumed a position of undisputed centrality. It has become a distillation, a compact, fleeting yet powerful image of a world irrecoverably lost, a world compromised by hatred and brutality, a world which must be approached with the armour of irony fully in place, and yet a world of irresistible allure. And it provides, no matter how tenuously, or how contingently, some signs of the survival of that world in dreams, in the imagination or in visions imprinted on my memory many years ago, a time when all experiences and sensations were new, fresh and shiningly clear.

Landing Music

The screen is blank, the golden images have faded. All that remains are the strains of sentimental Viennese music piped through the aircraft's sound system. We are obviously falling towards the source and origin of these sugary melodies. I try as hard as I am able to control my growing anxiety. Even though this 747 seems to be gliding down through the morning air with the ease and assurance of a powerfully muscled bird, ingrained misgivings, disciplined though not tamed by years of exposure to the perils of flight, assert themselves as the two realms, the celestial and the terrestrial, begin to come into conjunction.

In the night, above India, I could almost persuade myself that we were not suspended thousands of metres above the earth in a fragile metal cylinder. At that time we seemed to be in another existence, astral beings, safe, powerful and beyond harm, observing with indifference the faint pools of light floating in a sea of darkness. But when the ground looms large and menacing all around, as it is doing now, when you can see the miniature dots of cars scurrying along a busy highway, then anxiety becomes inescapably insistent.

My thoughts turn, therefore, towards that other aeroplane, and to that winter flight from Vienna and from the brutality this world had experienced, into the perpetual darkness of the northern night. I remember with an almost intolerable immediacy the lone, stark chimneystack that floated past every few minutes as the plane circled the town of Hartford in Connecticut, marking with clocklike insistence our approach to the seemingly inevitable death that awaited us below in the snowy whiteness. I recall too the terrible shudder and thud with which the plane, its malfunctioning undercarriage frozen and ice-bound, plopped into the soft thick snow, and how the young airhostess, who had maintained her regulation smile throughout the many hours of the emergency, fainted the instant all that creaking and jangling of metal had been silenced and we knew that we had been saved.

I am returning to the airport where that ill-fated journey began, and I am returning in a more general sense to my origins, in order to bring to it little bits of the Australia which I have come to know, and to explore again those two related worlds, Austria and Hungary, where, for me, life began. Does this palindrome-like trajectory demand, therefore, that this lumbering machine should fall to earth near some small town— perhaps Sopron, that quaint Habsburg town on the border of the two realms, where my mother grew up, which is situated a short distance from the airfield towards which we are rushing with complicated manoeuvres of diving and banking?

Commonsense insists, even at these moments of alarm, that such neat symmetry is appropriate only to the contrived world of fiction. But experience also tells me that life may at times be even more crudely and melodramatically contrived than the cheapest romance. Ancient fears know nothing of commonsense. They tell me with irresistible clarity and conviction that I should never have trusted my life to the guardians of this screaming and shuddering contraption, that I should have stayed at home and never considered going 'home' to the world that is no longer home for me.

It is much too late for regrets. We, even the flight attendants, are strapped into our seats. This clumsy machine is screeching towards disaster. We hit the ground with a roar of reverse-thrust and (miracle of miracles) the plane slows to a relatively sedate hurtle along the runway. It loses speed again just before turning towards the terminal. The landing music has been switched off. In its place an anodyne voice welcomes us to Vienna, reminds us to remove all personal articles from seat pockets and overhead lockers, and advises us to remain seated until the aircraft is stationary. With a slight hissing sound the plane comes to rest, and at that moment, on a utilitarian, rather dingy building, indistinguishable from air-terminals elsewhere in the world, I catch sight of the cursory but myth-laden identification: WIEN.

CITY OF DREAMS

MOZARTBALLS

Vienna, in this suave autumn of 1991, is obviously Mozart's city. One of the first sights to greet you in the arrival hall of the airport is a large likeness of the composer leering at you with a coquettish Mona Lisa smile. It is an advertisement for *Mozartkugeln*, a spherical chocolate confection with a soft nutty centre. I cannot help wondering whether 'Mozartballs' has the same connotations in German as in English. That may be the explanation for the enigmatic smile. It is a joke, moreover, that Mozart, who was not a little interested in all manner of obscenity and scatology, would have probably enjoyed greatly.

It is difficult to escape him anywhere in the inner city in this year marking the two hundredth anniversary of his death. Advertisements for all sorts of 'Mozart' comestibles stare from walls and shop windows. Souvenir shops are crammed with tee-shirts, mugs, beer-coasters, wallets, pouches, shoulder-bags and a hundred other items, all of them with his image painted, embossed, etched or engraved on them. Various tourist organisations entice visitors in fractured English to savour his 'immortal musik' as performed by players in eighteenth-century costume. This carnival of vulgarity almost drowns the serious and scholarly exhibitions, recitals and opera performances which are mounted to mark the bicentenary with appropriate solemnity and dedication.

The Viennese have obviously discovered a goldmine in these 'celebrations'. Never mind that two hundred years ago they probably hastened Mozart's death by deciding that they didn't care all that much for his music. Now in 1991 everybody is jumping on the bandwagon—the music shop crammed with compact discs of every note of music he wrote (and probably quite a few he didn't) is cheek-by-jowl with a confectioner's whose display honours him in all conceivable variations on chocolate, nougat, fondant, cream and custard. The city cannibalises its (for the moment) favourite citizen in order to extract even more dollars, marks and yen from the pockets of impressed and awed tourists.

The sensitive and the cultivated are naturally outraged by this undisguised commercialism, this blatant betrayal for thirty pieces of silver of one of the pinnacles of European culture. Yet Mozart himself may be held largely responsible for having become just another commercial commodity, something to be promoted and marketed like any other product. In 1781, just ten years before his untimely death in his thirty-sixth year, he finally broke with his employer, the Prince Archbishop of Salzburg, and embarked on a career as an independent musical entrepreneur in the imperial capital, the most important centre of music in Europe—except perhaps for Paris, which continued until well into the nineteenth century to occupy a position of barely challenged pre-eminence.

For a while the campaign worked. Mozart's subscription concerts were well attended; he attracted some pupils from the upper echelons of the Viennese bourgeoisie. Important pieces in the plan of battle refused, nevertheless, to fall in place. Despite the *succès d'estime et de scandale* of *The Marriage of Figaro*, neither a position at court nor any further commission for the court theatre materialised. The public wearied after a year or two of Herr Mozart's concerts where he performed his elaborate concertos in which he made sure that at the end each included a catchy tune derived from the dance music and popular songs of the melody-obsessed Viennese. They began demanding precisely what he had provided for them a year or so earlier: novelty. He was, therefore, the agent of his own destruction. He broke free of the demeaning world of servitude, a world where aristocratic patrons might not have cared very much for the music of their *Kapellmeister*, but didn't give a fig either for what the audience—their guests at suppers, soirées and fêtes—thought of it. Mozart had thrown himself on the mercies of the public and suffered the penalties of its fickleness and thirst for novelty.

His was, in truth, a sad fate. The public showed remarkably poor discrimination in scorning him and lionising the nonentities who became their darlings in 1790 and 1791. Yet it acted true to form—Mozart had appealed to those market-forces which are now being touted all over the countries to the east of Austria as representing a natural and desirable economic philosophy. He took his music into the market place, he sought the patronage of the public rather than the court or the nobleman's estate. The public sent him to his pauper's grave just as it is still capable of consigning to penury a former pop star or fallen movie idol.

Two centuries later Mozart is once again a highly lucrative commercial commodity. Salzburg has been raking in the profits of Mozart-mania for decades, despite the interruption of the odd war or two. Now it is Vienna's turn. Here marketing ranges from the boorish to the sophisticated. The bicentenary productions of the great operas are as much directed by the spirit of the cash register as the Mozart mugs, badges and pillowcases crowding the souvenir shops and street stalls.

Looking at all this tawdry merchandise with jet-lagged eyes on this bright autumn morning, I begin to wonder whether, as the last quarter of the Mozart Year approaches, the great public will once more grow weary of him, his music and his image. In 1992 it is Rossini's turn: will Vienna try to milk that anniversary too? Whatever the case, Vienna seems to have become a trifle more crass and vulgar as it celebrates the most elegant and fastidious of composers.

Despite this hard-headed commercialism, the city looks enchanting, in an amiably dotty way. One end of the Graben, a pedestrian thoroughfare devoted to plush cafés and murderously expensive shops, has taken on a fleeting resemblance to Palermo—due entirely to the grove of fully-grown palm trees in large tubs lining either side of the street. Vines and creepers luxuriating on the trellises of outdoor restaurants in the sidestreets transform this sophisticated city into a rural idyll. And there is kitsch everywhere: everything is both cosmopolitan and *gemütlich*, grandiose yet homely. There are cartloads of carved wooden objects for sale—smiling putti coyly presenting their rosy buttocks to general view; sweet-faced Madonnas cradling irresistibly cute infant Christs; assorted saints looking pious; reindeer, chamois, bears, cows with miniature cowbells around their necks: a sentimental Austrian menagerie. One shop displays a large china figurine of Julie Andrews in the act of climbing every mountain. Even the fast-food joints are a riot of heart-shaped carvings, blonde waitresses in dirndls and long-limbed youths poured into their lederhosen. A bewigged, satin-breeched young man is ready to conduct you on a walking tour of the places Mozart inhabited during his years in Vienna—and anyone familiar with those ten years of the composer's life remembers that he moved house with depressing frequency.

It is difficult to determine where the real life of Vienna goes on in the midst of this carefully stage-managed spectacle designed to relieve the hordes of tourists of their money. There are, it is true, apparently genuine Viennese people sitting in the outdoor cafés, many of them with mastiff-sized dogs unlikely pets in a city where most people live in small cramped, apartments. You begin to wonder whether these people are real. Obviously they are not waxwork models, like the dummy of Peter Altenberg that greets you as you walk into the Café Central, which is firmly closed this morning because a camera crew is busy filming a scene for what is, probably, a nostalgic costume drama. I conclude uncharitably that they are probably extras, walk-on players hired to populate a theme park. Perhaps it is only jet lag, as I wander around these streets, surprised that it is still only ten in the morning, that gives the place such a striking sense of unreality. And I suspect that that sense will increase throughout the next two hours until I am able at last to occupy the room in a modest but comfortable pension which has been reserved for me, except that—as the charming proprietor pointed out with a gesture that I last saw many years ago when I watched Elisabeth Schwarzkopf singing the Marschallin—rooms in Vienna are not available for occupation before noon.

It seems futile merely to stroll in the sunshine or to sit in a café waiting for the time to come when I shall be able at last to get some sleep. How better to spend two hours than by joining a serpentine queue for opera tickets? It is well after twelve when I reach its head. By then *The Marriage of Figaro* is sold out; I have to be content with *La Bohème* and *Lohengrin*. Back at the pension, light-headed with exhaustion, I notice a sign that hadn't been there last year. It announces in several languages IN THIS HOUSE MOZART COMPOSED *THE ABDUCTION FROM THE SERAGLIO*.

THEME PARK

Sunday morning. The window of my room, overlooking one of the great thoroughfares of the old city, provides an ideal vantage point from which to view this fantasia of sentimentality, nostalgia and displacement. All day the leaden late September sky (a remarkable contrast to yesterday's sunshine) has throbbed with the equally heavy-sounding bells of the nearby churches: the Michaelkirche just around the corner, the somewhat more distant Kirche am Hof, not to mention the cathedral itself, a stone's throw away in the other direction. Immaculately clad citizens flock to hear mass in these and in many other churches throughout the inner city—though whether it is religion or the music (mostly by Mozart, it goes without saying) that attracts them is hard to determine. Elsewhere symbols of imperial greatness loom in the autumn mists. Occasionally a ray of sunlight breaks through, illuminating, impartially, it seems, both the monument to Maria Theresia, the double-chinned Empress, and the nearby statue of the poet Schiller. Posters announce performances at the two opera houses, the three state-supported theatres, seemingly innumerable privately owned places of entertainment, various concert halls and churches. Early in the morning, just as on the morning of my arrival, queues form at the box office of the national theatres, where patrons eagerly inspect large

29

notices advertising the availability of tickets for these attractions.

And yet there is something jarring, rather peculiar about the obvious confidence and civilisation of this pompous but very beautiful city. What is the source of the prosperity that allows the Viennese to savour the delights of Demel's and Sacher's, the two fabled cafés, or to purchase the world's most desirable luxuries at outrageous prices in the elegant boutiques of the Kärtnerstrasse or the Graben? A large part of this affluence must be a direct consequence of the thousands of tourists roaming the streets of the inner city each day, reaching plague proportions in the high season, even in this year of economic distress and political threat, with the ominous shadow of civil war spreading over nearby Croatia. The streets are a babel of all the tongues and dialects of the world—after the first hour or two you don't register surprise at hearing a nasally Australian intonation expressing delight and astonishment or insisting that it's not all that different after all from Melbourne.

Vienna at the end of the twentieth century is a theme park par excellence; its citizens seem to have been carefully drilled to exhibit their culture and national characteristics (including their sneering disdain and contempt for foreigners). As recompense, it would seem, they may enjoy their traditional way of life in considerable affluence—animals in zoos are, after all, almost always well fed. Admittedly, other European cities are theme parks as well. In parts of London or Paris, Amsterdam or Rome it is often impossible to move for the waves of gawking sightseers jamming the footpaths, pedestrian malls and great civic spaces that once upon a time gave ample room for ladies and gentlemen of quality to stroll, to nod to each other in polite acknowledgment and to pursue the other civilised pleasures of the promenade. Life in those cities is obviously accompanied by the irritations of attempting to pursue an ordinary existence in the midst of the aimless wanderings of the jet-age 'barbarians'. There are, nevertheless, some remnants of an everyday life left in those places—at times grumbling and disconsolate, it is true, when people find themselves incapable of travelling on the Metro or the Underground, yet an ordinary life, for all that. In Vienna everything and everyone seem to be elements of the décor in a gigantic, staged extravaganza.

The place is, of course, wonderfully well maintained; in better shape, to be truthful, than Vienna's own funfair, the Prater, which is looking decidedly grotty by comparison. The city is, nevertheless, just as much a place of illusions and even perhaps of cheap thrills, a bold pretence that this dead city is still vibrantly alive. There is no cogent reason for the existence of Vienna except as an essay in sentiment and nostalgia. In the patterns of late twentieth-century political, social and even perhaps cultural life Vienna and Austria are both irrelevant, both victims of a grand predicament.

Austria's predicament is that it has lost its Empire. The scope and style of Vienna are ridiculously inappropriate for its population of a few million. Its grandeur may have impressed the inhabitants of Kakania, perhaps dampening their envy and restlessness by the assertion that this was their city too, a part of their proud heritage. Yet Kakania has been dead for many years—only the outward signs of its existence remain in this city as reminders of a vanished world. The result is an ever-present yearning for the past and an ugly cultural xenophobia masked by a welcoming smile. Austrian nostalgia, the pursuit of *Gemütlichkeit* visible in the streets of contemporary Vienna, did not exist so blatantly in the days of the Empire, when this small duchy stood at the centre of a vast and polyglot conglomerate of often unruly subject peoples. The transformation of the Holy Roman Empire into the Austro-Hungarian by the adroit House of Habsburg ensured that Austria could continue to enjoy its essential centrality, its conviction that it, and it alone, represented the essence of 'Europe', having successfully resisted those anarchic waves of republicanism and liberalism that flooded over many other states of the continent. The history of Austria throughout the nineteenth century reveals a striving to maintain such an insistence in the face of

Prussian ambition and energy. The disintegration of the Habsburg world in the years leading up to the Great War, observed with such malicious relish by Robert Musil in *The Man Without Qualities*, was the product of that rivalry, and also of the disastrous alliance between the newly formed German Empire (always seen by Austria as something of a parvenu) and the Habsburg realm, the old centre of the European spirit—that is to say of German civilisation and language. Before 1918 'Austria' was a cultural and idealistic concept that could embrace people in the most remote parts of this realm, like the people of the Bukovina commemorated by Gregor von Rezzori, or people like my grandparents, German-speaking Hungarians, Jews and Bohemians, who saw themselves as citizens of this world despite its many hatreds, rivalries and exclusions.

The paradox of contemporary Austria is that it has been obliged to transfer that imperial dream, its conviction that it is the leader of peoples and nations, into an entirely non-political sphere, or at least into a dubious political and cultural idealism. The people strolling around the immaculately swept streets of this theme park are, in a way, just as much displaced persons, exiled from their birthright, as those former citizens who were driven to the farthest corners of the world by fear, enmity and hate, people who elaborated a mythology of this golden world in countless cafés and espresso bars in Sydney and Melbourne, in Buenos Aires and Rio, in Johannesburg and Cape Town.

Vienna is wholly immersed in its past. The repertoire of the Vienna State Opera, that glamorous and prestigious establishment, is the most conservative in the world, with almost no departure from standard Italian and German works. Even in the visual arts, 'modern' in Vienna means Gustav Klimt, Egon Schiele and Oscar Kokoschka, artists firmly embedded in the culture of the *fin-de-siècle*. Concert-goers still consider Mahler a difficult modern composer. In no other city of Europe, not even in the architecturally richer cities of Italy, is the tendency to conserve, that is, to live in history, so evident as it is here.

The extraordinary number of dwellings Mozart occupied—generally because of his difficulties in paying rent—in the last ten years of his life are meticulously marked throughout the inner city. You may stay in this pension, where he wrote *The Abduction from the Seraglio*, or take coffee on the ground floor of a building where the G minor symphony was composed. Meanwhile the living culture of the German-speaking people is conducted elsewhere, in the cities of the newly reunified Germany, the world that Habsburg pride used to regard with undisguised contempt. To the citizens of Munich or to the inhabitants of the newly reunited Berlin (half glitz, half grot) Vienna is a cultural mausoleum dedicated to the old and hopelessly outdated fantasy of Kakania.

As you walk around the streets of Vienna, that world—the world of Mozart, Haydn, Beethoven and Schubert—seems to be a living reality. In the narrow passages of the old city the baroque palaces look down on the bustling world below with seemingly timeless serenity. Here is a sense of continuity, of the intimate and life-sustaining connections between the past and the present. A moment's reflection should remind us, nevertheless, of the lessons of the theme park. Vienna was almost wholly obliterated during the Second World War. Most of the city's famous landmarks were lovingly restored during the 1950s and the 1960s. My first memory of this city—for I do not remember the times I was taken there in my infancy to visit relatives or to spend a few days among the woody hills of the Wienerwald—is of the early winter of 1946, when my parents and I were making our way to our new life in Australia.

We spent those weeks of anticipation in a small hotel in the inner city. The three of us slept in one room, which was cast into a constant gloom throughout the dark winter days and nights. No glass remained in the handsome windows that looked, or should have looked, down on the thoroughfare below. They were boarded up with plywood, with one small rectangle of glass set into one of the panels. The only other source of light was provided by a naked low-watt bulb hanging from the ornate ceiling. At night it illuminated the heavy furniture and the great tiled stove—entirely useless because of the lack of fuel—with the exaggerated lighting effects of an expressionist film. Some years later I encountered those images again, in the old Regent Theatre in George Street, in Carol Reed's homage to the German expressionists, *The Third Man*.

The scene outside the hotel—fragments of which you could glimpse through the small piece of glass in the window—revealed the characteristic images of defeat. The shabby citizens of Vienna shuffled up and down the cobbled street, avoiding the piles of rubble that lay everywhere. Some were carrying shapeless bundles, others pushed carts filled with torn mattresses, pieces of an iron bedstead and other curious items. The occupying forces, chiefly Russians with their mouths filled with gold teeth, looked on with contempt. An air of utter despair hung over the city.

My parents pointed out two vast ruins at opposite ends of the central part of the Kärtnerstrasse. At one end only a few fragments of the elaborately patterned roof of the cathedral remained. At the other the great Opera House was an empty shell. Catholic Austria, the Habsburg patrimony that made Vienna the most violently antisemitic of European cities, and the chief monument of its culture (which so many Jews fostered and patronised) had both fallen victim to a dubious vengeance. Today the crowds milling around the church admire a building steeped in history. Visitors from the new world, especially the newest of the new, are visibly impressed by something so ancient, a monument that seems to have lasted so long, withstanding the ravages of time. Yet both the cathedral and the theatre have been rebuilt after their almost total destruction. These monuments of Austria's pride and achievement—both spiritual and cultural—may be regarded as gigantic essays in trompe l'oeil, an elaborate attempt to deceive, to gloss over a reality that no-one wants to remember, just as in a theme park you may find intricate reconstructions of days gone by or of worlds to come.

Contemporary Austria displays, in this sense, the folly of a sentimental education. The past has been sanitised, disinfected and altered to conform to a sentimental view of a culture or a heritage which no longer resides in reality but engages with images of fantasy. There remain, it is true, apparently substantial monuments—in both the material and the metaphoric sense—of the reality that shapes such nostalgia. Yet this city has, as the work of restoration on many an eighteenth-century palais reveals, an all too obvious sense of make-believe. As in all good theme parks the past is spruced up to appeal to the sensation-seeking tourist. In the great 'art' cities of contemporary Austria—Vienna, Salzburg and Innsbruck—no buildings may be erected that are out of harmony with their historical heritage.

As I scan the faces of the people strolling around the pedestrian malls of this meticulously reconstructed city, I do not discern any sense of the confusion that has been a traditional affliction or preoccupation in this world, the angst and scepticism that drove those trenchant critics of Kakania into their searing indictments of vanity and hypocrisy at a time when Kakania was still a reality, not merely a dream. In 1991 I see only contentment around me. Yet it seems a curiously shallow contentment, or so I persuade myself. But then one wouldn't expect to encounter misery in a theme park—the inhabitants of such places must always look clean, attractive and satisfied. And they must look as if they believe in the myths and dreams such places seek to promote. Why else would you bother paying the admission price—the outrageous cost of hotel rooms, of largely indigestible meals and cups of watery coffee? And Vienna is certainly a spotlessly clean city.

THE ETERNAL STORY

The bookshops of the inner city are sumptuously elegant. To those of us whose eyes are accustomed to garish dump-bins and promotional posters, lurid dustjackets and psychedelic paperback covers, these discreet temples of the printed word speak of restraint and ceremony. Solidly constructed and handsomely polished shelves and counters are almost over-burdened with novels and volumes of verse, essays and philo-sophical tracts, works on oriental art and Indo-European linguistics. There is nothing frivolous or vulgar here: this world seems to treat books with a respect which we, from the raw new world, may only regard with envy.

Scattered among these sober and chastely serious volumes are a number of somewhat more colourful books. Their dustjackets often show sepia photographs of portly gentlemen in severe military uniform, their faces all but covered by billowing beards and whiskers, monocles glinting in the sunlight or reflecting the flash of a magnesium flare. Bustled ladies step daintily from graceful carriages or stand ramrod-straight in imperial ermine. Here and there a panoramic photograph depicts a procession winding its way through the imposing portal of the Hofburg—cavalry, infantry, a military band, and in their midst, no more than blobs in these faded images, the rulers of the realm acknowledging the plaudits of the crowd who must have been standing in their serried ranks beyond the margins of the photograph, kept out of range of the commemorating camera.

These books are concerned with the illustrious House of Habsburg. Some recount its origins in the mountains of Switzerland. Others tell of its fortunes in the eighteenth century—the epoch of Maria Theresia and the expansion of the Empire. Most, however, concentrate on the seventy-odd years leading up to the gunshot at Sarajevo that marked the beginning of its end. Here is a myth world that gives substance to the nostalgia visible in the theme park outside the immaculately polished glass doors. These sober and scholarly volumes deal with the political, social and military difficulties of the last decades of the Empire. They analyse the stirrings of nationalism in North Italy, Hungary, Slovakia and else-where in a realm that stretched to the borders of the empire of the Russian tsars. The intellectual ferment of Vienna—and of Prague and Budapest—in the closing years of the nine-teenth century is discussed here with judicious restraint.

Flicking through these volumes reveals many footnotes.

It seems that what attracts readers to these solid historical discourses is the other face of the ubiquitous yearning for that golden past, a time when Austria was the proud heart of an empire, when Vienna's grandeur was justified because it was, after all, a great imperial capital. That face is the pathetic and scandalous life of the last Habsburgs, a tale ready-made for television epics and mini-series photographed in the places where these dramas were played out, and embellished with much swirling and twirling to the Strausses' innumerable waltzes, polkas and galops. All the ingredients of those sagas are contained in these handsome volumes—frustrated love, sexual rage, political intrigue, violent death. The cultivated citizens of this elegant city may enjoy all within the covers of these sumptuously produced tomes.

The border of the theme park is marked by the great semicircle of boulevards, the Ring, which replaced the old fortifications during the reign of Franz Josef, the Emperor of Peace. Here lies a different Vienna. Here live the scene shifters, the machinists, the set constructors and costume makers who keep the show functioning year in and year out. It may well be that the men, women, children and dogs who appear in the streets and squares of the park repair to this part of the city once they have clocked off duty, having spent the requisite number of hours eating cream cakes, strolling arm-in-arm down the Graben or the Kärtnerstrasse, not running around or making too much noise; sitting and heeling obediently, and certainly not straining at the leash; or else leafing through liberally illustrated historical volumes.

For me this is a much more familiar world. A long, wide street, the Mariahilferstrasse, running from the *limes* to the large open space (permanently in the process of being dug up, it seems) in front of one of the railway stations, is lined by shops, department stores, cinemas and pinball parlours of the sort you may see in almost every large city. Stiff shop dummies display the latest clothes—manufactured in Taiwan, Korea and even in the last remaining People's Republics—all designed to disintegrate after two seasons, by which time they will have come to seem as quaintly old-fashioned as the crinoline and the swallow-tail coat. An abundance of video equipment beckons consumers from shop windows heavily barred with lattice-work of iron. Through the plate-glass doors of the supermarkets you can glimpse shelves upon shelves of detergent powder and disposable nappies.

There are a few bookshops here squeezed between supermarkets and clothing emporia along the expanse of this noisy, traffic-choked street. Most of them have that depressingly temporary look familiar from the streets of Australian cities and towns, where a bankrupt shop is often cleared then filled with long trestle tables groaning with remaindered cookbooks, blockbuster novels that didn't make the big league, sex manuals and histories of Chinese traders in the thirteenth century or of the coalfields of Wales. Because this is Vienna, these establishments are a little less chaotic, perhaps even more permanent looking; their wares are, nevertheless, similar to the sort of stuff you may purchase in such places in Sydney or Adelaide, London or Manchester.

Prominently displayed near the entrance—according, no doubt, to the dictates of a marketing scheme concocted on Madison Avenue—are the ranks of lurid pulp trade paperbacks. If you have nothing better to do, you may amuse yourself by trying to work out the English titles of these Sidney Sheldons, Stephen Kings, Colleen McCulloughs, and Danielle Steeles. Nearby may be found less bulky but no less colourful volumes, obviously parts of a series, the covers of which depict sentimental pictures of sweet-faced young women wearing glittering tiaras and handsome young men in the dashing uniform of the Imperial Hussars. The likes of these books will not be found outside Central Europe. They are Austria's answer to Mills and Boon: Kakanian romances, Habsburg follies, chronicling the lives and loves of those glorious creatures who waltzed their way into oblivion in the Great War.

The last Habsburgs provide ideal material for the daydreams

of cheap romance. Their stories form one of those complex epics, with twisted branches and sub-branches, so much loved by medieval compilers of tales of love and high adventure. The trunk, the mainstay, he who supports the great weight of all these stories of tragic and doomed love, is the old Franz Josef, the Emperor himself. Not much can be made of the sober and serious life of this monarch who preferred a camp bed to the downy pillows of his many palaces, castles and residences. His dalliance with a discreet and respectful lady suggests domestic rather than erotic desires. The frustrated life and tragic death of his Empress provide, however, material for a succession of stories, sufficient in themselves to form a family of epic tales.

It is pleasing to find that in one of these bookshops—reflecting the tidiness of mind for which the Germanic people are renowned—the ill-fated Empress has a corner reserved for her, decorously separating her from her equally hapless relatives. Most of the titles, or if not the titles then the blurbs, set in large, florid type, manage to mention her pet-name, Sissy, much more charming and interesting, of course, than the icily formal Elisabeth. The illustrations on the covers of these little books—few of them exceed 150 pages—give sufficient indication of what the reader may find inside. On one, Sissy, in full riding habit, is seated on a fiery charger. A snow-covered plain stretches to the horizon. A sled, pulled by four prancing steeds, is hurrying towards her, conveying a lonely figure clad in black. This, as anyone familiar with Visconti's film will know, is the meeting between Sissy and her cousin, Ludwig of Bavaria, the Wagner-obsessed madman (or visionary) for whom she is supposed to have entertained an undying and unrequited passion.

Another image depicts her in the arms of one of those monocled or moustachioed warriors who appear on the covers of several books displayed on these shelves under the harsh glare of fluorescent strips. Elsewhere she is seen seated among a group of adoring and respectful peasants—probably the Hungarians she is said to have loved so much—while her gaze travels over their heads towards a small castle or hunting lodge in the background, the site, no doubt, of yet another hopeless amour.

She is depicted in imperial regalia at a splendid ball, or sitting by a window at twilight, a leather-bound volume open on her lap. And then there is the most evocative of these images: Sissy leaning decoratively on the railing of a steamer on a placid lake. Snow-capped mountains rise in the distance. A narrow headland is dominated by a mighty keep. Sissy, as always, gazes into the distance, dreamy, sensuous, a figure of mystery. Are we meant to see in that abstracted gaze a failure to recognise the crazed assassin who is, at that very moment, hurrying towards her?

The saga branches out to embroider variations on the lives of other members of this unhappy family: Franz Ferdinand, who enraged the Emperor by marrying the woman he loved, only to be gunned down in Sarajevo; Maximilian, Emperor of Mexico; cousins, nieces, nephews, relatives near or distant, people who once lived or those merely invented by the romancers' fancy have all entered into the neverending romance, the allure of which, judging by the number of books displayed in these harshly lit shops, can never pall for the citizens of Vienna. Anything, everything seems grist to the mill. Here Franz Ferdinand slumps in that open car in Sarajevo; there the Emperor of Mexico faces a firing squad of sombreroed anarchists. Elsewhere, young women are embraced by hussars, cavalry officers, a Cossack in one instance, beside moonlit lakes and dark forests, or against a panorama of Salzburg, Vienna or Innsbruck. The doomed family dances across the covers of these cheap, poorly printed and probably poorly written romances designed to cater for the fantasies of those who are obliged to live out their lives in poky flats overlooking gloomy courtyards or crepuscular light wells. None of this lucrative industry would be capable of surviving, however, had not one member of the imperial family taken his beloved to a small hunting lodge at a place called Mayerling to die in a suicide pact that has nourished countless romantic fantasies.

The story of Archduke Rudolf and Baroness Marie Vetsera is well known. The bored heir to the Habsburg throne, between bouts of drinking and whoring, the usual pursuits of unemployed royalty in the old Europe, met and fell in love with the barely seventeen-year-old Baroness Vetsera. Their meetings were brief and clandestine. According to Claudio Magris they were confined to the time it took to perform one of Wagner's operas, which the Baroness's mother always attended whenever they were performed at the Imperial Opera. That would have given the lovers at best five or six hours—though if Marie's mother's taste did not extend beyond the earlier and less demanding of the Master's works, their time would have been even shorter. Despite their precautions, the affair—as was inevitable—came to the attention of the court. What threats, ultimatums, cajolements or bribes were offered is not precisely known. Nor are the details of the events at the hunting lodge on the night of 29 January 1889 quite clear. What is known, however, is that the next morning, the young Baroness's body was discovered in her bed, while nearby in a pool of blood lay the body of the Archduke.

These events make up a sordid tale: an impressionable girl, a dissolute prince of the blood, intrigues, spying and treachery. It has been transformed nevertheless into a romantic myth: Marie and Rudolf, at least for Austrians, have joined Héloïse and Abélard, Romeo and Juliet, Tristan and Isolde as martyrs of tragically doomed true love. And so their story reappears, prettified, disinfected and sentimentalised, on the covers of these cheap little romances in the bookshops of Mariahilfer-strasse. Marie is always depicted as the epitome of angelic sweetness, fragility and dedication to love. Rudolf, who inherited the squat, almost peasant-like physique of the male members of his family, is pictured (of course) in dashingly Byronic guises. As always, the ugly, the brutal and the dissolute are transformed into the noble, the sentimental and the heroic by the strong drug of nostalgia.

The pulp industry that fills these bookshops is no different from the merchants of escapist romances elsewhere in the world. The difference lies in the curious though very strong sense of location that colours these books ranked neatly on their imperial shelves. This is your history, they seem to be saying

41

to the dumpy ladies who are standing in front of these shelves pondering their choice. Perhaps the Viennese . have been persuaded that their history, their glorious past, is not the familiar story of brutality, chicanery and hypocrisy that seems to be the fate of all people and all régimes. History has been converted for them into romance. Nostalgia has transformed a brutal past into a seductive dream. Everything is dedicated to feeling, sensation and sentiment. Mayerling happened only a little over a hundred years ago. You may easily visit the place and shed a sentimental tear over Marie and Rudolf. The Habsburgs are gone—though perhaps one day they may come back—but the 'Burg is still there. Romance and passion may be found beneath the surface of a dull world—you only have to search for it, these little books seem to be saying.

An intangible yet obviously strong bond appears to bind this world to its fantasy past. The citizens of the theme park appear to have accepted these illusions as reality. Sentiment, nostalgia and the allure of the relatively recent past, even where it led to suffering, defeat and death, define for these people the essence of being Austrian. To the east the former Soviet Empire is disintegrating just as their own Empire—one that had ruled over most of those territories and people—disintegrated when the Elisabeths, Rudolfs, and Ferdinands were felled by their own hands or by the assassins' bullets. But why concern yourself with the horror and brutality in what is still called (in this year of the palindrome) Yugoslavia? Why should you be distressed by the fate of the orphans of Romania? The real life is here, in the eternally fascinating story of Sissy on her horse, Marie in the arms of her Rudolf, and Maximilian, eyes clear with courage and defiance, standing before the firing squad.

HAPPILY EVER AFTER

The Volksoper is a dull-looking building near a clattering and clanging tramway viaduct. It is, as its name suggests, a theatre for the masses. In the past its repertoire was devoted almost exclusively to that peculiar genre, Viennese operetta, which was (and remains) a vehicle for conveying the most outrageous fantasies of Kakania. To the accompaniment of catchy tunes and rousing choruses, these absurdly escapist musical plays celebrate a fantasy in which no-one dies in a hunting lodge or falls victim to the anarchist's bullet, but lives happily ever after.

Viennese operetta reached its apogee in the years between the gunshot at Mayerling and that of Sarajevo—though examples of this essentially imperial entertainment for the masses continued to be composed beyond the years of the Great War, into the 1920s, and indeed almost until the grim days of Vienna's fiery death in 1945. Their plots—if they may be graced with such a term—almost always end with the triumph of love. Whatever the complications, misunderstandings, or obstacles that keep the lovers apart for an hour or two, all is well by the time the rousing finalé is reached. With much swirling, clinking of glasses, rushing around the stage and with as high a note as the singers of these confections are capable of reaching, a typical Viennese operetta ends with marriage, happiness and celebration.

It would be difficult to see any connection between these trivial and escapist fancies and the world of experience. Operettas may be set in Paris or Peking, Vienna or St Petersburg, but their true location is always a never-never-land where any occasion will do for singing and dancing. Many of them reflect, nevertheless, the fantasies of Kakanian amity and benevolence, and seem to subscribe to the fiction that this troubled world was, when all is said and done, one big happy family, an idea assiduously promoted by its rulers even at a time when that fiction could no longer be sustained anywhere but in the theatre. There at least the pretence could be continued.

Until the approaching war made travel between Budapest and the provinces difficult if not impossible, my parents spent each Easter with my mother's family in Sopron, a picturesque border town some fifty or sixty kilometres to the east of Vienna. Sopron remained an essentially Austrian town even after the partition of that part of the world at Versailles caused it to become—to the dismay of many of its inhabitants—the westernmost city in the newly independent state of Hungary. During our last visit, my parents took me to the little municipal theatre to a performance of *The Gypsy Baron*.

I remember almost nothing about that performance. My sole memory is of a scene in a forest clearing—crudely painted flats and backcloth—with a group of gypsies seated around an obviously fake campfire. In their midst stood a black-haired figure, with a large gold earring in one ear, a short jacket with elaborate frogging slung casually over his shoulders. He sang a lusty song—with many refrains I remember—in which the chorus of gypsies participated enthusiastically.

The Gypsy Baron was first performed in Vienna in 1885. It seems obvious that by that time the Habsburg propaganda about the essential unity and harmony of the Empire had appealed to the promoters of popular entertainment, who could see solid profits flowing from its promulgation. *The Gypsy Baron*, like many subsequent examples of the genre, seeks to transcend the national, ethnic or tribal rivalries that have always tormented this world. Hungary was the most troublesome territory of the Empire, not necessarily because the Hungarians were more fervently patriotic and more gallant than their neighbours—though they liked to think that they were—but because they were the most numerous. Gypsies, according to Viennese mythology or prejudice, were a particularly Hungarian phenomenon—another cause of dissatisfaction to Hungarians who were convinced, of course, that gypsies belong properly to that more easterly part of the continent which we now call Romania. Barons were, on the other hand, one of the high (though not too exalted) ranks of the Kakanian nobility. A gypsy baron, a contradiction in terms according to many Austrians, represents a reconciliation of the two most important and influential territories of this Empire. If a gypsy may become a baron, even if only on the operetta stage, Austrians and Hungarians, Bohemians and Slovaks, Serbs and Croats may also live peacefully under the aegis of the double-headed eagle.

In these entertainments the impossible idealism of this world—an idealism that probably no-one took seriously by 1914—was given a spurious validity. Their titles reveal all. The Hungarian Emmerich Kalman, composer of a series of phenomenally successful Viennese operettas, seems to have had a particular gift for finding subjects and titles to promote that dream. One of his operettas, still in the repertoire of companies all over the world is usually known in English as *The Gypsy Princess*. The German title, *Die Csardasfürstin*, yoking together the *csardas*, the most popular of Hungarian dances, with an exalted rank of the Austro-Hungarian nobility, is particularly eloquent, speaking of those pious fantasies that these trivial entertainments embody.

Here at least the fond hope of the Habsburgs, that they could somehow forge a harmonious supranational community out of people who had in certain instances been enemies for a thousand years or more, received a tiny fragment of confirmation. Operetta became an astonishingly popular form of entertainment in almost every one of the Habsburg lands. In the theatre, provisionally and briefly, a Hungarian or a Ruthenian could agree with the implicit assumption that under the benevolent dispensation of the Father–Emperor (who could make barons out of gypsies) this was the best of all possible worlds. Outside the theatre, though, the fiction was much harder to maintain. As I stand in front of the Volksoper, waiting for the traffic lights to change, I begin to wonder whether operettas are still being performed in Zagreb and Sarajevo, cities where the old hatreds of this world have been given once more a new lease of life.

THE LAST BANANA

A tram rattling through the grey streets of the real Vienna, away from the theme park, the kitsch, the sentimental fantasies, takes you to the edge of the Wienerwald, the Vienna Woods, site of another set of nostalgic dreams. The woods begin at Grinzing, nowadays no more than a suburb of the metropolis, its houses displaying plaques commemorating those famous citizens of Vienna who lived along these twisting lanes. A hundred years ago Grinzing was a village surrounded by the vineyards that supplied the vine-covered taverns which purvey the local vintage throughout the late summer and the long autumn of this part of the world. In the gaps between the villas of the rich and the famous you may glimpse vine-covered hills, heavy with yet-to-be-harvested grapes.

The taverns come to life late in the day. Throughout the balmy nights of late summer, and under the chilly skies of autumn, the people of Vienna drink, eat, sing and dance, surrounded by carefully contrived rusticity. The good life, pursued so assiduously amidst the imperial grandeur of the inner city, here takes on another colouration, a fantasy of the simple rural life, its joys and its wine, idylls of well-being and companionship—in other words, wine, women and song, and tales from the Vienna Woods. The celebration of new wine and rustic simplicity is a profoundly characteristic Viennese pursuit. No other metropolis has striven so hard as this city to evolve a fantasy of rural life amidst the marble and granite of imperial pomp. Vienna constantly conjures up images of the countryside, even in the heart of the inner city. At one corner of the great irregularly shaped space around the cathedral, an ancient piece of wood preserved behind shatter-proof glass displays hundreds of embedded rusty nails, which had been driven into the living tree by shepherds and countryfolk to commemorate their visit to the imperial city.

Nowhere else is this sentimental amalgam of city and countryside more poignant than at Grinzing. Here town and wooded hill meet in an ordered, carefully landscaped union.

Nothing here seems real: the meticulously preserved village atmosphere, the crooked lanes, the charming taverns are as contrived and decorative as the vine-clad slopes towards which most streets and lanes seem to be leading. Here is another stage set, a cunningly crafted trompe l'oeil designed to bemuse and beguile, and to remind you of the potential that exists here for a joyous marriage of country and city. In other cities the countryside intrudes, sometimes with disturbing and disconcerting effect, nowhere more so than was the case in Canberra before the lake was filled, when sheep grazed peacefully but incongruously on patches of dry grassland between buildings of monumental pretentiousness. Here, in Grinzing, it is otherwise. The little town is prettified, the fields and woods are manicured—perfumed, you are inclined to think, as were the cows in the toy-dairy of the Austrian princess who became, to her misfortune, Queen of France.

From Grinzing you must take a bus to the hills known collectively as the Vienna Woods, an ascent both literal and symbolic into a higher level of sentiment and nostalgia. There images of conviviality are replaced by the sweet allure of fresh air, sunshine, the scent of pines and the exhilaration of physical exercise. Meticulously marked and signposted tracks indicate paths that beckon through this tamed wilderness. Here you always know where you are going; each track ends at a convenient *Gasthof* where food, drink and good cheer await the weary traveller. The terrors of the dark forest, where Hansel and Gretel might encounter the perils of the Gingerbread House, where bloodthirsty dragons or malevolent magicians often lurk, have been tamed and civilised. Danger and menace have been converted into playfulness. You may imagine that you are wandering through a dark wood where all sorts of dangers are to hand—but it is all pretence, like so much else in this city and forest, an elaborate illusion to provide carefully controlled thrills.

On this sun-drenched autumn afternoon the paths are crowded with people. Several are dressed in the required paraphernalia of such outings: in this world every activity has its appropriate costume. Lederhosen and dirndls, worn in the inner city only by purveyors of fast food, seem almost obligatory here. These strollers are playing out a domesticated, nostalgic version of a great institution of the Germanic world—the walking tour, that ritualised enactment of the great *Wanderlust* which took generations of young Germans on energetic, hilarious rambles over the Fatherland in commemoration of the wanderings of their ancestors through the menacing forests of Gaul. There they experienced that sense of community, the absorption of the individual into the tribe, which reveals the darkest corner of the German soul—beyond individuality, pity and compassion, driven only by the instincts of the herd and the mass.

On Kahlenberg, the sunny summit of these woody hills, all is peace and contentment. The couples strolling arm in arm do not seem to be driven by the demons of the blood. Yet beneath the amiable holiday mood, an urban pastorale with alpenstocks embellished with plaques commemorating walks achieved and mountain peaks conquered, sinister possibilities glimmer. This world is capable of masking ugliness and brutality, converting them into nostalgia and sentiment. Mayerling is not very far from here. At that site of the sordid attempt to cover up the deaths of Rudolf and Marie, a shameful exercise was conducted which came to implicate many members of the Kakanian aristocracy. The indecency with which Marie's body was secretly bundled out of the lodge, denying her family access to it or permission to bury it decently, was the sorriest manifestation of the edifice of hypocrisy and evasion that was erected over that pathetic death tryst.

This world is very practised in such hypocrisy. It is only too willing to insist that black is white, that things are other than they seem. It is able, therefore, to convert the ugly, the shabby and the brutal into beauty and nobility. These days waves of visitors come to worship at the tomb of romantically frustrated love at Mayerling, and to marvel at the shrine into which that unhappy place was converted in a supremely hypocritical act of legerdemain.

And so it is with the couples and groups walking in the autumn sunshine. The art of pretence, near neighbour of hypocrisy, has become extraordinarily refined. It is, no doubt, wonderful to pretend that you are wandering in the wild woods where spooks and monsters might be lurking—but, of course, you are merely strolling along the well-made tracks of yet another theme park, a carefully contrived illusion of unbounded nature situated at the terminus of a suburban bus route. In a similar way Austria—and indeed much of the world it once controlled with imperial pride and arrogance—insists that brutality and hatred do not exist here, can never have existed in such a blessed place. The great Austrian hypocrisy that burns across the pages of Schnitzler and Zweig and of Musil and Thomas Bernhard, which made Wittgenstein hate his native land with corrosive passion, manifests itself as clearly here, in this sanitised wilderness, as it does in the poisonous duplicity of Viennese, Austrian, indeed Central European social and political life. The smile that kills and the strangling embrace are fundamental attributes of this world. Cruelty and coldheartedness are masked with the smiling face of civility.

For all that, these woods, this city and this society are alluring, presenting images that soothe, entice and constantly whisper that this is assuredly life at its very best. For me, in my inappropriately antipodean clothes, among these dedicated walkers and vacationers, that sense is particularly poignant. This is a world and an existence into which I could so easily melt, and become absorbed by its charm. Except that I know that that charm is no less treacherous now than it was on an autumn afternoon in 1937, a time I cannot remember—a time before memory—yet a time which has entered into the fabric of my life, adding, in a small way, to the network of influences that has determined what I have become.

On that Sunday, during what was, as it turned out, my parents' last visit to Vienna before our return to the blackened shell of the city in the freezing November of 1946, we joined the throngs of people flocking to Grinzing and Kahlenberg to catch the last bit of sun, the last whiff of fresh country air before winter closed in. My parents probably realised that the winter which was about to enfold them was to be far longer and more severe than the natural winter of God's creation, and that it was, moreover, to be an infernal winter which would come to a fiery end. So it was here, at Kahlenberg, according to a mythology lovingly cherished through the dark years of the war, that they bought the last banana that I, an eighteen-month-old toddler in a stroller, was to enjoy, until nine years later, in 1946, on our journey to America and to that forced landing in the snows of Hartford, we saw bananas again, at a little airport in the Azores, where our plane made an unscheduled landing to ride out the storms raging over the North Atlantic.

THE GREAT WHEEL

In her stuffy, overfurnished flat in Budapest my father's mother kept a china cabinet filled with small silver trinkets. There were windmills and rustic cabins, farmyard animals, goose girls and goatherds, haycarts and wagons, barrows and buckets. The silver was chased and embellished, shining brightly where the polishing cloth came into contact with the metal, darkly shadowed in folds, creases and recesses. Here was a miniature world of Central Europe's nostalgia for the simple life, transformed into costly objects for display in bourgeois households. This sentimental evocation of idylls in lush forests or beside bubbling streams was rendered into kitsch in the same way that, half a century after the time when I used to play with those knick-knacks, the kitsch of modern Vienna, its Mozartballs and dirndls, transforms the commonplace into a sanitised urban fantasy. Good taste, costly materials, pictur-esque romanticism form a continuing strand of illusion throughout the culture of the countries that had fallen under the sway of the Habsburgs. The rulers of that cumbersome Empire employed romantic, nostalgic illusionism in marble and granite in the cities they built along the banks of the Danube, and throughout the institutions they founded and fostered. The descendants of people who had once lived under their rule persist in pursuing those romantic dreams in the grim realities of the end of the twentieth century.

One object among my grandmother's collection of trinkets did not fit in with the genteel nostalgia and subdued romanticism those silversmiths sought to convey for their middle-class patrons. This was rather larger than the other pieces, and was also relatively crudely made, more impressive for the amount of precious metal it contained than for its craftsmanship. It represented the *Riesenrad*, the gigantic Ferris wheel in the Prater, Vienna's amusement park, which was to achieve fame in *The Third Man*, when it became the site for Orson Wells's famous quip about the Swiss and cuckoo clocks.

The presence of that rather vulgar object among my grandmother's household gods tells the tale of the accretion of mythologies in the culture of the Kakanian bourgeoisie, a world that disappeared, along with my grandmother and millions of others, in the conflagration of the Second World War. She was a typical product of the Habsburg world. She was born at a time when Vienna was still the centre of the Empire, the node or navel of a cumbersome political edifice which was already falling apart at the time of her birth, and was to disintegrate entirely in 1918. For her, as much as for my mother's family who lived on the edge of Hungary, in a province which was, until the end of the Great War, a part of Austria, Vienna occupied a place in private and public mythologies similar to that of London in the imagination of early Australia.

By nationality, my father's family were Hungarians, they had lived for many years in or around the place that became Budapest through the yoking together of a Habsburg fortress-town on one bank of the Danube and a nondescript village on the other. Before that, members of my family had lived in various provinces of the Empire, or in one of the German states. They did not, indeed they could not, identify with any of the nationalist movements based on what we would now call ethnicity, for their background and their attitudes were, within the narrow confines of that Danubian world, entirely cosmopolitan. Inevitably they were obliged to have at least a working knowledge of German, not merely for reasons of livelihood but perhaps more significantly, because the family almost always included members whose first language was incomprehensible to several of their relations. Within the network of social and family ties in that world, it was not unusual for a young man in Budapest to marry a distant cousin in Prague, or (as was the case with my father) a young woman whose family was basically German-speaking—even though by my mother's generation all had received a bilingual education. Just as German provided the lingua franca in this world, so Vienna came to represent a sort of super-capital for people living in the cities, towns and villages of the Danube basin. It was where you went for holidays, especially your honeymoon, it was where you took your children to show them the marvels of civilisation—*your* civilisation—or to purchase bananas, and it was the place where you relaxed the strict standards of good taste that governed your essentially provincial life, to buy questionable objects like the silver *Riesenrad* that occupied pride of place in my grandmother's china cabinet.

Despite their looking towards Vienna as the centre of their civilisation, as the measure of elegance, culture and learning, my family did not have anything more than a mild sense of exile in the cities and towns of Hungary, Bohemia, Moravia or Slovakia where most of them had lived for generations. They had a complex, layered sense of patriotism. They felt more or less at ease among those 'nations'; they identified with many of their aims and aspirations; they observed their customs and rituals—my mother loved to dance the *csardas*—and they felt that they had put down roots in that world, despite ominous rumblings from ultranationalist groups which consistently questioned that right. Above, but also including, that sense of local patriotism was another level of allegiances and sentiment—symbolised by my grandmother's purchase of the silver wheel—which made them see themselves as the inheritors of Habsburg civilisation, a way of life that transcended the national and racial diversity of this world and embraced peoples and nationalities within the ample bosom of the Empire.

In this dual citizenship, which allowed my family to look to Vienna as their cultural and social home, but also allowed them to regard themselves as fully-fledged citizens of Hungary, the question of race played an essential and yet in one way entirely insignificant part. The urban bourgeoisie of Vienna, Budapest, Prague, as well as of course of the great German cities, contained sizable Jewish elements. Many practised the ceremonies of Judaism—as the great synagogues erected in those cities witness—but just as many had lapsed, or at least continued to observe its stern dictates only in a superficial and half-hearted manner. Though there were exceptions to be found everywhere, in general for these people Judaism had decayed from an all-embracing social, cultural and personal structure into a mere religion, something to be tucked into a corner of your daily life, or even to be abandoned entirely. Many intermarried with people of other faiths.

One of my father's cousins, a Roman Catholic, succumbed to religious mania in a way that proved embarrassing for her acquaintances and disastrous for her children. She was one of the family eccentrics. When she visited my parents in Budapest, she usually caused a sensation by falling on her knees outside every church she passed in the inner city (and there were many) whenever she accompanied my mother on her ritual shopping expeditions. So thoroughly had she been absorbed by Gentile society that she forced her children into the two great institutions of the Habsburg world. She connived and cajoled until her son was accepted by one of those brutal military academies Musil evoked in the terrible pages of *The Young Törless*. He committed suicide in his second year. The daughter was packed off to an upper-class convent where she was raped by the invading Soviet forces in 1945.

Many of these people suffered the inconveniences of being

Jewish or, perhaps more precisely, of being deemed Jewish. But they were all adept at clever footwork, at those arts of survival which all—Jew as well as Gentile—had to practise in that world of hurdles and barriers, a world where a 'Keep Out' sign always implied that there was a way round. Many, Mahler is the most celebrated example, formally embraced Catholicism in order to gain entry to restricted professions, others merely avoided pursuits not open to them. Before the long disaster that began in 1914 and came to a fiery climax in 1945, this world offered plenty of opportunities for intelligent, resourceful and cultured people. They shut their eyes to the dust rising from the advance of those ultranationalist movements, in Austria as much as in other parts of the Habsburg world, which were to bring about their destruction. But at the time when my grandmother purchased her silver Ferris wheel, she and her family felt comfortably at one with the world in which they lived. They were protected by their Hungarian nationality and by their membership of that great society which found its centre in the imperial city that boasted, apart from other marvels, an amusement park erected on the site of a former royal hunting ground.

In the Australia of the 1950s, as I was beginning to learn something about the way of life of the country in which I had settled, I came to recognise curious analogies between the attitudes and standards of my grandparents' world (by then almost entirely obliterated) and the nostalgia of many Australians of the time towards a distant land. The people of the dusty outer suburb of Sydney where we spent our first years were fierce in their Australian patriotism. For them that land, or rather the corner of it they knew, represented an earthly paradise, the nonpareil of existence. Though they treated us with suspicion and at times open hostility, they were, nevertheless, anxious to demonstrate to us the physical, social and material wonders of a land of unbounded promise. They seemed incapable of imagining any other existence, any social or cultural system which could be superior to theirs.

And yet, anomalously, they often spoke of their desire to

go 'home' to England. Now that the war was over and the sea lanes were open once more, it may be possible, they said, to save enough money to go home for a few months, before it was too late, before they grew too old or infirm. We assumed that these people who spoke longingly of England and filled their houses with its nostalgic emblems—Toby jugs, plates decorated with views of Westminster Abbey, Canterbury Cathedral or Windsor Castle—were exiles aching for a lost world, just as we had begun to yearn for Europe, despite the horrors and brutalities that drove us to seek shelter in the most distant part of the globe. Yet those people were mostly, with very few exceptions, second, third or even fourth generation Australians. The 'home' they spoke of and dreamt about was a mental construct, even a lovingly cherished fantasy. They celebrated Australia with fierce and at times narrow-minded enthusiasm, but they called their streets Pembroke, Oxford and Norfolk, and their houses Sandringham, Windermere and Arden. They lived in two worlds, loyal to each, unaware, it seemed, of the gulf that separated them.

The social and cultural complexion of the Australia of the immediate postwar years mirrored the dual allegiance of my grandmother's world. In each case people felt part of a large cosmopolitan world which was fully their birthright. Beneath such pride, maintained despite occasional instances of prejudice and intolerance—against Jews and other undesirables in the Habsburg world; against their colonial cousins by the British—lay a more immediate, though somewhat ambivalent attachment. My family felt at home, comfortable and safe in Hungary, but they must have known that a fierce and increasingly strident ethnic nationalism, the claim of the Magyars that they and they alone were the only true Hungarians, posed a challenge to that safety. Australians of the years after the war did not feel, or at least would not admit, that their occupation of the land was in any way contingent or even perhaps provisional. Nevertheless they were, despite their noisy protests, uneasy inhabitants of a frequently hostile land, visitors often unwilling to commit their lives unconditionally to the world they celebrated, the world they claimed to be the best of all possible worlds. They looked to a distant fantasy-land as the source of cultural and spiritual values; their desire to 'go home' answered the deepest mythic needs. That world, they were convinced, would rejuvenate them, bring them into contact with their origins and the life-sustaining forces of their heritage.

In Vienna, in this autumn which is still indistinguishable from high summer, when the golden light illuminates the handsome baroque palaces as much as the kitsch, the vulgar and the crass, I am more aware than ever of the similarities between my two worlds. Australians who were adults at the time when my parents and I arrived in that sleepy suburb of Sydney thought of themselves as much heirs of a proud tradition as did my grandparents and their parents before them who regarded themselves as the beneficiaries of a great social and cultural empire. For my grandmother Vienna was not as distant and out of reach as London was for the citizens of Sydney in the late forties. And yet she entertained just as many fantasies about the true source of the culture and the society which sustained her, and she too indulged in her own version of nostalgic kitsch when she placed that model of the *Riesenrad* among the tasteful objects in her china cabinet.

It is curious and ironic, I realise, as I am standing, here in the Prater, in front of that wheel, watching it turn slowly against the soft blue sky, that I should have left one nostalgic world for another; that the culture of the Australia in which I grew up had icons and totems which answered the same dreams as those silver objects in my grandmother's glass case, especially the clumsy representation of the great wheel of Vienna. And for me the wheel has, in a way, turned, for looking at this slowly revolving contraption that nothing could persuade me to board, I am conscious again that I am about to return to Hungary, not for a few days and in the isolation of my emotions and memories as nine months ago, but as a minor public personality, invited to teach young Hungarians about the literature and culture of the place I now call home. I also realise that I have no memory of Vienna in summer time or in autumn. I have stood in front of this great wheel several times in the past, and thought, on each occasion, of what it represented in my grandmother's private and perhaps faintly eccentric mythology—but it was always immobile in hibernation. Now it is moving, and from somewhere in the amusement park the breeze wafts in my direction a strain or two of 'The Blue Danube Waltz'.

A PIECE OF CAKE

Walking along a narrow cobbled street—more alley than street—behind the cathedral, I am pulled up short by that most evocative aroma: sweet vanilla and pungent coffee. It is a commonplace scent, perhaps the characteristic smell of Kakania; it floods over you every time you walk through the glass doors of one of the great cafés of Vienna or Budapest. Rarely, however, is it as enticing as it is now, flowing through the open door of a small café on this autumn afternoon. My dream-sensation of melancholic wellbeing returns with almost urgent immediacy. I cannot resist walking into the café, even though I've only just had a sandwich at the buffet of the art gallery, having been wearied by endless rows of bulbous women, eviscerated martyrs and dead pheasants.

This is a very modest café. Half-a-dozen small marble-topped tables are ranged along one wall of the narrow room. The wall opposite is occupied almost entirely by a glass-fronted counter, displaying on mirror-backed shelves a variety of cakes, gâteaux and pastries. These have an invitingly homely look, very different from the sculpted extravaganzas offered for the delectation of their patrons by the great cafés of this city. If those establishments emulate the salons of aristocratic mansions—marble halls, Chinese rooms, wintergardens—this small café resembles the drawing rooms of bourgeois apartments seventy or a hundred years ago. The fierce though faded flocked wallpaper certainly looks old enough to be considered antique, while the lace curtain draped over the window at the front has lost most of its pattern through repeated darning. The crystal chandelier hanging from the ceiling has been rendered opaque by decades of steam, coffee fumes and tobacco smoke.

At this early hour of the afternoon, the place is practically deserted, though in an hour or two it will no doubt be jam-packed, as all Viennese cafés, large and small, are crowded at the appropriate and traditional time of five o'clock. Now there are only two customers, *habituées*, it would seem. They are elderly ladies of indeterminate age, for both of them are heavily made up, with obviously dyed hair or perhaps wigs. Their gnarled and knobby fingers suggest that they are very old indeed. The waitress, who is probably the proprietor, stands beside their table, one hand resting on the back of one of those spindly chairs which provide the usual furnishing for such establishments. As a concession to the season, no doubt— though the day is warm, even oppressive—she wears fur-lined felt boots over black stockings.

The three women are deep in conversation. I sit down at one of the tables at a discreet distance from them. The waitress acknowledges my presence and resumes the briefly interrupted discussion. There is, of course, no hurry—everyone in this part of the world seems to have ample time. The rhythms of café-life admit no haste. I have learnt to accept this convention, even though I live in a country where people are usually impatient and often in a hurry. I have not yet learnt, however, the art of staring vacantly into the middle distance, at which Europeans seem so adept as they sit in cafés, hanging on every word spoken at the next table. I know that it is quite proper to listen to these conversations as long as you maintain the fiction that eavesdropping would never enter your mind. Lacking that skill, I now do what I always do in such circumstances: I become wholly absorbed by the pages of my address book.

The ladies' conversation is hard to follow. They speak in the slurred and mellifluous Viennese dialect which almost constitutes a distinct language. All I am able to catch is a few words. They are sufficient, nevertheless, to give some indication of what they are talking about. It seems that they have been occupied by this topic for some time; it may indeed be that I have strayed into an instalment of a long-running, real-life serial. Certainly, what I glean from their rapid and largely incomprehensible conversation seems to have the ingredients of a conventional soap opera. The centre of attention is a young woman, the daughter of one of the customers. Her husband seems to be an out-and-out rotter. I understanding nothing of the long litany of his crimes and outrages, but the exclamations of the lamenting mother's companions clearly indicate their gravity. I begin to wonder whether this is a tale of marital infidelity—but it could just as easily be a matter of money, for I am able to catch the words 'twenty thousand schillings' which form a sort of leitmotif throughout these lamentations. Perhaps it's both, for now I begin to hear sneering references to 'that kind of woman'. Even if feminist theory has penetrated this most conservative society, it has obviously made no impact whatever on these elderly members of the Viennese middle class.

Now, after what has obviously been the proper lapse of time, the waitress excuses herself and shuffles over to take my order. I ask for coffee, knowing that you mustn't immediately specify which of the many kinds of coffee available in these establishments you would prefer. Instead, it is necessary to engage in an elaborate ceremony of negotiations, eliminating one by one the various options—iced or hot, long black or short, with warm milk or cold, with whipped cream or with brandy or rum, or perhaps that peculiar mixture of coffee and drinking chocolate that some people in this part of the world seem to enjoy so much.

Having satisfactorily concluded these negotiations, she now asks me, with a formal smile, what I would like to eat. Nothing, I reply, only coffee. The disappointment on her face is unmistakable. She gestures towards the glass-fronted counter. Can't she tempt me with one of her wonderful cakes or pastries? And, lowering her head, dropping her voice to a whisper, she suggests a piece of her *Sachertorte*. This, she assures me, is *echt*, the real thing, the genuine article, made in the house—I won't find any better in all of Vienna. It seems churlish to refuse. As she disappears behind the counter to draw the coffee and to dispense the cake, I fancy that I detect a look of triumph on the faces of her customers, who had suspended their litany of woes to observe our negotiations. This foreigner will now find out what a real *Sachertorte* tastes like, their expressions seem to suggest.

Every café in Vienna serves a chocolate cake of that name. Yet not many years ago the world's press carried reports of a complicated court battle between the owners of Demel's, the most sumptuous of Vienna's cafés, and the management of the Hotel Sacher over their respective rights to use that most distinguished appellation. Commonsense would have suggested, of course, that the hotel's richly brocaded and outrageously expensive café should have the sole right to that name. The litigation was concerned, however, not with commonsense but with the complicated toing-and-froing many years ago of pastrycooks between café and hotel. Who invented *Sachertorte*? the learned judges were asked to determine. Further, does the inventor retain the right to the name, or does it rest with the place of invention? I cannot remember the outcome of this complex legal process, which amused the international press for a week or two before some other quaint and trivial story came to occupy its attention. Perhaps, it occurs to me, the case is still *sub judice*, pending a determination which could well establish a precedent of great culinary import.

What is perhaps most surprising is the ordinariness of that disputed delicacy. Wherever *Sachertorte* is served in Vienna, it is always the same: a dense chocolate-flavoured cake, with a trickle of jam in the middle, glazed with a thin layer of shiny chocolate. To my possibly unrefined palate, this fabled confection seems indistinguishable from the products of those packets of cake-mix that crowd the shelves of supermarkets. Can this be the cause of such heated litigation? Is it for this that cafés all over the city risk goodness-knows-what fines and penalties as they continue to tempt you with their own *echt* version of the famous confection? Perhaps *Sachertorte* is charged with a mystic significance that we outsiders cannot comprehend. That may be the reason for the fierce rivalry between Demel's and Sacher's, why countless establishments flaunt legal restraints, finding a characteristically Kakanian way around the 'Hands Off!' sign.

The waitress returns with my coffee and a slice of cake. She places these offerings on the marble table-top with ceremonial deference, and, as though this were one of those vast crowded cafés where once in a blue moon even the best of waiters might get into a muddle, announces one black coffee and one piece of *Sachertorte*—with cream, she adds. I lift the fork to taste a morsel. The elderly ladies have stopped talking again, and are looking at me with almost coquettish smiles in anticipation of the sensation am I about to experience. The taste is indeed wonderful, a rich, nutty, chocolate substance, much more moist and aromatic than such cakes usually are. It is, moreover, quite unlike any *Sachertorte* I have ever been served in the cafés of this city.

It would be inaccurate to say, though, that I had never tasted anything like it in my life—as the coy smiles of those ladies seem to be suggesting. This confection seems identical to a cake my mother used to bake, the recipe for which was lost when she died, consisting, I recall, of eggs, chocolate, ground hazelnuts but containing no flour. She always insisted that this was the real *Sachertorte*, a recipe given to her by the Ursuline nuns of Sopron who had educated her. She couldn't remember how those supposedly devout and otherworldly women came by that closely guarded secret—which even the two warring establishments, Sacher's and Demel's, seem to have lost judging by their contemporary offerings—but she maintained, to the end of her life, that the wonderful cake she used to serve in Sydney, in a world seemingly light-years removed from Sopron and Vienna, was the only real, genuine, indeed *echt*, version of the celebrated delicacy. Sitting in this homely café in a sidestreet of the old city, savouring the wonders of what is (I

am persuaded) obviously the genuine article, smiling at the two
ladies who look as if they are about to burst into applause,
I experience a wonderful sense of contentment, even perhaps
of peace.

The afternoon is wearing on. More customers arrive, all
elderly, stocky and short, overweight because they have
indulged no doubt in too much genuine *Sachertorte*. They greet
everyone politely, smiling, sometimes shaking hands, and
dispose themselves at the remaining unoccupied tables. The
place is positively buzzing: the waitress is obviously going to
be rushed off her fur-clad feet for the next hour or two.

MUSIC LOVERS

Busts of Mahler and Richard Strauss stare suspiciously at each
other across the vast marble-clad foyer of the Vienna State
Opera. The Bohemian Jew turned Catholic and the Bavarian
who fashioned several heady, though entirely spurious musical
fantasies of Vienna, were both directors of this great institution. That position is the most glamorous public office in
Vienna. Its incumbent is perhaps even more respected than the
prelate who presides over that other great theatrical establishment, the cathedral, situated at the other end of the Kärtnerstrasse. Between them, cathedral and opera house define the
polarities of Austrian culture as it was espoused by the citizens
of Kakania despite the many differences of race, religion and
nationality. For me, the descendant of those people, it is
unthinkable to visit Vienna without at least looking inside the
Stephansdom and, more importantly still, without going to
the opera.

Cathedral and opera house were both meticulously rebuilt
after the disaster of the Second World War. The hordes of
tourists rolling like a relentless wave from one to the other
marvel at the preservation of anything so ancient as that
venerable house of worship and at the spick-and-span freshness
of the century-old theatre. Yet both are restorations, nostalgic

reconstructions, not so much of the physical buildings that stood on these sites, as of the dreams and aspirations of a sentimentalised past. The present theatre, though somewhat different from the original structure, preserves the social, cultural and even spiritual assumptions on which the regal or ducal opera houses of Europe—from London to Moscow, from Stockholm to Lisbon—were based. In its present incarnation, the Vienna State Opera House is as much an essay in nostalgic kitsch as the tawdry tourist wares displayed in booths and shop windows everywhere in the city. When the reconstruction of the theatre commenced in the early 1950s, certain modifications were made to the design to improve the backstage facilities and to ensure the greater safety of patrons in case of fire. Almost nothing was done, however, to the auditorium or the public spaces of this monument to alter the concept of a theatre as it evolved in the seventeenth century.

The only ticket I could afford for tonight's performance of *La Bohème* is in a side box in the third tier, just below the level of the balcony. Moreover, my place is in the second row of chairs—those in the front row are much more expensive. I find that it is not so much a chair as a high stool with a footrest. It affords an excellent view of the boxes on the other side of the auditorium, but of precious little else. I notice, however, that the front places are still empty, even though it is only five minutes before the performance is supposed to begin. Meanwhile the young woman sitting beside me shows me how to stand on the footrest and thus obtain a partial view of the stage. It becomes clear to me that this can be sustained only in short bursts.

I am obviously suffering from the inconvenience of occupying a lowly place in the elaborate hierarchy of a theatre lovingly rebuilt by an apparently democratic state in imitation of the royal theatres of a vanished world—except that the royal box has been supplanted by a sort of enclosure, capable of containing a clutch of cabinet-ministers and their consorts. When the theatre opened its doors for the first time, it was, of course, the Imperial and Royal Court Opera House, the chief

theatre of the Habsburg realm. Though capable of accommo-
dating some 1500 patrons (most, though by no means all,
seated), and requiring, even at that time, the patronage of a
bourgeois (in many cases Jewish) public, this theatre was
nevertheless conceived as if it were the plaything of an absolute
monarch. The best place in the auditorium, indeed the only
place affording a full view of the stage spectacle, was the royal
box, at the centre of the horseshoe-shaped auditorium, and at
a height mathematically determined to allow its occupants to
savour the full effect of perspective scenery. Every other place
in the house is inferior—the farther seats are removed both
vertically and horizontally from this cultural holy of holies,
the more their inferiority is emphasised by the restricted view
of the stage they offer.

Royal entertainments, practised in most of the European
courts since the seventeenth and eighteenth centuries, set the
pattern for the architecture of European opera theatres. All
were built on a horseshoe-shaped pattern which made the
occupant of the ceremonial box—king, duke or elector—the
centre of a cultural ritual. The lines of perspective converged
on his august person. The entire spectacle—the ceremony of
art—drew its sustenance from his presence. Opera became an
expression of royal power and therefore (at least in the rhetoric
of absolutism) the mirror of a nation's greatness.

Opera houses are placed at the focal points of those cities
of Europe where dreams of political power were expressed as
celebrations of art. The more absolutist the régime, the more
prominence these secular shrines tend to occupy. Garnier's
pompous edifice in Paris dominates a conjunction of boulevards and streets; even now, more than a century after its
construction, one is aware that streets, houses and ways of life
were obliterated to make room for this statement about the
grandeur not so much of France, as of Napoleon III's vision
of a France ruled by an Emperor, the autocrat in a frock-coat.
Paris's new 'democratic' Opéra de la Bastille, erected with
obvious though perhaps unconscious symbolism in the Place
de la Bastille, a reminder of the many varieties of absolutism,

betrays an equal sense of imposition—the destruction of the mean, the decrepit and the familiar to make room for that grandiose emblem of the republic of *gloire*. Only in London, a city always suspicious of its sovereigns' claims of absolutism, is the opera house tucked away in a sidestreet near what was until very recently a vegetable market.

In Vienna the opera house stands at the very centre of the great semicircle of Habsburg boulevards known as the Ring— while, on another plane of urban perspectives, it stands opposite the cathedral, linked to it by the city's, perhaps Europe's, most elegant and expensive thoroughfare. Empire, Mammon and the Church provide the reference points for this temple, which serves more than the worship of Polyhymnia, muse of the sublime hymn. It is the focus of ambitions and dreams of power, a substantial symbol of the reconciliation between absolutism and the people, and an insistence that the state is built not on subjection and servitude but on willing submission. The Father–Emperor, in his royal box at the point where the lines of perspective meet, may thus be confirmed as guardian and protector, the source of both glory and goodness. In one sense, the spectacles of nobility and honour (the conventional subjects of eighteenth-century *opera seria*) were addressed to him and him alone. The sovereign looks upon the magnanimity of Idomeneo or the clemency of Titus, while Idomeneo and Titus, (and countless other pious, magnanimous and clement monarchs) lift their eyes towards him, and discover their likeness there. They see and are observed by their heir and epitome in full face; the lesser beings, ranged around royalty, may catch no more than sidelong glimpses of glory and magnificence. It would not be seemly for such creatures to look upon full majesty. The lowest of the low, at the very back and sides of the highest gallery, may count themselves lucky to be vouchsafed a vision of the laurel crown on the head of Clemency or Magnanimity.

By the time that this theatre was built and the Central European mania for opera entered my family's life-stream, such baroque exultation had long become a thing of the past. The stage was occupied not with spectacles of heroic altruism but with the indiscretions of the boudoir and the treacheries of lust and passion. Yet inside the gilt auditoria of the opera houses of the Habsburg world, the hierarchical stratification of the eighteenth century persisted, though in a significantly altered guise. Although these theatres were still known as royal or imperial during the closing years of the nineteenth century, when my grandmother, the owner of the silver Ferris wheel, went on her honeymoon trip to Vienna, ordered the heavy furniture which forms one of my last material links with that world, and accompanied her new husband to the opera, they depended on the patronage of the metropolitan bourgeoisie to enable them to perform night after night throughout a lengthy season. During the great age of Viennese opera from the 1880s until the years of the Great War, the bourgeoisie, and perhaps even more importantly the Jewish bourgeoisie, provided sustenance for and determined (to a large extent) the aesthetic policies of such institutions.

In Vienna, in Budapest and Prague, and in the other large cities and provincial centres of the realm, going to the opera became a social ritual with its individual and characteristic codes and conventions. To attend the opera was a mark of cultivation, and also an indication of your standing within the complex hierarchy of bourgeois society. Gradations were subtle and seemingly infinite. A clear distinction existed between those who had taken out subscriptions and those who merely bought tickets for individual performances. The part of the house where patrons sat announced their social status to the world at large.

The night of the week for which you had obtained a subscription, the part of the house you occupied—whether in the stalls, or in one of the boxes—were both governed by social position. The choice of night and place was not a matter of money; you did not, as in those vulgar societies of the new world that the citizens of the Habsburg Empire looked on with such scorn, buy the most expensive seat you could afford. That might be done in one of the popular theatres where all was show and flounce, where you could display your often newly found wealth. At the opera it was different, you sat in that part of the house to which your status entitled you. It was not a matter of prohibitions; no-one said, for instance, to my aunt's husband, who was a dealer in horseflesh, that he may not sit in one of the grand boxes of the second tier in Vienna or Budapest, though had he done so he would no doubt have received some very haughty looks from his neighbours. Rather, he knew that he would have been uncomfortable in close proximity to people who were above him on the social scale, who seemed to belong to another order of existence, and with whom he never had any dealings. His clothes, his physique, his manner and his deportment would have indicated that he was not one of 'them'. He was far more comfortable in the third tier, or perhaps in the back of the stalls, among people of his own kind.

Decades after the disappearance of that world and those people, I wonder, as I sit on my uncomfortable stool in a side box on the third level, whether such distinctions still exist, whether time has swept away those elaborate social gradations, just as it seems to have transformed the royal box into a sort of ceremonial corral. And I also wonder what my family would have thought of one of their number occupying such an inconvenient place. Where did they sit when they went to the opera in Vienna? There is no way I shall ever find this out. Yet what little I know of that vanished world suggests that their proper place—like that of the dealer in horseflesh—was probably at the back of the stalls, or perhaps on the third tier, but, of course, in the front and not as far to the side as I am, here in Vienna, fifty or more years later, and in another sense at a distance of light-years away, wondering when the performance will start—it is already half past seven—and whether, with a bit of luck, the front seats are going to remain empty.

As the house lights are beginning to dim, the missing occupants arrive, squeezing through the narrow space between the chairs to occupy their seats at the front of the box. The woman is young and elegantly dressed in a black gown with elaborate silver-thread embroidery. Her long blonde hair falls in a voluptuous curve down one side of her head. I notice that she wears very little jewellery but, like many European women, she uses what seems to me far too much perfume. Her escort is a good deal older. Stocky, bearded, with rimless glasses, he is wearing a black bow tie with a lounge suit. This seems to me a vulgar habit, but I have noticed during various visits to Germany and Austria that the practice is quite common: perhaps it represents a social convention I know nothing about.

They settle into their chairs—blocking entirely what little view of the auditorium there had been—just as the performance begins. I cannot actually see the curtain rising over the jaunty music that begins Puccini's sugary tale of midinettes, bohemians and consumption, but I can hear its swish, and I can hear that the quality of the orchestral sound has changed now that the large space of the stage is no longer covered by the heavy curtain. Standing on the footrest as my neighbour had demonstrated, it is possible to see about half of the stage, perspectives all askew, as the merry artists prance about on Christmas Eve, cold, hungry but indomitable in spirit. Often they disappear into the invisible corners of the stage, and I realise that it is far too uncomfortable to remain perched like a parrot on this footrest.

The couple in the front of the box do not seem to be paying much attention to the performance. She, it is true, has her face turned towards the stage, chin resting on her hand, but I do not think that she is taking any of it in. Her partner is sitting in such a way that the only thing he could be looking at is the brocaded partition that separates our box from its neighbour. He is entirely absorbed by planting light kisses on the lady's free hand and arm, which he is holding in a way I have seen shopkeepers and auctioneers holding for inspection large precious objects—vases, bronze figures—with reverence and with extreme care lest they fall and shatter.

Meanwhile on stage the poet is now alone, having promised presently to join his companions in Christmas merriment. The moment has come for the arrival of Mimi the consumptive seamstress, and it is as well, therefore, to stand on one's perch again to catch a glimpse of her. She arrives with her candle: the singer possesses a fine voice and sings with considerable feeling and expression, but she is heavily built and not in the first flush of youth. It occurs to me that perhaps this is a performance better heard than seen, and I decide therefore to sit down once more, especially as the precariousness of my position could make me lose my balance and topple onto the pair in front.

They, for their part, are totally absorbed by their curious ceremony. She has not moved at all: impassive, abstracted, her face still turned towards the stage yet paying no attention to it, there is no movement of her head, no ripple in her flowing hair that would suggest that her eyes are following the singers as they move around the stage. Her lover, on the other hand, has progressed from her arm to her neck. He is still holding the arm as though it were some precious fragile object, a holy relic perhaps, and this obliges him to rise slightly from his chair so that his lips might touch her nape to place the lightest of kisses on it.

The lovers on stage have departed into the moonlight and the first act has come to an end. Applause and curtain calls. There is, however, no interval. By an imperial edict of the late nineteenth century, still honoured in republican Austria, performances at this theatre must conclude no later than 10.15 pm. For that reason, the four acts of *La Bohème* are performed here with only one interval. Nevertheless a pause is necessary while the elaborate scenery of this thirty-year-old production is changed. The house lights are raised to a dull glow, providing enough illumination for you to consult your programme or the contents of your bag, yet indicating clearly that it is not time to go out for a drink, to smoke or whatever other pursuit is appropriate for intervals during performances of opera. This is a time for polite, murmured conversation over the hammering and thumping coming from behind the curtain. The lovers in front of me do not converse but continue their silent pantomime, a courtship ritual like those of insects that you can see, much magnified, on television. They are wholly absorbed by this ceremony, she in her stillness, he in whatever elaborate code governs the path his lips trace around her hand, arm, neck and shoulder. Dedicated to their ritual, they seem beyond place and time, trapped in a private and exclusive universe.

The second act begins, and I resume bobbing up and down. But I find that my attention is distracted more and more from festivities in the Café Momus. This is one of those plush productions from the sixties, when vast amounts of money could be spent by directors and designers to fill the ample stage of this theatre. Several square miles of Montmartre seem to have been transferred to the Vienna State Opera, at least as far as I can judge from the segment visible from my perch. A milling crowd fills the terraces of streets at the back, while at the front of the stage, outside the café, Mimi and the bohemians, Musetta and her wealthy admirer sing the familiar music. It is all very lively, colourful and not a little hectic. Yet I grow increasingly absorbed by the lovers sitting in front of me. They have now progressed to the next stage of their curious and mysterious ritual. The gentleman's left arm is now twined around the lady's back and, fingers clenched, he is stroking her cheek with his nails, while his right hand is placed firmly under her armpit. He now looks like a musician playing some exotic stringed instrument, except that no sound, no response emerges from it: she is sitting as before, frozen in her posture—a wax dummy, a mannequin, a plaything.

This pantomime continues throughout the performance. They are still at it when I return to the box after the interval; they do not cease for the melancholy parting of the lovers in a bitter, snowy dawn, or for their reunion in the artists' garret where they first met, or for Mimi's pathetic death in the arms of her lover. As before, nothing distracts them from their absorbed ecstasy. And then, at the end of the performance, as the applause begins, and as the singers, including the resurrected Mimi, come to take their bows in front of the plush curtain, the couple rises briskly from their chairs and squeeze their way out as efficiently as they had when coming in.

Throughout the years I have lived in Australia, a land where musical culture, especially opera, is not very firmly entrenched, where audiences often seem unaware of the conventions of good manners and respect to which art claims to be entitled, I have often thought about these older societies where the arts are valued, where audiences are well-informed and well-mannered, where they will not start chatting about their problems with dishwashers or differentials at a moment of sublime beauty. Yet here, in the world that had become an object of veneration and longing throughout an antipodean exile, a quite different possibility now presents itself. Central Europe's much publicised respect for culture, its putting the things of the spirit and the mind well above the claims of Mammon may be one of the lies, one of the instances of dishonesty that have marred the political and social life of this part of the world. Opera as the communal symbol of a coherent society, where all respected their proper places in that order—whether in the stalls, the boxes or the balcony—yet came together under the one roof in celebration of the finer things of life, may have been no more than a ruse, a pretence to mask instincts which, in the final count, had little to do with those reaches of the mind. It is for that reason that the boxes in these theatres used to be furnished with a curtain that could be pulled down, obscuring the occupants in their cosy cubicle, and why in some of these theatres—as in the opera house in Budapest during my childhood—a couch was placed at the back of the box, well out of sight.

It is just after ten o'clock as I leave the theatre. Perhaps, it occurs to me, that imperial edict about the time by which performances must end had little to do with public convenience, with ensuring that patrons may catch the last horse-tram or whatever conveyance was in use at the end of the nineteenth century. It may well have been designed in order to allow ample time for silent lovers to reach the climax of their performance in some overfurnished apartment in the heart of the imperial city.

71

RELIQUARIES

Vienna's churches echo with memories of the opera. Even the interiors of venerable gothic piles underwent thorough modernisation in the seventeenth and eighteenth centuries to transform them into God's theatres. The churches constructed in that epoch are often indistinguishable from the court theatres of the age. The Karlskirche, a basilica dedicated to St Charles Borromeo, 'Reliever of the Plague,' the masterpiece of Fischer von Erlach, the virtuoso of the Austrian baroque, reveals its essentially theatrical design from the moment you set foot inside the porch. It is a miniature foyer—your eyes scan its wall and corners in search of the cloakroom and buffet. The church itself is embellished with every variety of coloured, veined and patterned marble. The high altar is displayed behind an ample proscenium arch, its curtain raised to reveal a stunning spectacle of marble, gold and bronze. The organ gallery, protected by an elaborately carved balustrade, occupies the position of a royal box. The architect's flamboyant manipulation of space, light, colour and texture contrives to suggest tiers of galleries and boxes rising in a semicircle around the altar.

The various strands that constitute the dreams and fantasies of this world come together more clearly in this place than anywhere else in the former imperial capital. Here distinctions between vulgarity and refinement, between the secular and the spiritual, between substance and shadow all vanish. A temple dedicated to the worship of an all-powerful Creator, before whom all human vanity and ingenuity must be humbled, is an extravagant display of the human arts of construction, decoration and illusion. It is a baroque Tower of Babel, a challenge to the Almighty to excel, in his own theatre of nature, the ingenuity and brilliance of the Habsburgs' architects, painters, sculptors and masons. The Karlskirche, like the other flamboyant instances of the South German baroque, seems more a monument to human megalomania than an expression of humility and adoration.

Religion and even spirituality in this world have little to do with the mysterious bonds of meditation and prayer that bind creature and Creator. There is not even the incense-heavy mystery of the churches of the eastern rite, enamelled saints and prophets glowing darkly in a vague, indistinct sea of burnished gold. Here everything is light, pomp and spectacle. The emphasis is always on communal celebration, not on private worship. God and the Emperor seem to have been on equal footing here, notwithstanding the pieties of humility God's anointed might have declared while kneeling before the shrine of the Invincible. Church and state merge within the operatic interiors of these buildings just as cathedral, palace and opera house define the cardinal points of the imperial capital.

In another, though cognate, sense these shrines of regal might and magnificence are also treasuries and armouries, guarding securely the wealth and the armaments to ensure that this realm, its monarchs and its people may continue to enjoy their unique privilege as those most favoured by God. No doubt in some ecclesiastical office somewhere in this city there must be a register listing the holy and venerable relics cocooned in their reliquaries of gold, crystal, precious gems and the rarest of marbles. How many splinters of the True Cross or how many thorns of the Passion are listed in that register? Does anyone have an accurate count of saints' bones, nail clippings, hair, bits of parchment-like skin, dried organs and viscera? Is there a fragment here of the swaddling bands in which the immaculately conceived Virgin wrapped her infant son, the Incarnate God? Is a piece of the scourge with which he was flayed after his betrayal by the Jews, preserved in an imperial or episcopal chapel? How many ampoules of his most precious blood lie hidden in chests and tabernacles?

These relics, objects of worship and veneration, provide guarantees of salvation or at least of remission. The holy places of Vienna are a pharmacopoeia for the next world, a spiritual pharmacy containing the best and most costly drugs to ensure immunity against perpetual damnation, a powerhouse of weapons with which to fight sin and the devil. These engines may be turned, nevertheless, against God too. So much of his power is concentrated in this realm, and so many of his lieutenants too (albeit in bits and pieces) that their possessor might well attempt to vie with the all-powerful, denuded as his treasury is of its potency.

The iconography of baroque absolutism (in Austria as much as in the rest of Europe) was obsessed with apotheosis. On the ceilings and in the domes of civic halls, rooms of state and audience chambers in this city, the Franzes and the Josefs, the Ferdinands and the Rudolfs are depicted borne aloft in glory, their ceremonial robes billowing in the breeze, flights of angels guiding them through the swelling clouds. The deification of kings and emperors may have been more than a poetic fancy, a metaphor for their terrestrial greatness. Perhaps they believed that through the possession of so many of God's treasures, and because of the pomp, pride and circumstances of the temples they had constructed—temples of art and power as much as temples of religion—they could challenge God and displace him on his throne.

Berggasse is a thoroughfare dedicated to a shrine for darker dreams. There is nothing magnificent, imperial or even imposing about this drab street of solidly dull blocks of apartments and shops catering for the mundane necessities of everyday life—a flyblown grocery, a couple of bootmakers, a down-at-heel café or two. The Vienna of pomp and circumstance seems light-years, not merely hundreds of metres, away.

It is not difficult to imagine ghosts wandering towards the tightly-barred entrance of Number 19, where a small brass plaque advertises the opening hours of the Freud Museum. It is many years since those creatures of fable—Dora and the Wolf-Man—sought admission to the sanctum of cigar-smoke, priapic figurines and Oriental carpets. The shrine is now empty, its god or oracle fled long ago. What you may admire for the modest entrance fee of a few Austrian schillings is as much a dim echo of the past as the remnants of Mycenae or the bare ruined choirs of the English countryside. The museum is a reconstruction—as is so much else in this city—an attempt to pretend that time has not passed and is, in a sense, stationary. The memorialisation of Freud is as irrelevant to the Vienna of today as the careful preservation of a pompous palais, an exuberant church interior, or those relics slumbering in their costly repositories. When, as an act of almost incredible generosity, the Nazi masters of the city exiled its octogenarian citizen, even allowing him to take with him his tools of trade and household gods—instead of reserving him for the inevitable fate of his kind—it pulled down the shutters over a heritage it could never recover.

Freud is in all probability our most accurate guide to Vienna at the greatest moment of its cultural history. That moment did not have the grandeur or bombast of the mighty imperial dream. It did not conquer nations with the sword or preside in strutting arrogance over a motley array of subject peoples. Rather it had the greatness and allure of decay, of a world in disarray and on the brink of disintegration. Freud thought that he had discovered the universal secrets of human behaviour, the wellsprings of what had previously been called the soul. Yet what he chronicled in his painstaking and obsessive studies of bourgeois neurotics and paranoiacs was the malaise of an age and of this particular world, rather than the secrets of all humanity. The pantheon of obsessions, repressions and neuroses he uncovered and interpreted—the tormented fantasies of those who shuffled along the cobblestones of Berggasse—represent the glory of that world, an imaginativeness which was capable of producing images that have fascinated the modern world, and have provided raw material for great writers as much as for amateur psychiatrists.

Freud liberated Mitteleuropa to itself. He allowed it to celebrate its most characteristic preoccupations as valuable cultural assets. Before Freud, because of the aristocratic and imperial insistence that neurosis, obsession and indulgence in erotic fantasy were bad form, the bourgeoisie of this world had to sweep its most persistent preoccupations under the cultural carpet. You entertained fantasies of killing your father or sleeping with your mother in the silent confessional of the bedroom. Then came Freud who allowed such sinful thoughts and forbidden desires a public face. He made them respectable: the innermost life of the Viennese middle classes, (their most cherished possession, truth to tell) could henceforth be displayed in the terms of their own culture—which those people always treated with the utmost respect. The fantasies of the bedroom and the bathroom—like Proust's little secret chamber at Combray—now had the cachet of respectability: they could be discussed in terms of Oedipus and Hamlet, Leonardo and Michelangelo. The characteristic self-absorption of this world—reflected perhaps by the curious design of Germanic lavatory-pans noted many years ago by Erica Jong in *Fear of Flying*—could form the basis of public concern and high art. Mahler's symphonies are inconceivable in a world innocent of Freud; without that spirit Mahler would have become no more than a bombastic Smetana. The atmosphere of Freudian Vienna was the licence which allowed Mahler to indulge in the vulgarity, neurosis, sugary sentimentality and endless repetition of often childish formulae and devices, and to transform them into sublime art.

Freud believed to the end of his life that his work was scientific and therapeutic. Its real value and object, however, were much more cultural and artistic. It gave shape and definition to the obsessions of this world—the tightly shuttered, overheated salons and bedchambers of bourgeois Vienna and of the domains of the Habsburg world—making its petty jealousies, snobberies and rivalries seem significant and momentous. A shabby domestic squabble could assume the proportions of an epic tale; an adolescent's clumsy explorations of sexuality could be seen as replicating the Fall of Man. What the old culture of patrician and aristocratic Vienna considered beneath contempt, much preferring the glories of the battlefield and the intrigues of the boudoir, became the preoccupations which its practitioners and consumers considered high art. Each time a Viennese or Hungarian matron experienced the anguish of jealousy provoked by the antics of an errant husband—

which was the case with my grandmother—she could comfort herself that she was reliving the greatest of mythic events evident both in the tales of antiquity and in the latest best-selling novel on the shelves of fashionable booksellers.

That dream spread beyond the confines of Vienna and of the Habsburg world. No figure of the late nineteenth century or of the early twentieth provided novelists, playwrights, poets, film-makers, musicians and painters with as much material as Freud. With the passing of time he himself became the subject matter of fictions as highly-coloured as the fantasies of his own patients. The novels in which he appears as a character form an impressive list in English alone. He has even crossed the equator, together with the other cultural baggage of the old world that arrived at various times on the shores of the antipodes. Brian Castro's *Double-Wolf* manages to tell a tale in which the seedy guesthouses, cafés and second-hand book-shops of Katoomba rub shoulders with the stuffy consulting room of Berggasse 19.

For the Vienna of 1991 Freud is no more a real presence than he is for the Australia of the time. Though this is the site of the beginning of those mysteries that have spread to most corners of the globe, its significance and potency are no more striking or glamorous than those of other deserted shrines. The rooms are largely empty. A discreet notice advises the pilgrim that Freud's possessions, the arcana of his ministry, the relics of the new religion, are preserved in Hampstead, that place of Egyptian exile from the homeland. Instead of the actual and presumably potent cult-objects we are greeted with a series of photographs, reproductions of letters, testimonials, a few books and pamphlets and a number of lesser holy objects—pens, inkwells, spectacles, cigar-cases. But the essential items of the mystery, the consulting couch, the statuettes, are elsewhere: they fled with their oracle. The strange emptiness of the Freud Museum in this dour thoroughfare is an eloquent reminder of the emptiness of the city itself. It too is an attempt to reconstruct a lost past. It too has to be content with the reproduction in place of the original.

Having lost the rich stream of neurosis, obsession and myth-

77

making that primed the pump of its culture—the painters, poets, musicians and writers of the *fin-de-siècle*—Vienna has sunk into the desuetude of imitation, reproduction, nostalgia and kitsch. It is no longer that hothouse where a basically Jewish bourgeois culture ran into headlong conflict with the older values of Catholic Austria. The spunk has gone from this world, leaving behind merely pale imitations of its former glories.

DEFENCE OF THE REALM

One of my last days in Vienna brings me back to the opera, for the five hours of Wagner's *Lohengrin*. The experience of my earlier visit led to a decision of considerable gravity. Yesterday I joined once more the queue that forms on most days at the box office and exchanged my seat in the third tier for one in the stalls. The expense is probably unjustifiable, but (I comfort myself) five hours is a long time and, moreover, the opera is to be performed by those stellar names that you usually encounter only on record labels. Those expectations are frustrated as soon as I look at the ominous slip of paper inside the programme: the world-famous conductor and two of the principals are indisposed; they are to be replaced by three no doubt excellent performers whose names are, nevertheless, completely unfamiliar to me. I wonder what terrible affliction has visited this august establishment, and whether the change of cast is at all connected with the world-famous conductor's spectacular row with the management—which has even attracted the attention of the arts columnists in distant Australia.

Wagner described *Lohengrin*, probably his most popular work, as a 'Romantic Opera'. Dyed-in-the-wool Wagnerians usually sneer at this relatively immature opera, but for most audiences, such as the well-dressed Viennese gathering here on this late afternoon in autumn, it represents the most accessible of the composer's demanding music—even though it goes on hour after hour after hour. Vienna did not take readily to

Wagner's overblown music-dramas and he, in turn, poured all the scorn of his contempt on this frivolous public. He smarted from their rejection of *Tristan and Isolde*, that 'undemanding' love story he had written to woo their patronage. Budapest, a decidedly provincial town during the last quarter of the nineteenth century, developed Wagner-mania earlier than this much more sophisticated and musically cultivated city.

Yet Vienna also succumbed to the sinister magic of those outrageous essays in self-aggrandisement, dangerously addictive drugs which, once tasted, can never be abandoned. As the first, high notes of the prelude begin sounding on the violins, I, only a halfhearted Wagnerite, and one more conscious of the tedium of *Lohengrin* than of its magic, find myself entranced by this absurd tale of maligned maidens, knights of the grail, dark enchantments and miraculous restorations. As the wonderful sonorities rising from the orchestra pit fill the auditorium—this is after all arguably the world's finest orchestra—I become a willing accomplice in an act of artistic vandalism. I know that these bombastic music dramas—among which *Lohengrin* may indeed be the most refined or at any event the least barbaric—represent a perversion of all that music, culture and civilisation should strive to achieve.

The cult of Wagner emerged in step with the rise of Fascism, National Socialism and the other ultranationalist totalitarian movements that swept over much of Europe. The spirit of *das Volk*—the people, the tribe—could be heard pulsing through the Master's music. This was not the carefully crafted, elegant music of patrician culture. It had nothing to do with the classical virtues of restraint, moderation and economy of means. Instead it unleashed demons lurking within the listeners' veins. It did not appeal to the intellect or even to the sensibility, but principally to the emotions—raw, unmediated, residing not in the individual consciousness but in the consciousness of the tribe.

Wagner broke with the conventions of opera both spiritually and physically. The Festival Theatre at Bayreuth, built to his own specifications and embodying his ideals, has none of the social gradations of theatres like this one in Vienna. Its rows of seats rise without interruption from the first row to the last: there is no gallery, no boxes, apart from a couple of discreetly placed private recesses which were reserved for his family in the original design. The justification for this in the rhetoric of nineteenth-century cultural politics was the example of ancient Greece, where the design of the great amphitheatres— at Epidauros, Delphi and in many other places throughout the peninsula—did not establish social distinctions between various groups within the audience by erecting physical barriers. Gone too were the elaborate decorations in gold, marble, plush and paint that contrived to turn many of the opera theatres of the 'old' Europe into jewelled cases to display the audience as much as the spectacle on stage.

Bayreuth may have been intended as a reproduction among the green Franconian hills of the virtues of the Attic world. It is, for all that, a setting for shamanistic rituals. The mature music dramas (even *Lohengrin*) deliberately and consciously set out to subject their audiences to trials calling upon all their physical (and also spiritual) resources. You have to give up your whole being to *The Ring* and *Parsifal*. You cannot squeeze in a performance between dinner and seduction: *Parsifal* keeps you captive in the theatre for six or six and a half hours; even *Rhinegold*, the shortest of the tetralogy of music dramas comprising *The Ring*, requires almost three hours to perform, and there is no break for an interval in that score. Wagner demanded— and obtains from enthusiasts—the sacrifices of the devout.

Such sacrifices and discomfort (the seats at Bayreuth are not padded) are appropriate to acts of religious mystery and worship. The audience willingly subjects itself to these hardships because it is no longer composed of individuals, each with his own consciousness of the demands made upon him, but of a group, an entity, a Gestalt perhaps, totally absorbed by the revelation it is privileged to witness. The music dramas are static and statuesque. Very little 'happens'; there are usually only one or two personages on the vast, cavernous stage. They are gods, mythological beings, above and beyond ordinary emotions and preoccupations, obsessed and tormented by grand, abstract concepts—Fate, Godhead, Duty and Love. Their lengthy monologues and slow-moving vocal disputes deliberately shun movement and vivacity. The music itself achieves its greatest effects through lack of variety. The endlessly recurring thematic units (the notorious leitmotif) the deliberate rhythms, the emphasis not so much on melody as on massive blocks of sonority all contribute to this replacement of entertainment (the disgraceful frivolity of opera, according to Wagner) by ritual. The audience at Bayreuth (as in other theatres where the Wagner cult came to flourish) are too disciplined to sway and chant in shamanistic ecstasy; there is, nevertheless, something of the possessed in their demeanour as they sit immobile on their hard wooden seats for two-hour stretches at a time in a darkened theatre.

Wagner's sounds and the images he conjured, those transparent poetic and theatrical emblems, became the holy relics of that nationalist movement which emerged in the beer halls of Munich at the same time as his works discovered those enthusiastic audiences which had largely eluded him for most of his creative life. Its thumping rhythms were heard on the streets of Munich, Berlin and Vienna as full-throated youths yelled for the cleansing of decadent and foreign pollution from the holy German realm. The bombastic praise of German art as the citizens of Nuremberg gather in the festival meadow at the end of *The Mastersingers* was heard again at the vast rallies conducted in that most German of all cities. Wagner accompanied the march of intoxicated hordes, heeding the call of the race deep in their pulse, sweeping aside the bourgeois and therefore decadent virtues of compassion, tolerance and magnanimity to defend the realm of purity. He liberated ancient forces that had lain dormant in the blood of the German race, which had been shamefully subjected to the domination of decadence from the west—the frivolous French—and from the east: the Jews, gypsies, Slavs and other denizens of the Balkan peninsula, the threat Oswald Spengler had seen flooding over the great Central European site of civilisation.

Many answered that call to arms which spread from Bayreuth, the holiest of shrines in this new religion, to the other opera houses of this world. From those places intellectuals, pundits, the politically ambitious and dedicated spread the gospel to those millions of people who did not usually venture into theatres and opera houses. A cultural phenomenon became political; it accompanied, indeed it was probably instrumental in generating, that terrible cleansing of the German lands, the holy realm of the *Volk* half a century ago, the effects of which still echo in this world. For that reason many people—and not merely Jews—still refuse to attend performances of the Wagner operas. Until very recently not a note of his music was heard in Israel.

That is one account of the Wagner cult, a convenient historical fable, an easy division into 'them' and 'us', an occasion for expressing a sense of cultural superiority: why subject yourself to the bombast, vulgarity and tedium when there is Bach and Mozart? The other is more embarrassing, easily swept under the carpet, yet—especially in this theatre in Vienna—one that cannot be ignored. Wagner's followers were by no means exclusively racial and political ideologues, men and women devoted to their holy cleansing mission, whose belief and dedication were reasserted each time they participated in the rites of the Master. Such people were, in all probability, a small (though by no means uninfluential) minority. In all likelihood there were not enough of them to fill the theatre at Bayreuth for the four weeks of the festival. Wagner attracted, from the closing decades of the nineteenth century until almost the middle of the twentieth, a bourgeois public who could not in many cases deliver guarantees of Teutonic or Aryan purity. The French, still smarting from their recent defeat by the Prussians, began flocking to Bayreuth as soon as the theatre opened in 1876. During the following decades the urban middle classes of Central Europe, many of them Jews, or at least people who would find themselves Jewish by virtue of the Nuremberg Racial Laws, flocked to theatres in order to be embraced by the gorgeous sonorities and mythic abstractions of Wagner's music dramas.

They attended performances of these works—which were to become the psalms and anthems justifying their destruction—in their own jewelled, marble-encrusted theatres. Few if any made the pilgrimage to Bayreuth. My father—a more ardent Wagnerite than I am—made that journey, from Sydney, only in the last months of his life. When he returned he said that he much preferred the 'old way' of performing his favourite operas. The 'old way', as practised here in this theatre, in Budapest, and in the Leipzig and Dresden of his student days in the 1920s, was an uneasy but seductive marriage of the essential superficiality and frivolity of the opera house—its flounce, its display, its rigid social hierarchies—and the deeply subversive intent of those works to which that public flocked with such enthusiasm. The citizens of Budapest and Vienna willingly disrupted the normal patterns of their lives to arrive at the theatre in the afternoon (as I have done today), foregoing the ceremony of the visit to the café, the evening meal, all the rituals of their middle-class existence, to submit themselves to the enchantment of the composer many of them referred to as the Master. During the intervals they hurried to the elegant buffets to sustain themselves with delicate sandwiches of caviar, salami, and mayonnaise. They would have scorned the sausages consumed in the long intervals of Bayreuth by the true devotees as outward and visible signs of their membership of the tribe.

This afternoon, in this theatre where members of my family used to fall under the sway of these insinuating, infuriating and yet irresistible conjuring tricks, I am more aware than ever of the anomaly of their willing complicity. Even *Lohengrin*, perhaps the least ideological of Wagner's works, should have been sufficient to fill them with alarm and apprehension. They should have realised that their caste-ridden rituals of bourgeois life were directly challenged even by this 'romantic opera', a heady world of magic and enchantment.

Lohengrin begins in Brabant, on the banks of the Scheldt— Wagner's plot is drawn (remotely) from a medieval chivalric romance. Henry the Fowler, defender of the realm, is rallying the warriors of Brabant to join him in opposing the Hungarians, that barbaric race from the east, who are threatening these lands, the centre and focus of Christendom. I wonder whether those people—my father, his relatives, the inhabitants of that world—ever listened to these words. Did they pay attention to King Henry's call-to-arms, or was this only a lot of noise to them, a preparation for the heart-rending romance that, for them at least, was the justification for their five hours of discomfort?

The well-dressed audience around me doesn't seem too interested either. They are sitting politely, attention fixed on the huge expanse of the stage where, in a curious steely-blue twilight, the ranks of warriors loudly proclaim their loyalty to King Henry, Christendom and virtue. I wonder too whether any erotic adventures in the darkened boxes accompany this rousing chorus. Now a menacing figure, accompanied by a woman of obviously evil intent, begins to level accusations at the heroine: she has murdered her brother, he says, in order to seize for herself the duchy of Brabant. At this moment there is a notable change in the attention of the people around me, of the whole audience it seems. They are much more alert, concentrating on the soprano who now comes forward, to the accompaniment of sweetly chaste sounds from the orchestra. Every breath in the house seems to be held as the singer begins her account of a dream in which a knight clad in silver came to rescue her from her predicament.

These people obviously know *Lohengrin* very well, and they know too that this is the moment at which the singer—whoever she is—is to embark on the great trial of her career, having stepped in to fill the role vacated by the world-famous exponent of the part. For them, it occurs to me, this is just another opera, an absurd fantasy, an occasion for fine singing. I can sense their attention waxing and waning throughout the long performance. When the hero arrives in his swan-drawn boat—indeed to rescue the maiden—they are obviously impressed by the skill of this celebrated tenor who is not (thank goodness) indisposed. They are less attentive at the beginning of the second act, where the sinister baritone and his full-voiced wife plot the maiden's downfall by persuading her to break her rescuer's prohibition that she must never ask him his name. Everyone seems to enjoy the wedding march (*that* wedding march) in the last act, and by the time of the final scene, when the people of Brabant are once more gathered on the banks of the Scheldt so that the grieving Lohengrin might bid farewell to his errant wife—she had, after all, asked him his name— many seem to be looking forward to the end of the performance. No-one appears to be much interested in King Henry's lament that the knight will not be joining him in the crusade against the Hungarian barbarians.

The people gathered here this evening, remnants of Kakania, might just be redeemed by their frivolity. As this long performance draws to its close it occurs to me that no-one— either on stage or in the audience—is taking any of this very seriously. The production is, to say the least, bland. The design and the costumes are atmospheric and picturesque. The director seems to have been content with marshalling his large forces— principals, supporting cast, chorus and extras—on and off the stage with as little fuss as possible. There is no interpretation evident, not much emphasis on the text except to sustain the fairly thin narrative strand. It is all faintly old-fashioned, justifying itself by the gorgeous sound emerging from the stage and the pit, as may well be inevitable in a theatre where you have practically no view of the stage from many of the seats.

This blandness, the refusal to take *Lohengrin* as anything but a romantic fable with some marvellous music, may imply that the old ghosts, the fire in the blood, are things of the past. Perhaps we are lucky enough to be living in a time that has gone beyond those outrages to which the citizens of this city assented as enthusiastically as their German brothers and sisters. This *Lohengrin* is a pretty, decorative affair, as befits a theatrical performance in a theme park. It may therefore be that the irritating and in many ways risible life of that theme park, which has been increasingly grating on me during my days here, is a way of neutering its inhabitants, ensuring that they will never again rise to the call of the demons of the tribe.

That proves to be a cheering thought. Yet no sooner has this possibility occurred to me than I realise how mistaken it is. It may be very comforting to think of Vienna, and of those parts of Kakania that came under its spell, as the reservoir of the old aristocratic values which tried—vainly as it turned out—to stem the tide of demagoguery. It has been said often enough that Austrian antisemitism was fundamentally social, not political or malevolent. The princes of the blood might have scorned an eminent family like the Wittgensteins because Jewish blood coursed through their veins, but they would never, the legend insists, have sought their destruction. That may have been true of the rulers of this realm—though an innate scepticism makes me doubt that assertion. It was patently untrue of those urban mobs who howled for the final solution propounded by the Führer, who was nurtured in the pleasant city of Linz. The ugliness of the twentieth century emerged as much out of this Austrian world as it did out of the German soul and blood—and there was, moreover, the spring of 1938 when the citizens of this country eagerly embraced unification with the Reich.

Thinking harder about my family's seemingly innocent infatuation with Wagner's music (especially *The Ring*, my father's favourite) than I ever have in my life, the possibility seems inescapable that these people were to a large extent accomplices to their own destruction. Their blood may have also been stirred by these heady images of a primitive life, one far removed from the stuffy proprieties of their well-uphol-stered world. They too may have yearned for the cleansing and the new beginning, and for the twilight of their own gods. Perhaps they imagined that they had become so assimilated into the 'Aryan' world of Central Europe that they did not recognise themselves as the enemy—those threatening forces swarming in the east. I am ashamed to remember, at this time of pre-paration, of transitions, when I am preoccupied by the prospect of travelling to Hungary in a day or two, that my family regarded with utter contempt those barbaric people, especially

Orthodox Jews with their long sidelocks, who lived to the east of their tight little world.

Perhaps my father, the great Wagner enthusiast, escaped my grandmother's cluttered apartment, with its tasteful furniture, exquisite bibelots (except for that vulgar Ferris wheel), the ceremonies of bourgeois life, to liberate himself to the irrational, the antithesis of that cosy world, as he succumbed to the magic of *The Ring*, of *Tristan and Isolde* and even *Lohengrin*. Like so many people in that world he may have persuaded himself that he was a fully integrated citizen of what was still—despite the rearrangement of the political deckchairs at Versailles—old Kakania, where rivalries and differences were contained in an harmonious realm, where the various ethnic, political and religious forces politely agreed to respect each other's differences. He did not realise, it seems to me, that those enthralling music dramas challenged his very right to exist, let alone his right to spend many nights in these theatres as he fell under the sway of the Master's magic. He believed in all sincerity, perhaps even without giving it a conscious thought, that the world which sustained and protected him was an orderly bringing together of all levels of society, without in the least transgressing boundaries and divisions as in the great opera houses of Kakania where stalls and gallery, boxes and standing places were decorously ranged around the royal box, the node and centre as well as the guarantee of that life.

A SEASON IN HELL

She is sitting on a low wooden bench, arms spread out to support her as she leans back, looking at the infernal triptych before her. This picture gallery tucked into a corner of the Academy of Fine Arts contains the usual collection of respectable masterpieces—melancholy landscapes, a regulation Madonna with Child or two, several still lifes with fruit, loaves of bread and slaughtered hares—appropriate paintings for the young ladies and gentlemen studying in this imperial academy

87

to admire and emulate. One exhibit is, however, entirely out
of key with all this propriety: it speaks of another world, a
terrible and obscene vision of suffering and torture. It is a large
triptych of the Last Judgement, almost certainly the work of
Hieronymus Bosch.

The gallery is all but deserted. The woman on the low bench
is the only occupant of the room dominated by Bosch's sadistic
fantasia. From the doorway, as I am struck by my first
encounter with that hideously compelling vision, I become
aware of her immobility. She is dressed in the autumn uniform
of the Viennese middle classes, a well-cut 'English' raincoat,
a silk scarf around her neck, an expensive-looking skin handbag
placed on the bench beside her. She sits there, enthralled it
seems by that terrible image, immobile, absorbed, apparently
unaware that there is anyone else in this dusty room with
creaking floorboards. I approach the painting, and so catch
sight of her face, her colouring and the cast of her features—
all of these suggest that this lady is one of the few Jews of
Vienna.

Europe's churches and galleries are filled with depictions of
the Last Judgement. Most are grandiose affairs: important
billows of smoke and flame; millions of the damned swarming obediently to the imposing portals of hell; Christ and his
angels seated in their full judicial dignity. Such a judgement
is delivered in no petty court; this is the ultimate tribunal—
malefactors might well feel some pride in having come under
its jurisdiction. Those canvases and frescoes seem to be saying:
if you have to be condemned, this is a good way to go. Bosch
knew otherwise. There is no glamour in death, cruelty and
torture, only obscenity. His Last Judgement is a carnival of
horror, a sadistic Disneyland filled with squawking imps and
with devils relishing the most ingeniously homely tortures.

At the top of the central panel Christ and his kneeling
apostles, Mary, Joseph and God the Father look down on the
scene of torture below them. They are indifferent, isolated and
remote, surrounded by a sunny glow of light. The damned and
the tortured, their tormentors and executioners are equally

oblivious of the majesty revealed above them: they are wholly absorbed in their task of killing, maiming, suffering, screaming and dying. A huge nicked knife, wielded by toad-like and ape-faced monsters is bearing down on a group of naked wretches writhing on the ground. Above them three of their comrades are impaled on the bare branches of a tree—one, a soldier still wearing his helmet, is attached by a branch driven through his testicles. In the background another is impaled on a long drill, a thin shaft protrudes from his anus. Below him a huge metal-plated war-machine, a sixteenth-century Sherman tank, advances with a sharply-pointed serrated knife protruding like a metal phallus. The head of a sinner is just visible below the rim of a barrel filled with an evil-looking toad-infested liquid. A reptilian devil, clutching at the knife that has been driven through its neck, breathes fire and smoke at the almost submerged wretch.

Seated in front of a small fire of twigs, a web-footed she-devil with a headcloth, her face indistinguishable from Tenniel's Red Queen's, is frying a sinner in a large skillet. Two eggs lie on the ground beside her—her own offspring, or ingredients for an *omelette au pécheur*. Below her a duck-billed creature, a platypus with human legs, is carrying a malefactor trussed on a spit. On a stony ledge a group of blacksmith-devils are nailing horseshoes to the feet of the condemned, hammering them on anvils and tempering them in a furnace. Beside them, through a fissure in a rocky outcrop, a drawbridge is being lowered. Toad-faced devils are about to push a naked figure down the sharply inclined plank towards a row of spikes. Another figure is already impaled on the spiked wheel placed beneath this horrible slippery-dip.

Dominating the panel, behind a sinner fastened to a gigantic lance, an arrow piercing him through his navel, two large machines serve as instruments of mass-torture. Here is the triumph of technology, a celebration of the efficiency of mechanised torment. One of them resembles a diving-bell. The wretch trapped behind an oval lattice of steel works a spiked treadmill with bare feet. Two armed fiends are holding another

naked sinner by his legs over the rim of a metal bowl placed
on top of the machine. His task is to pull on the heavy chain
tied to the neck of the sufferer on the treadmill, thus forcing
him to continue with his labours. Behind this contraption two
of the condemned are working a spiked disc—one seems more
fortunate than his companion: he wears heavy, knee-high
boots. The spiked disc is attached by gears to a heavy millstone.
Arms and legs of about-to-be-pulverised wretches are in the
process of being dragged under it.

In the background, receding towards the horizon, towards
the shining sky where an indifferent deity looks upon this scene
of retribution, more mundane images of torment are faintly
visible where the glow of volcanic fires illuminates images of
hanging, drawing and quartering, of garrotting and eviscer-
ation, of beheading and breaking on the wheel, of being shot
to death with arrows. On the margin of the earth, where its
blackness meets eternal light, the horrors are no longer visible,
being represented by sinister blobs and lines as the strange
images of death depicted on the panel recede into infinity.

Such a carnival of torture requires a large, busy workforce
to ensure its efficient operation—just as the theme park of
Vienna needs all those strollers, café-patrons, spruikers and
windowshoppers, dogs and blue-uniformed attendants (like
those guarding this gallery) to keep the show on the road day
after day, year after year. The worker-devils in this painting
come in all shapes and sizes—skeletons, monkeys with the
heads of toads, a pot on legs, dragons and lizards with human
hands, a hooded head without trunk or limbs, propelled on
two large, well-shaped feet. Another wearing a bulbous hat
has the face of a sage elder; he is supported on two frogs' legs
growing out of his ears. Some are busy plying their trade, even
though many should be writhing in agony, having had spears
and knives stuck through their bodies. Others are hurrying
towards their next task, or perhaps they are on their way to
clock off—as with the egg-monster, lizard head visible through
a crack in the shell, two muscular booted legs in hose also
breaking through, an arrow piercing the carapace. A cross

between a chicken and a hippopotamus is leading her young past the torment and the carnage. A long-billed demon is labouring on crutches, bearing on his back an unfortunate stuffed into a wicker basket. On the roof of the brothel an ape-fiend strums on a lute held over his head, worn like a piece of fashionable headgear.

One of the side panels, placed on the left hand of the indifferent Christ, shows us hell itself. Here the tormented are crowded into narrow spaces, the fiends are not merely the toy-figures of the central panel—though there are many of those present—but also huge creatures, menacing heads looming over the carnage. Near the entrance to hell, an archway decorated with a frieze of frogs, a turbaned figure with horn-rimmed spectacles—inspector or scientific researcher—observes the busy traffic. A huge, kneeling demon has all manner of creatures crawling over his body.

Above the entrance to hell, supported by its massive masonry, a pavilion is filled with a sea of naked, writhing humanity. A curious pot or lantern on top of this tent-like structure has flames and smoke spewing from arched vents. A demon kneeling on this furnace has a long trumpet sticking out of his backside on which he plays, no doubt, merry farting tunes. The pavilion, scholars of Bosch's iconography tell us, is a bath-house. This is a place of torment for adulterers, fornicators, dealers in flesh. Bath-houses in Bosch's time were, like modern massage parlours, places where sexual practices and fantasies had free rein. The sinners boiling in this infernal bath-pavilion are accompanied by a female devil wearing the characteristic headdress of prostitutes, by musicians, by devil-bawds and demon-procurers.

For me, and I suspect for the raincoat-clad woman who is still sitting on the low bench, transfixed by this vividly coloured, comic-strip vision of hell, that bath-pavilion suggests another, though more recent, infernal iconography. Most of the sufferers, the tormented humanity depicted in this obscene vision, have the same expression. The creature being fried by the Red Queen in her pan, the one suspended by his testicles, the face floating in the barrel of toads, the operators of the treadmill and the crowd jammed into this pavilion are all frail, naked and expressionless. They seem beyond pain, beyond the cry of protest, beyond offering any resistance. Few of the crowd flowing towards the pavilion, driven by demon-guards, seem to be trying to escape in a futile attempt to avoid the inevitable. Only the woman standing at the front of the boiling bath, her hands covering her eyes, mouth torn with a scream, seems capable still of registering outrage and fear. The rest are passive, resigned, or at best are content to extend their arms in supplication.

Eyewitnesses have remarked on the docile way the con-demned shuffled to the shower blocks of the Nazi extermin-ation camps, leaving their clothes in neat piles in the designated places before entering the narrow chambers. They knew where they were going. Few believed the anodyne fiction that the filth and grime of their long journey in cattle-trucks was about to be washed off by cleansing water before they embarked on their new life of work and freedom. Yet few raised any protest, only one or two tore at their guards or battered on the heavy iron doors as they were bolted shut on those masses of writhing flesh. Neither desperation nor heroic defiance characterised the large majority of people who had been tormented, humiliated and murdered in the most savage ways in those camps or elsewhere throughout the long and continuing history of human cruelty.

Bosch's triptych tells the truth about cruelty and barbarity: they are not grand, spectacular or theatrical. They are, on the contrary, mean, grotesque, even comic. The painting is filled with bizarre demons—several, like the platypus in tails, may even strike some as cute. Torment and extermination require efficiency and co-ordination—the processing of people at Auschwitz and Treblinka was decades ahead of its time in the application of management techniques. Factories of death, just as other factories, depend on the collaboration of all concerned. Bosch knew that truth as well as the supervisors of the twentieth-century death camps knew it. Some of them may, indeed, have learnt a thing or two from this painting in a gallery dedicated to Europe's great heritage of art, when—perhaps as uniformed or sailor-suited children on a cultural excursion— they were conducted through these rooms steeped in Kakania's traditional respect for culture, for the finer things of life.

INSCRIPTIONS

I

On monuments and buildings; on the bases of statues and above ceremonial gateways; inside the cupolas of churches and the foyers of the great theatres; in the extraordinary reading room of the National Library, a baroque fantasy with trumpeting angels and learned emperors carried aloft by the muses; on shopsigns above the establishments of the great merchants of the city: pastrycooks, purveyors of hunting perquisites, gentlemen's outfitters, silversmiths, bootmakers; on blocks of stone or marble set among the cobblestones of squares and streets, Vienna is a city of inscriptions. In flowing Latin or pompous German they commemorate a proud history. This chiselled chronicle of cultural and military greatness perpetuates the memory of all who had ruled over this centre of a great realm. Their statues and memorials gaze upon the imperial city with pride, arrogance and satisfaction. They made this world great, and its greatness, even in the age of Reeboks and McDonald's, is confirmed by the indestructibility of chiselled stone. The greater glory of the Franzes and Josefs, the Ferdinands and Karls, the Eugenes and Ottos, of Maria Theresia, the double-chinned matriarch, and also of God, is guaranteed for generations to come.

II

The Gloriette is an elaborate folly, a type of Brandenburg Gate, on a grassy knoll above the royal palace of Schönbrunn. Formerly the summer residence of the Habsburgs, built, the guide book tells us, by Maria Theresia with a particularly

feminine sensibility when compared with the baroque extravagance of 'male' Vienna, Schönbrunn is now a suburb of the
city, easily reached by the plebeian Underground. Once it used
to be in the countryside, away from the hurly-burly, the noise,
the foul odours and the intrigues of the capital. Even today
though, the place has something of a rural atmosphere. One
side of the Gloriette looks upon the formal gardens leading
to the palace below. From the other side a carefully contrived
wilderness seems to stretch for miles, but probably only as far
as a busy suburban highway discreetly screened by lush trees.
The Viennese have brought the art of illusion, of façadeism,
to high perfection. For what amounts to a few cents, visitors
may purchase a ticket from a booth carved out of the side of
the Gloriette, allowing them access to the top of the structure.
It is a good place from which to view, and better still to
photograph, Maria Theresia's yellow summer palace—the
colour scheme of which gave identity to the architecture of the
Habsburg world in cities as far away as Milan and Bucharest—
and the gardens in front of it. The top of the winding staircase
is secured by a heavy painted metal door, now bolted open
with a sturdy chain and padlock. Its surface records the dreams
of immortality carved by the Lisls and Rudis, by the Giannas
and Giacomos, by the Brads and Leannes who have come here.
And in the middle of the door, writ large in bold lettering as
befits the pride of place, the royal centre, that to which all
must pay homage: AUSTRALIA RULES.

III

Just inside one of the entrances to the Westbahnhof, where you
have to catch most eastbound trains, including those for
Budapest, a plaque surrounded by vending machines and
advertisements for *Mozartkugeln* records that from this station
hundreds of thousands of people were conveyed eastward, to
death.

RETURN OF THE NATIVE

History According to Karl Marx

When history repeats itself, Marx said, it turns into farce. This is the second time in a year that I have set out for Budapest from this railway station in Vienna where a modest plaque commemorates the infamous eastward migration. The earlier occasion was high drama. I was about to approach the forbidden land, that city and country which I had avoided for the best part of fifty years, not daring to go back, partly because of the grave political risks I would have encountered during the Cold War and in the years of the Berlin Wall, but also, and much more importantly, because I did not want to come face to face with memories, attitudes, a personal and a communal history which I had swept under the carpet, or pretended to myself had never existed.

With the pathetic fallacy beloved by neoclassical theorists of tragedy, that journey was undertaken beneath gloomy winter skies, in the gathering dusk of a December afternoon. The platform resembled one of those classic scenes of flight and panic that are etched on the imagination of the twentieth century. A sealed Russian wagon was filled with impassive but alarmed faces staring through the grimy windows. The carriage in which I had reserved a seat was already full to bursting— a good half-hour before departure time—by sullen or excited swarthy people surrounded by cardboard boxes.

There was an air of anticipation and fear as we approached the Hungarian border. Communism had been dead for only a few months; no-one believed that the political system had really changed, that border guards would have given up their jackbooted ways. When they came clumping through the train, they did, indeed, look like incarnations of totalitarian brutality. Grim-faced, they inspected our passports with slow deliberation. I experienced again a long-forgotten panic when

I saw them looking at the page on mine that said 'Place of Birth: Budapest, Hungary'. They bore off several of the swarthy people crowding the corridor—their cardboard boxes travelled on unaccompanied.

Today the sun is shining. The people on the platform are relaxed, even smiling; most of them look, and probably are, 'western'. The train pulls in more or less on time. Though the compartment fills up a few minutes before the punctual departure, there are no usurpers, no cardboard boxes. The fat American lady in pink jeans and her lanky husband, whom I had seen smiling at each other on the platform, settle into the window seats. Each burrows into what looks like a blockbuster novel, though the front and back covers are missing from both. The businessman sitting opposite me begins to fuss with a sheaf of computer print-out; I retrieve for him a stack of glued-together British passports which has fallen out of his briefcase and landed under my seat. An Italian couple are poring over a green-covered book entitled *Ungheria, Oggi ed Ieri*. Outside, the grey buildings of an unfashionable district of Vienna look almost cheerful in the autumn sunshine.

We roll towards the border through a pleasant landscape: neat fields, neat houses, neat church spires. The border station no longer looks grim and threatening, as it did in the winter darkness nine months ago, like a spectral sequence in a black-and-white spy thriller. Now, in the afternoon light, it is merely shabby and ill-kept. The border guards are cheerful and relaxed, unlike their surly comrades on my earlier visit—though in all probability they were merely tired and cold. These guards don't pay much attention to my passport once they see that my visa is in order, nor to the businessman's sheaf or those of the Italians. Yet there is a minor fuss when the American man hands them two passports. Where is the other person? they ask in Hungarian. Incomprehension. For what will prove to be the first of many occasions in the coming weeks, I am obliged to step in as a reluctant and unhappy interpreter. The British businessman (who, I suspect, is of Hungarian origin) looks at me suspiciously, but, being British, he keeps himself to himself.

It is up to me therefore to convey the information that the lady has gone to the lavatory. For a moment a hard-set look passes across the guards' faces, as they issue the stern instruction that she is to come out.

Having had their ultimatum translated for him, the American goes off to fetch his wife; the guards take possession of their passports. He is away for what seems a very long time. The guards are getting restive, and I am beginning to wonder whether they are about to assume their former nasty habits. They hold a brief conference, and one of them walks down the corridor towards the lavatory. No sooner has he gone than the pink lady and her husband return from the opposite end of the carriage. Now the guard who had stayed behind in the compartment goes off in search of his colleague, carrying with him the protesting Americans' passports. The Americans, confident members of a society who think you may cock a snook at borders and wander off to the loo passportless, betray some signs of alarm. Perhaps they are momentarily touched by fear and suspicion of those dark countries behind the Iron Curtain, fears and suspicions which had kept me for so many years from venturing behind it. Perhaps they too feel that just because someone has said that the Iron Curtain no longer exists does not necessarily imply that the cruelties and the exercise of arbitrary power which had been conducted behind it for decades will have ceased altogether.

Nevertheless, as in all good farces, confusions and perplexities are resolved once all the actors are gathered on stage. The border guards, the Americans and their passports are all reunited, mild reprobation is conveyed through the medium of the interpreter, the solitary figure—Jaques, Malvolio—who always stands to one side when everyone else is celebrating that all's well that ends well.

We are on our way once more. The countryside, now that we are inside Hungary, doesn't look much more forbidding than it did in Austria. The houses may be a little less well kept, the cars tootling along the road beside the track are not as glossy as those on the other side. Everything here seems very ordinary and speaks of the commonplace. There appear to be no ghouls or monsters. For all that, I feel myself growing increasingly apprehensive the closer we come to Budapest. Soon, within the hour no doubt, I shall have to get out of this well-upholstered compartment; the evasions of my days in Vienna will have to come to an end, and I shall have to face once more the difficult and distressing task of entering a society where my identity is not what I would like it to be. Once again those fears that beset me as SQ24 was heading towards Vienna are very real and pressing: will people in Hungary assume that I am one of their own, that I have come home? Will my belief that I am Australian be challenged and perhaps denied here, the place where I was born? Will I fall into some sort of existential void out of which I shall not be easily (if at all) able to extricate myself?

The moment of severance (or of commitment) is obviously near. There, on the horizon, the hills behind the city are clearly visible. There is the communications mast and there the ugly monument to the Soviet troops of 1945. The train sweeps in a large curve around the city. It crosses the Danube. The river sparkles in the sunlight; the domes and spires of the city glow in the afternoon sun. It is, I tell myself, a beautiful sight, just as the Americans are saying loudly to each other, 'Well, look at that, isn't that something?'

There is no time for reflection. We arrive at the station; this time I know exactly what to do. I know that you cannot change money (at least legally) there, but that a few Austrian banknotes will work wonders. I know that you mustn't look curious or expectant as you walk along the platform if you wish to avoid the attention of touts and shysters. I know where the taxi rank is and walk confidently towards it, as if this were the place where I have always lived, the place where I belong. I brush aside brusquely, and in Hungarian, the one miserable creature importuning me in broken English to exchange currency. I have reserved a room in a small hotel at the top of a steep hill; I therefore select a taxi which looks as if it will be able to make it up there. I ignore the loud protests of other drivers, those who claim to have had precedence in a non-existent queue. I don't even bother to ask the driver whether he'll accept Austrian currency. Having done a quick mental conversion at the unofficial rate of exchange, I merely hand him the appropriate amount at the end of the trip, with, of course, what is for me a modest but for the driver an impressive gratuity. The people in the hotel welcome me in minimal English and, to my horror, I hear myself conversing with them in Hungarian, exchanging greetings and pleasantries, and complimenting them on the nice room they have reserved for me.

A View From the Bridge

When people speak of the beauty of Budapest they almost always have the Danube in mind. Standing on one of the bridges spanning that broad stream, looking at the panorama glowing in the late afternoon sunshine, I too am impressed by what is one of the world's great vistas. To the left the hills of Buda rise in tiers, like the galleries of a great theatre. On my right, upstream from the most imposing of these bridges, (a graceful structure suspended on intricately ornamented chains that give it the name 'Chain Bridge'), beyond the row of solidly handsome buildings lining the embankment, the great, vaguely oriental dome of the Parliament seems one mass of burnished gold. In the distance the green shadow of St Margaret's Island, a woody park with hotels, restaurants and swimming baths, floats on the slowly flowing water.

In Budapest the Danube is the focus of the city; Vienna, by contrast, has turned its back on the river—it flows forgotten, out of sight, leaving behind merely a dreary canal clipping the edge of the old city. The scale of London is far too great for the Thames to be an essential presence in the way that the Danube is in this city, even in those parts where it is out of sight. Only the Seine, snaking its way through Paris, binding together the elements of a complex urban world, has something of the impact that the Danube makes on Budapest. The Danube is, however, a much broader stream than the Seine, more imposing—and Budapest does not have the kind of glories which vie in Paris with its more modest river. Here the river is all.

The Danube is the reason for the existence of this city. Thirty or forty kilometres upstream, at the border of what is still known in 1991 as Czechoslovakia, the eastward flow of the river takes an abrupt ninety-degree turn to the south. As it changes direction, it flows through a series of high hills which once provided an excellent strategic position from which to guard or control its placid lower reaches. The hills continue on what becomes the western bank after the river performs its change of direction. On the opposite, that is the eastern, side the flatlands stretch seemingly to the end of the world.

Various people settled among those hills overlooking the great plain on the eastern shore. The Romans came and left behind a modest amphitheatre and a few broken columns—they even established a settlement farther downstream on the other side. Towards the end of the first millennium King Stephen established Christianity; a royal court of sorts came into being among those hills in a place that was eventually called Buda. Four and a half centuries later a brilliant culture flourished under Matthew Corvinus, whose name shares, with the evangelist, that of the gothic church (much restored, and another latter-day fantasy), the stone spire of which dominates the skyline above the river. That short-lived period of learning, civilisation and peace was brought to an abrupt end by the coming of the Turks. They turned churches into mosques and built their shallow-domed bath-houses over the thermal springs which, since at least the time of the Romans, have been much exploited features of this locality.

Two centuries later the Turks were driven out by the Austrians. The Habsburgs eventually built their large royal palace on one of the promontories above the river more as a symbol of power and perhaps of arrogance than for any strategic purpose. By the time the slow construction of that ungainly pile commenced, the flat reaches of the opposite bank, hitherto trading posts, fishing settlements, even resting places for the odd nomadic group, had begun to assume the characteristics of a town—Pest—to become by the end of the nineteenth century a burgeoning, cosmopolitan centre of trade, commerce and intellectual ferment.

Looking towards Pest on this golden afternoon, when the pall of noxious fumes hanging over the city turns the sun's slanting rays into great gilded beams, what I see is the result of an extraordinary growth in the last years of the nineteenth century and the first few of the twentieth. There, opposite the Habsburg fortress town of Buda, which even in my father's youth in the twenties remained to a great extent a conservatively Austrian town, emerged the chaotic, noisy, competitive and ambitious society of Pest, made up of the many racial and national strands of Kakania, that blossomed with extraordinary energy at the turn of the century. By then the two towns had been formally joined together, and their names had changed from Buda and Pest to the composite Budapest. But that ferment, the heady energy that made people speak of this city as another Chicago or New York, was much more characteristic of the flat expanses of the eastern bank. Streets, avenues, massive apartment blocks mushroomed there as more and more people flooded in from all over the Empire to exploit the golden opportunities offered by that brave new world. The patricians of Buda looked down on the anthill of Pest with bemusement and growing distrust.

Pest was my family's world. They lived among those bustling streets in a polyglot society that was a microcosm of the variety of Kakania. My grandmother, at the time of her wedding trip to Vienna, when she purchased her furniture and some of her household gods (including that Ferris wheel), must have seen avenues and boulevards being laid out, massive buildings rise out of the ground almost overnight, bridges constructed across the broad expanse of the Danube. Her parents, and also my grandfather's no doubt, attended performances at the Opera House, smaller than Vienna's, though

103

much more elaborately decorated, as soon as it opened its doors. She may also have attended the celebrations in 1896 to mark the millennium of the foundation of the Kingdom of Hungary and probably admired the great new public space, with its ornate sculptures and monuments, built to commemorate that great event. For her, as for her younger son, my father, living in Budapest meant inhabiting that raw, complicated but exhilarating world that sprang up on the flat lands opposite the staid Habsburg town where the remnants of Roman, Magyar, Turkish and Austrian history seemed increasingly anachronistic, irrelevant to the real source of Budapest's energy and potential.

The pomp and arrogance of Habsburg hegemony among the hills of Buda riled Magyar nationalists of the nineteenth century. The abortive revolution of 1848 was directed against the usurpers and invaders in their fortress that dominated, symbolically and physically, the great river. Even after the reconciliation of 1867, when the country's Habsburg masters gave Hungary a measure of autonomy, and began thereby to elaborate that pious myth of a supranational state which soon devolved into the fantasies and absurdities of Kakania, nationalist sentiment smouldered beneath the surface of an apparent calm. By contrast, the inhabitants of the other bank embraced the social and cultural implications of the Kakanian myth. The construction of the huge bulk of the Parliament on their side of the river may have been dictated by no more than contingency—Buda was much too hilly to provide a site for so large a building. Yet, everyone recognised the implied symbolism. Here was a splendid structure, the world's first building to be centrally heated. It was obviously the outward and visible sign of the emergence of Budapest as one of the great cities of the world. It graced moreover the energetic and dynamic skyline of Pest, the metropolis of the future, the epitome of the newfound peace and prosperity—which was to come to an abrupt and bloody end as a consequence of the gunshot in distant Sarajevo.

As the sun disappears behind the steep hills of Buda,

enveloping in long shadows the buildings clinging to their sides, I am reminded that even for my parents that part of city remained somewhat alien, as it had been for my grandparents and, no doubt, for their parents before them. Buda was site of the conflict between Magyar and Austrian. My family, inhabitants of the multilayered world of Pest, stood aloof from those disputes: they could not identify wholly with either side, were suspicious of each. If their sentiment inclined towards either it would probably have been towards the Austrians—despite their arrogance, and indeed bigotry—because my family and people like them looked beyond the confines of those 'nations' that made up the Habsburg realm towards that cultural cynosure some two hundred kilometres away, Vienna, the city of their dreams. They were in essence internationalists, not by virtue of an ideological conviction, but because they thought they were citizens of a vibrant and energetic world where the opportunities for the good life were unbounded.

In Pest, over which the shadows of the Buda hills are now advancing, just as the terrible tide of German bigotry and Magyar nationalism crept over it during my childhood, their lives revolved around the institutions of their world—especially those sites of public ceremony, the cafés, the opera and the theatres, which gave that world shape and substance. Memory tells me that my parents rarely crossed the river. They lived in Pest, or for some years in a suburb on the Pest side. Scraps of family mythology I remember suggest that on summer nights they would sometimes visit riverside restaurants in Buda, to eat the fiery fish stew, the local version of bouillabaisse, and to dance to the music of the gypsy bands. I can recall one or two occasions on which I crossed the river in one of the white paddle-steamers that used to ply between the two banks, to be taken to visit the Castle, to be shown the 'ancient' church of St Matthew and the few streets of seventeenth- and eighteenth-century buildings nestled around it. I remember that on one occasion there was a great fuss because my parents refused to take me on the funicular that runs from the embankment to the Castle—they considered it unsafe, citing an accident that was supposed to have occurred a quarter of a century earlier. On the whole, though, we kept to our side—the Pest side of the river—at first because the patterns of our life as they had evolved through the years made Pest their focus, later because of war, persecution and peril, and finally, in the days after the siege of the city, because these bridges, now enveloped in the autumn dusk, lay as tangled masses of metal and stone in the waters of the Danube.

THE UNDERWORLD

At the foot of one of the bridges across the Danube, a pedestrian underpass leads to the streets and boulevards of Pest. In an attempt to enhance the appearance of this short tunnel—usually the haunt of gypsies begging for alms and delivering blood-curdling curses on those that refuse—its walls are lined with enlarged photographs of nearby streets and squares taken at the turn of the century. They show the bustle of a newly-emerging metropolis; in an entirely intangible way they remind me of photographs taken in Sydney at about the same time. There is the same sense of rawness—in the eyes of the hurrying pedestrians as much as in the appearance of shopfronts and the sides of buildings as they were caught by the camera. For all their period charm, intended no doubt to evoke an older, more leisurely world, these images speak of the new, the emerging and also of the unformed.

Several of these photographs show quite clearly the names of various merchants and tradesmen—butchers and cobblers, upholsterers and grocers—painted on large boards above the windows or doors of their establishments. Most of them are German names, and many, at least of the superior variety of merchant or artisan, bear the discreet emblem of the official favour bestowed on them by His Majesty, the k.k. monarch, Franz Josef. Here were His Imperial and Royal Majesty's Hungarian bootmakers, grocers, wine-merchants and station-ers, all catering for His Majesty's needs whenever, as King of

Hungary, he resided in this part of his dual realm—which, in reality, did not happen very often. These nostalgic images serve as reminders, in this grim underworld of begging gypsies, of that Kakanian past which now, in the second year of the new dispensation, is becoming a matter of sentimental preoccupation for the citizens of Budapest.

Beyond the subway other emblems of the Kakanian past are visible. The semicircle of boulevards, modelled on Vienna's Ring, once more bear their former imperial names: Elisabeth and Theresia; Franz and Josef—though in another subway under one of these boulevards, at one of the large Metro stations, the exit signs still direct the unwary towards thoroughfares named after Lenin and his ilk. The broad avenues which fan out from these boulevards—inspired by Baron Haussmann's Paris—once again commemorate Hungarian statesmen and patriots approved (or at least tolerated by) the Habsburgs. This part of the city is a cartographic fantasy of Kakania, with former street names boldly cancelled in red (like 'no smoking' signs) acting as reminders of the forty-year-long usurpation by heroes of socialism.

There is nothing beautiful about the present-day aspect of these streets and avenues. Budapest bears all the depressing signs of a half-century of neglect—which followed the severe destruction of war—bred out of the grim assurance of Hungary's political masters during those decades, unscrupulous men who knew that they were not answerable to the people under their subjection, and felt no obligation therefore to repair the city's crumbling fabric. They also knew that they had the guns—readily used in 1956—to discourage any grumbling or potential revolt. In this Indian summer of 1991 the handsome chestnut trees lining the broad avenues of the inner city may momentarily disguise the crumbling façades of monumental buildings poorly restored in the years after the war. The illusion is, however, shortlived. As your eye travels from the luxuriant foliage to the blackened, grimy walls lining these streets, you seem to be looking at obscure but menacing hieroglyphs of destruction and neglect. A poorly patched window embrasure here, there the telltale scar of a collapsed balcony, and everywhere the pockmarks of bulletholes chronicle the outrages and indignities suffered by this city during a tragic century.

The roadways are choked by a neverending stream of noisome traffic; ancient cars, that obviously have rarely been washed or properly serviced, dodge in and out of each other's way, seemingly heading for the inevitable collision and avoiding it, in most instances, only by a hair's breadth. The occasional crunch of metal, the frequent screech of tyres and the many dented mudguards testify to the risk of travelling by car along the streets of Budapest. Meanwhile these antiquated Trabants and Ladas, interspersed here and there with gleaming Porsches and other four-wheeled icons of Budapest's new life, send out plumes of noxious smoke. Mixed with the foul odours rising from vents and apertures, this provides the characteristic aroma of modern Budapest.

The streets are almost always crowded with shuffling, ill-clad people. They mill around bus stops or congregate in the large underground halls leading to the Metro lines, which are filled, in this era of the new dispensation, with hawkers and stallholders spruiking their wares at the tops of their voices. The footpaths are littered with discarded newspapers, empty cigarette packets. Eyes must be kept on the ground—not only to avoid excrement left behind by the city's countless dogs, but also pools of vomit and urine. There are many misshapen people and also even more drunkards than you are likely to see in most cities of the 'western' world.

After darkness falls, prostitutes start their beat along certain well-known stretches of the great line of boulevards. The homeless begin to bed down on park benches and in the doorways of public buildings. Waves of yelling youths and drunken conscripts, roaring sentimental ballads which pass for folksongs, roll along the footpaths, sometimes spilling over into the roadways, into the path of the screeching, rattling traffic. You grow uncomfortably conscious of a young man following you a few paces behind; your grip tightens on your wallet in the pocket of your trousers. If your path takes you into one of the ill-lit and largely deserted sidestreets or alleys, the still emptiness is even more alarming than the bustle of the great avenues and boulevards—you hope fervently that the youth who has been shadowing you in the crowded street has gone on his way.

Budapest at the end of the twentieth century is not a theme park. It is driven by the terrible realities of a world that has been at the centre of the great upheavals of a brutal epoch. Amidst such realities there seems little room for fantasy. Accordingly, Budapest, in its grime and anarchy, is much more like the cities of the familiar world than the elaborately staged spectacle of Vienna. It is dirtier and much more decrepit than London, for instance, yet in both places urban decay is ever-present and palpable. Like London, like Munich, like much of Sydney and Melbourne and even prim Adelaide, Budapest is one of the infernal cities of the modern world. Here the canvas of filth and corruption may have been painted in more lurid colours and with bolder strokes. There are, nevertheless, the same icons of decay visible as in those cities of the 'developed' world.

Fantasies, however, are beginning to emerge. Coming out of the pedestrian underpass with its sepia images of Kakanian Budapest, you find yourself at one end of a short, narrow street, nowadays mercifully free of the wheezing cars that choke the rest of the city. This is, and had been in the years of my childhood, the most elegant shopping street in town. Its glories always paled beside those of the Graben and Kärtnerstrasse, points of comparison for a world that rarely looked beyond Vienna to the great cities of Western Europe for its inspiration. Yet there were glories sufficient to satisfy people like my mother, much of whose life during her five or six years of metropolitan affluence before the coming of war revolved around this street and the lanes leading off it. Her days were marked by pilgrimages from one to another shrine dedicated to beauty and elegance. The route may have varied from day to day and from season to season, but her devotions conducted her in an ever-changing pattern to the dressmaker and the milliner, the shoemaker and the furrier, the cosmetician and the coiffeur. Whatever path her peregrinations described, the final goal, and resting place after such exertions, was invariably the large café, the most elegant in Budapest according to the social code that governed her life, at the top of the ample square at the far end of this street.

Some echoes of that long-vanished world remain. A few of the boutiques display goods of a kind not seen in the dusty and flyblown shops and department stores in other parts of the city, though the windows of some of these boutiques carry discreet signs announcing that their merchandise is available only to holders of hard currency. For that reason, perhaps, the street is filled with jeans-clad youths whispering to anyone who looks like a tourist, offers to exchange currency at rates almost double the official.

The crowds of tourists—mostly Germans, but even here the occasional Australian intonation can be heard—pass in great waves up and down the street. They seem to pay little attention to the dozens of young men importuning them to exchange money, or indeed to the shopwindows filled with goods of unimaginable luxury to the eyes of the citizens of Budapest. To them it's all familiar; the magic brand names—Gucci, Christian Dior and Armani—are household words, common-place domestic objects. Yet even if they were attracted by these glittering emblems of affluence, they would find it difficult on most afternoons or evenings to inspect at leisure the shop windows where these rare objects are displayed. Both sides of the street are lined with people (mostly peasant women, kerchiefs tied round their heads) holding out for inspection embroidered tablecloths, bedspreads and sheepskin jackets from Transylvania. With ululating voices they praise the exquisite workmanship of these unique objects and implore the kind lords and ladies strolling along the street to buy from them, so that they may feed their starving infants or care for their aged mothers. The lords and ladies understand none of this, apart from guessing that they are being invited to purchase goods identical to those displayed in the windows of the large folk art emporium prominently situated in the middle of this street.

The women stand immobile, hour after hour, in the two long rows stretching the length of the street. With extended arms they display their wares as though they were precious relics or trophies. The eyes of some are glazed with fatigue, others are nervously agitated as they seek their prey, while their chant ripples along the street like the lamentations of the damned. 'Buy, noble lord, buy, for the pity of God' mingles with 'Buy, gracious lady, buy, for my blind mother's sake' in a strange cacophony of counterpoint. Its echoes and murmurs bounce off granite and plaster walls, cobblestones and plate glass. These immobile figures are terrible presences, the living dead, past whom the waves of sightseers slowly flow like the damned streaming into hell.

In this underworld, this world without hope, a few shining emblems, accessible to all, serve as reminders of another world where life is rich and filled with boundless promise. In a side lane behind one of the rows of lamenting women a large, rounded yellow M beckons crowds into a brightly lit interior where Big Macs and Cheeseburgers are dispensed by gaily dressed boys and girls, as wholesome and smiling as the confident teenagers in the many American sitcoms Hungarian television churns out with blissfully unsynchronised dubbing. While Vienna looks towards its sentimentalised past for spiritual nourishment and the indulgence of fantasies, this second city of the former realm of Kakania has its eyes firmly set on the wonders of the west—that indeterminate but magical world that begins at the Austrian border. McDonald's stands as an icon of the distant, intangible good life—the world where there is no sorrow or poverty, no brutality or suffering, a world where Reeboks and Levis are plentiful and cheap. As yet there are merely glimmers of that world to be seen in the streets of Budapest—a McDonald's here, a news-stand selling *Playboy* there, a branch of an Austrian chain of supermarkets groaning with imported foodstuffs next to a booth dispensing Coke. These images of hope illuminate the lives of those condemned to dwell among the crumbling decay of a city which, from some vantage points, sparkles with breathtaking beauty.

FAMILY REUNION

A family reunion, after a long separation, should be an occasion for rejoicing, for the deepest emotional satisfaction. That, at least, is the lesson of literature. Experience, as is often the case, gives the lie to such dreams. Finding my one remaining Hungarian relative, a person to whom I was very close in the early years of my life, produces awkwardness, even embarrassment. And we come to realise, after the first few minutes in which we catch up on forty-five years of family history— births, marriages and deaths—that there is little left to say. We have grown apart, separated by time, distance and language: my Hungarian is a blunt, outmoded instrument; my cousin's command of English is, to say the least, limited. Across that gulf we must try to establish again a relationship that in the normal course of events would require decades to reach maturity.

The bonds that existed between this woman and me when we were young were much stronger than an account of our consanguinity would suggest. Though only a few years older than I am, she is my mother's first cousin—the product of a late marriage and of seventeen childless years—which makes her into some sort of surrogate aunt. We were, however, treated almost like brother and sister by a family in which there were no other young children. Years before her birth, my cousin's parents helped to bring up my mother, whose father had died when she was a toddler. My mother, in turn, regarded her first cousin—who was born a few years before her own son—almost as a daughter, to be indulged, protected and cherished. My cousin spent many months at a time living with us. A bond developed between the two of us of which only a few scattered images remain. One, perhaps the most eloquent, resides in that penumbra of the memory where fantasy and experience

112

intersect. And yet, within the first hour of our reunion, she provides me with proof that this haunting memory isn't merely a product of fantasy or nostalgia. Scrabbling around in an untidy drawer, she produces a photograph taken when I was about three years old showing the two of us, on a day of blinding summer light, splashing about in a wooden laundry tub filled with water. The memory of that scene swells in my imagination: I can smell the heat of that long distant day, and the odour of freshly mown grass.

That provides a deeply satisfying moment. Otherwise we are both somewhat stiff, even perhaps formal, a barrier separates us as much as it separates me from her husband, whom I had not met until now. Three middle-aged people sitting in a pleasant, sparsely furnished living room on the top floor of a dreary, barracks-like block of flats built during the socialist fifties, play out the elaborate pretence that they are not strangers, that their lives are still somehow connected by intimate ties. Such a pretence cannot be sustained for long. Soon awkward silences and gaps in the the conversation begin to appear. My cousin, sensing that something is required of her, but not knowing what to do, sighs and says, crossing her arms behind her head, 'Well, well, life's strange, isn't it?'— and then goes into her tiny kitchen to do something about dinner.

Over that evening meal—cold meat and salad, as is the custom in this part of the world—the fiction that we are somehow close, intimately connected is gradually abandoned. We realise that we are strangers, acquaintances at best. Yet on this evening, I come to discover in this middle-aged woman and her wheezing asthmatic husband something of the history of this sad country in the last half-century.

Eighteen months or so after our arrival in Australia in 1947, my parents contrived to obtain an entry permit for my mother's elderly mother. At the same time they tried to persuade this cousin, who was then sixteen or seventeen, to join us in Australia. I do not know how seriously she considered their offer, but ultimately, after the exchange of several slow-moving letters, she refused: her mother (my grandmother's younger sister) was already showing the symptoms of the breast cancer that was to take her life a year or two later. For some years we kept in touch with my cousin: the occasional letter would arrive telling us of her studies at school and university, and eventually of her early marriage and of the birth of her daughter in 1953 or 1954.

Then came the terrible days of October 1956. The newspapers carried ominous banner headlines and, after those inevitable days of delay in a world without the electronic transmission of images of horror and brutality around the globe in seconds or minutes, pictures of the fighting in Budapest. Seeing those images and reading the reports carried by eyewitnesses and by those who had managed to escape to the west in all that confusion, my mother became increasingly alarmed about the fate of her young cousin. With frenzied determination she sought out every agency that could possibly provide her with information about her relative. News organisations, the embassies and consulates of European nations, the various churches were all sympathetic but proved incapable of helping her. Finally, in about 1958, word came by way of the International Red Cross: my cousin and her family were well but wished to have nothing to do with capitalist lackeys.

Many years of silence followed. Letters were returned marked 'unknown at this address'. Then, in the late 1960s, a postcard arrived, showing the socialist paradise of a Black Sea resort. The brief message announced that my cousin and her family were enjoying a well-earned vacation. In the next few years more postcards, even the odd letter (from the address where she had not been known some years earlier) arrived. They were always vague, noncommittal, usually concerned with news of her daughter's progress through the various grades of school. My father visited them briefly when he returned to Budapest for a few days a year or so after my mother's death. He reported that they seemed reasonably comfortable and happy: the daughter had married and had just given birth to a daughter of her own.

A desultory correspondence followed. I wrote to my cousin when my father died. I sent her the occasional photograph of my wife and children. When I spent a few days in Budapest in 1990 I tried to telephone her a couple of times but received no answer—I assumed that she had gone away somewhere for Christmas. As it turned out her telephone number had changed but no-one at the large hotel where I was staying bothered to tell me, after I had asked the concierge to check the number, how to find out about new and altered telephone numbers. That is how it came about that this family reunion did not take place until today, and only after I had spent several frustrating hours trying to raise the altered numbers service of Budapest's antiquated telephone system. Now, sitting around the dining table in my cousin's small flat, I realise that I know almost nothing about this woman and her family, who are my closest surviving relatives. And, growing conscious of the reserve that greets any mention of those forty years of Hungary's communist past, I begin to suspect that I will be vouchsafed very small glimpses only of my cousin's life during those years of silence.

As the Soviet empire in Europe crumbled away and countries formerly under its sway asserted their independence, the news was greeted with jubilation in many parts of the 'free' world. These oppressed people, who had shown their unquenchable desire for liberty in 1956 and 1968, and later with the rise of Solidarity in Poland, would at long last know freedom. The yoke of tyranny had been thrown off; a bright new day was dawning for those tragic and long-suffering nations as the map of Europe was being rapidly redrawn. In Australia, in this extraordinary year of 1991, the doors of the Hungarian Embassy in Canberra were thrown open to receive, in an act of reconciliation, compatriots who had fled the oppression and brutality of that régime. That gesture, charged with symbolic import, was no doubt repeated in embassies and consulates the world over. Optimism and goodwill were in the air. A line had been drawn through a brutal history; henceforth amity and brotherhood would rule all Hungarians.

Such myths are as simple as the rhetoric in which they are couched. Reality is more complex, and one probably significant part of it is to be encountered here, in this small flat in a grubby and pollution-choked thoroughfare, where this grim and decrepit building, with huge cracks running up its façade, proves to be the best maintained structure in the street.

My cousin begins to talk about their hard life. She is a retired history teacher. Until a year or two ago the pension she and her husband received was sufficient to allow them to make ends meet. They had to be careful, of course, but then who doesn't? There was enough for their daily needs. Not any more. She has had to go back to work part time—thank goodness they had friends in the ministry who could pull some strings. At this point her husband says that he should go back to work too, electrical engineers can always find something to do. That provokes an outburst from my cousin: he certainly can't go back to work, being as ill as he is with asthma, and last winter he had pneumonia twice! He shrugs, and says something entirely characteristic, it seems to me, of the spirit of Kakania, which must still be lingering in these decaying streets and avenues. 'Oh well', he says, 'it's probably better to get pneumonia at home: the flat will certainly be cold enough when the heating's cut off'.

Their story is a familiar tale. You cannot spend even a few days in this city without becoming aware, from snatches of conversation overheard in the streets and in buses, from the monologues of taxi drivers or from the dismay and disbelief of people in supermarkets when the cost of their meagre purchases is totalled, that the new forces operating in this country are imposing hardships on many citizens. Abroad, in places like Britain, America and Australia, the change in political régime was seen in idealistic and largely sentimental terms. Everyone would now have freedom, everyone would enjoy the benefits and blessings of a democratic and open society. Few of these people, the odd idealistic intellectual apart, see those changes in such terms. For most Hungarians the change was neither political nor ideological but predominantly economic: the substitution of the market-driven policies of the capitalist world for the old, discredited command economy of the communist era.

Some, my cousin tells me, are doing very nicely, thank you very much. I know immediately what she has in mind. A monied class is beginning to emerge in this city in a way that was not apparent nine months ago, at the very beginning of this new world for what is still at times referred to as gallant little Hungary. Then there were no young men in screeching Porsches to be seen. None of the women in the two or three elegant cafés that remain were seen wearing the outrageous quantities of jewellery now to be seen as these members of the new upper crust sit, hour after hour, consuming delicacies, emblems of social superiority in this world. None talked loudly then, as many do now in cafés and on the streets about their acumen and cunning in outwitting their business rivals, about the huge profit they made from bringing a second-hand Mercedes, purchased in Austria for next to nothing, across the border, and selling it to some sucker here who just had to own one.

And, as was inevitable, there are many more poor people now—pensioners, those on fixed incomes and, of course, the unemployed and the homeless, a situation, my cousin says, they had never known. Have I seen those young people roaming the streets of the inner city? she asks. Did I know that they are homeless children who sleep in culverts and viaducts, some of whom deal in drugs or sell themselves for sex? I tell her that it's nothing new to me—that's what it's like at home. That word gives her a momentary pause, but then she shakes her head and smiles—oh no, that can't be true, my home is, after all, in the west, things like that don't happen there no matter what they were told in the past.

Both of my relatives grow more animated as they continue telling me about the problems and confusions of this society, those problems and confusions that are visible even to the casual visitor in the streets of the city. I do not hear anything about freedom, liberty or democracy; all I hear from them are the all-too-familiar preoccupations of my own world: the appalling amount it costs nowadays just to keep yourself fed and clothed. Do I know how much it costs now to have a pair of shoes heeled? (The figure mentioned seems—from the perspective of exchange rates—risible, a mere nothing, the cost of a ferry ride.) Did I know that education, even at primary school, is no longer free? And you have to pay for medical services! The litany continues, mixed with stories of the way people are making vast amounts of money from the newly deregulated financial structures. Where will it end? they ask, shaking their heads.

My cousin suddenly becomes very agitated, her eyes are flashing with fire—I recognise in her those mysterious characteristics that are carried through a family's genes, changing and altering with circumstances, yet surviving and persisting despite all sorts of vicissitudes. Why did they stay in this godforsaken place? she asks the walls, the abstract watercolour above the settee, those emblems of western affluence, the colour television set and the video recorder, and even the large pot plant in front of the window—probably placed there to block out the view of a crumbling building on the opposite side of the street. Why, oh why didn't they get out in '56, when there was a chance? Indeed, they were about to go, they'd all but arranged it, but lost their nerve at the last minute. If only they'd had the courage! But no, they stayed, stayed here in this terrible corrupt world, a world going from bad to worse, a world with a curse on it.

Her husband, the more ironic and phlegmatic of the two, tries to dampen her frenzy. For people like them, he says, it's rotten everywhere. They're the sort that always gets it in the neck—the clever and the unscrupulous survive anywhere. Might as well make the best of things; after all they're a damn sight better off than many others—and he begins to reel off a list of names, a disaster attached to each, in order to calm my cousin whose emotions seem to be in danger of getting out of hand.

There is, however, no stopping her. This is a family characteristic I recognise only too well. It does nothing, though, to diminish my embarrassment. These people, despite the ties of blood and sentiment, are strangers to me; I do not know how to respond to this dangerous heightening of the emotional temperature. I look away as she continues her tirade of lamentation—now concerned with her fears for her daughter and granddaughters—and my eyes light on the shelves of books that cover most of the walls in this small flat. And there, straight in front of my gaze, I notice the dull red lettering on a row of books bound in the coarse linen cloth used in these countries. They announce: Marx, Engels and Lenin. The realisation strikes me that I am in the company of people who had been attracted to the now discredited ideals of communism, who may even have been members of the Party. Their bitterness is perhaps a result of seeing the disintegration of the Party and the enthusiastic way their compatriots have embraced the infernal doctrines of capitalism.

Several Australians of my acquaintance would recoil with horror from that realisation or possibility, as though these people were afflicted with the plague. Yet it is difficult to see in these ordinary, fundamentally middle-class people the brutal steely-eyed ideologues of western mythology. It would be far easier to regard them as pathetic victims of that heartless system—except that if they give any appearance of being victims, the fault seems to lie with the present régime as much as (if indeed not more than) with the past.

It is certainly the present with which my cousin is preoccupied in her agitation. I cannot follow the fine details of her tirade for I know almost nothing of the political intricacies of the previous forty years. The theme of her nervous, edgy monologue is, however, clear enough: the country is screaming to the right. All sorts of nasties are crawling out of the woodwork, war criminals, former Nazis (the word she uses actually refers to the Hungarian variant of National Socialism

119

that flourished in the forties), rabid nationalists and religious bigots. The Catholic church is all-powerful, and she repeats something that also played a part in my parents' mythology, concerning the wartime activities of a celebrated Hungarian prelate, beatified in the anti-communist hagiography of the Cold War years. Being a highly emotional person, she is almost shaking with distress; tears well up in her eyes as she tells me that her one hope is that her daughter's family, who are about to spend nine months in London where her son-in-law is to take an advanced degree in Economics, will stay in the west, will try their luck in England or in America. This world, she says, sweeping her arms around the small living room, will always be a world of hatred and brutality—and now someplace or other the gas chambers and ovens are probably ready, waiting for the first cattle-trucks . . .

The scene—for this family reunion has assumed the proportions of a scene—is embarrassing and painful. It would be only too easy to accuse my cousin of neurosis, of that emotional imbalance characteristic of our kind of people and also (at least according to popular belief) of women of her age. She has gone, as they say, completely over the top, totally out of control. Her husband looks at her with a mixture of pity and irritation; he has probably witnessed many such outbursts in the past. Yet underneath the excess, the self-dramatising, I recognise many years of bitter experience. Her outburst is not merely the displaced fear of a neurotic; she is haunted by phantoms that may have assumed, in the course of the years, shapes even more grotesque than they had possessed in the past. They are, nevertheless, phantoms of a particularly insistent kind. She may, for all I know, be entirely mistaken about the turn Hungarian politics is taking in this new order. But that seems not to be the point. Rather, an understanding of a sort comes to me about the likely nature of her life during those years when she resisted my mother's sad, and equally alarmed and distressed, attempts to establish contact with her young cousin, whom she loved with an almost maternal intensity. I imagine I can reconstruct some of her life in the last three or four decades—years about which she seems so reluctant to speak, evading all attempts on my part to discover why her husband has not been able to work for many years, or what type of work she did in the gymnasium, a secondary school for gifted young people, where she was the head of the history department, or why she retired at (for this world) an early age: in short all those mundane details of our life about which we normally display no reluctance to speak.

On the way back to the hotel, sitting in a half-empty tram—for it is late at night now—I try to picture my cousin when young in those years just after the end of the war, as she was trying to pick up, or indeed start, her life from the ruins of the old. Alone with her ill mother—her father was one of those who had disappeared—she somehow managed to finish school and gain a place in a university. That much I know; the rest must remain conjecture, though a conjecture (I am convinced) with a good degree of probability. Perhaps she felt that a new order was about to begin. The rhetoric of the time promised that the old world of privilege and brutality would be swept away, to be replaced by those shining ideals: equality and justice. She may have seen in that promise a possibility of hope, that she would no longer be persecuted, exploited and reviled as her family had been throughout the years of her childhood. The death of the old world would have been welcome to her, for she was too young to retain any of those sentimental dreams that people like her parents and grandparents, and to an extent those like my mother, entertained about the spurious benevolence of Kakania—a benevolence that somehow compensated for cruelty, injustice and the wanton use (or abuse) of privilege.

A photograph taken at that time shows her as a confident young woman, eyes shining, the skin on her broad Slavic cheeks (another rogue gene that has woven its way through my mother's family) is smooth, youthful, indeed almost childlike. Her smile seems entirely spontaneous—no photographer's coaxing could have produced such openness. She is leaning towards the camera, her shoulder ready to advance into a new world. Perhaps she believed that she could help forge that world, and in so doing put behind her the horrors and the unhappiness which had been her lot—as of millions of others—in the past. Optimism seems to shine out of that photograph: the great communal good which she was ready to help build would compensate (she may have thought) for a dead father, a dying mother and a ruined world.

How long did that illusion last? I imagine her eagerly engaged not merely in the labour of building a new society but in those earnest and dedicated discussions—at school, at university, later at her place of work and at meetings of the local cadre—where the mysteries of the new religion would have been celebrated with absolute faith and dedication. But it could not have lasted. Soon she must have started to notice, no matter how devout she may have been, the sad but inevitable gulf between brave ideals and the realities of life in the new paradise. When did she first suspect that those urging her to greater and greater exertions on behalf of humanity—rather than those outmoded concepts of the state and the nation—were often lining their own pockets at the expense of those whom they attempted to fire with internationalist zeal? When did she realise, at last, that all that had really happened was that the old order had reshuffled itself, adopted new slogans, made a few minor changes in the cast, and continued untroubled on its way?

Disillusion and disenchantment must have come to her. Perhaps it came in 1956, perhaps earlier. By middle age—as was inevitable—she would have looked on the world with much more cynical eyes. Yet, I begin to think in these midnight meditations as the tram is approaching its terminus, even though she came to recognise the sham, the venality, and the corruption in those pious and rousing slogans and exhortations, the ideal itself may have remained fresh and seductive. For the alternative, which (she imagines) she sees blossoming every-where in the birth of yet another new world, is a return to the nationalist bigotry, to the terrible millennium-old enmities that have always torn this world apart. I do not think that she has become disenchanted with the holy texts that line the bookshelves of her flat, only with the way they have been compromised in a world that always compromises the noblest of ideals. I ask myself whether she is subtle enough to realise the inevitability of this outcome—one which will occur with any religion that is prepared to make no allowance for human imperfection. I suspect that she cannot reach that level of abstraction because she sees only the imperfections of this particular world, where she has lived out her life of many disappointments.

I cannot entirely disagree with her. It is appropriate perhaps, though hardly wise, for those of us living in the fabulous world beyond the Austrian border to see the great ideological battles of the century in terms of those simplicities which our politicians and demagogues are intent on offering us. Inside one of the former satellites of the Evil Empire, it does not seem entirely axiomatic that the alternative to that earlier belief or conviction is to be preferred. Under 'socialism', after all, no-one starved or went unhoused. The sad fact may well be not that people like my cousin were wrong, mistaken or even evil, but that their ideals were, as always, exploited and abused by the brutal and the unscrupulous, who are now busily reconstituting themselves in this new dispensation.

As I was saying goodnight to my cousin, before walking down innumerable flights of stairs with her husband so that he could unlock the heavily secured gate, she turned to me and said 'You know, I was terribly lonely. You had left; your grandmother went to join you; my mother died . . . There was no-one, no-one at all.' She sighed as she pecked me on the cheek. And I realised that for this middle-aged woman whom I had last seen as a radiant girl, the great political conundrums of our century were inseparable from the sorrows and the few triumphs of her life. I came to understand that she had been living in history much more intensely than we in the lotus-land of the antipodes could imagine—and I, for my part, could feel no regret that I had missed out on that slice of the troubled history of this sad little country.

THE CLANGING DOOR

Budapest's theatres are numerous, excellent and inexpensive. The rate of exchange admittedly distorts the cost of a ticket— I paid a little over three dollars for an excellent seat in the stalls for tonight's performance of *Richard III*. For Hungarians that is a more substantial sum, the equivalent of the cost of a day ticket on the city's splendid public transport system. During the long years of grim socialist conformism the theatre provided performances of high quality at minimal cost. Theatre tickets and tram and bus fares are, indeed, just about the only prices not to have skyrocketed in the twelve months of freedom this society has enjoyed.

Shakespeare's play is being performed in a vast theatre built in the last years of the nineteenth century. Formerly it was a home for musical plays, popular dramas and comedies. It was one of the theatres people like my mother considered fashionable; a certain social cachet adhered to attending a performance here. Nowadays, together with four or five other theatres, it presents repertory seasons of classical drama from Aeschylus to Beckett. The richness of the theatrical offerings in this city is astonishing. In the space of one week, or ten days at most, you may attend performances of five of Shakespeare's plays, three or four by Molière, the works of Ibsen, Chekhov, Pirandello and Osborne as well as plays by Czech, Hungarian and Russian dramatists whose names are unfamiliar to me. You may, in addition to all this, see *Cats* and *Joseph and the Amazing Technicolor Dreamcoat*, not to mention the ubiquitous *Les Misérables*. The two opera theatres—one a jewelled, diminutive version of the great theatres in Milan, Vienna and Paris, the other a frightful barn constructed in the 1930s along the best Fascist architectural lines—give performances for most of the year. An operetta theatre is reserved exclusively for those Kakanian fantasias which seem to have withstood, here as elsewhere in Central Europe, the passage of time and changes of régime. Two marionette theatres stage puppet versions of remarkably sophisticated works—at one they are currently giving performances of Goethe's *Faust*, which is itself indebted to a series of popular puppet plays.

There are those who say that the golden age of Hungarian theatre is coming to an end. Now that the press and media are no longer controlled by rigid and ever-vigilant censorship, the excitement has gone out of the theatre's ability to deliver subtly coded commentaries on the corruption and injustices of a totalitarian régime. There is no longer any thrill in recognising dangerous parallels with situations everyone knows about (but no-one dares mention) in innocently classical fables—the story of Hamlet and of Phaedra, of Oedipus and of John Gabriel Borkman, or indeed of Richard Crookback himself. People much prefer to spend their evenings in the strip clubs and sex revues cropping up all over the place.

The theatre is nevertheless crowded this evening. This is a celebrated production, first staged during those turbulent months when the movement for reform was coming to a head, when it was not clear whether Gorbachev would honour his implied promise not to interfere in any bid for self-determination by this country, or whether the tanks would roll again, as they did in 1956. In those days, several people have told me, the murderous political rivalries of Plantagenet England provided a brilliant mirror for the time. By now the production is said to have gone soft, lost much of its punch, being merely a competent performance of a classic. It is, however, still capable of attracting large crowds; the auditorium is almost full ten minutes before starting time, and it is then that I discover that I'm sitting in the wrong seat. With murmured apologies I squeeze my way into the single empty seat directly in front of the one I had been occupying.

An elderly gentleman on my left says something sardonic about people getting confused about where they're meant to sit. Though he probably means only to be jocular, I find myself bristling, and once more embark on the carefully rehearsed spiel about having spent most of my life in Australia, about the confusing way theatre seats are numbered etcetera. He seems quite interested. Where do I live? he asks. I tell him I live in

Sydney. Does he know it? Well, he's heard of it. Then he begins to quiz me about my profession—a common Hungarian trait this—about where I live, about my family and so on, to such an extent that I'm beginning to think that he has overstepped even this society's generous tolerance of inquisitiveness. I answer him as briefly and as noncommittally as I am able, for the thought has crossed my mind that he may be a police informer, even though the current official doctrine insists that there are no longer such informers in this free society. That is a proposition, it occurs to me, with which my cousin would no doubt disagree violently.

At this stage our conversation takes a bizarre turn. My neighbour mentions the name of a former colleague of mine, nowadays a reasonably well-known public personality—though hardly, one would have thought, of international renown. Then, taking out his wallet, he shows me a passport-size photograph of a man of Chinese appearance. Do I know who this is? I shake my head. Well, I should know, he tells me, mentioning the name of a famous heart surgeon recently gunned down in a street in Sydney, not far from where I live. He says that he owes everything to that man—he saved his life, and now he doesn't know what will become of him and of all those people whom that wonderful man restored to life. And then, switching into English, he confesses that he has been teasing me, and introduces himself. He owns, he tells me, a pharmacy in the Sydney suburb of Glebe.

During the two intervals of the play we chat in the foyer, smoking our cigarettes. Should he be smoking? I ask. No, he says shrugging his shoulders. But why not? You shouldn't believe everything doctors tell you. Our conversation is pleasantly desultory. My companion's accent is marked by those open vowels and trouble with elisions that make it difficult for Hungarians to learn idiomatic English. Frequently, he slips into Hungarian, appropriately enough, it occurs to me, in our no-man's-land between two cultures and societies.

I ask him what he thinks of the play. It's impressive, he says, these people certainly know how to act. I cannot but agree with him, for this long, well-paced performance is acted with wonderful professionalism. Yet it is not the quality of the acting but the curious excitement in the auditorium that impresses me. In this production, Shakespeare's murderous tale of ambition, cunning and political chicanery is anything but a piece of quaint historicising. Rather, it is raw, immediate and—despite the new order that is allegedly flourishing here—still capable of being deeply disturbing.

One side of the stage (which is clad in rough wooden boards) contains a large metal door. It is the sort of door you see protecting dangerous places. Its heavy metal bolts speak of secrets. It is to this door that a succession of fallen figures are led in the course of Shakespeare's tale of murder, revenge and counter-revenge. Behind the door is the execution chamber. As the mighty are led into that unseen, secret place, there is a sickening sense of anticipation as we wait for the thud of the headsman's axe. They went in proudly or defiantly; they emerge as parcels wrapped in blood-stained hessian. As the complicated and incestuous rivalries of York and Lancaster run their course in this sardonic vision of political brutality, where the victims are almost as corrupt as their predators, the opening and shutting of that door and the thuds echoing behind it act as eloquent commentaries on the terrible lessons of political life. How many in this audience, I wonder, have seen such a door opening and shutting, receiving the latest victim of a brutally pragmatic régime?

We, in the happy west, in that world of wealth and plenty most people here dream of with longing and envy, do not admit to such realities. Perhaps our world also has its heavily bolted doors, its secret chambers. They have not, however, become parts of a mysterious public mythology, as they have here, where everyone in this theatre knows what that door signifies. And the reason for that must be that our world—which we so often censure for its brutality and exploitation of the weak and the defenceless—is less brutal, less cruelly indifferent to injustice, suffering and barbarism than this world had been until a short time ago.

Performances of *Richard III* in the English-speaking world often toy with similar icons of tyranny and brutality. There is nevertheless something contingent and even faintly obscene about such posturings. Here in Budapest it is otherwise. When, at the culmination of a sequence of sickening murders, assassinations and executions, the body of the vanquished Richard is hurled into the pit that had received those hessian-bound bundles, I sense something that I have never experienced previously with this play. It is just and entirely proper that the deformed usurper should have come to such an end, despite his attractive roguery, despite the keen edge of sarcasm with which he played his deadly games. In a more stable and possibly more effete society we may entertain notions of Shakespeare's celebrating this lord of misrule. Here there is no room for that luxury—as there probably wasn't in Shakespeare's world either. Here people know that such figures must be cast into the pit that had also received his victims. What is not clear, though, is whether they realise that the very fact of vengeance, the entirely proper extinguishing of a force as obscene as Richard, inevitably means that that nauseating cycle, the opening and shutting of the metal door, must continue through the as yet unwritten pages of their history.

At the end of the performance, as we walk into the still-balmy evening air, I exchange a few words of farewell with the pharmacist. He tells me that he must hurry to his sister-in-law's, where he is staying. He has to get up early in the morning to go riding. He knows someone who can pull a few strings to get him a fine horse most mornings. They usually telephone in the afternoon to make the arrangements. He had heard from them today. So he'll be up at the crack of dawn for a good canter—a fellow has got to get his exercise, after all.

DIPLOMATIC INCIDENT

The Australian Embassy in Budapest is housed in a handsome turn-of-the-century mansion overlooking a large park in Pest.

It was built by one of those bankers and industrialists whose energy and ambition transformed this city, a sleepy and prim amalgam of a small town and several villages, into a bustling, thriving, cosmopolitan and, as always with the nouveaux riches, slightly vulgar metropolis. That ambition and thirst for wealth came to seem threatening to the often impoverished members of the Hungarian nobility who had established their townhouses on this side of the river, and also to the German-speaking society huddling around the Castle above the opposite bank—people whose families had settled there after the expulsion of the Turks, more or less as colonial administrators, the upholders of the political arm of the great dream of Kakania.

For me, this part of the city is familiar territory, at least in mythological terms. I spent the first few months of my life in a flat in an avenue near the park, and the worst years of the war in a building just around the corner from here, but in a much more plebeian quarter. Two streets away is the institution where I received the only formal education—two or three days—before I started school in Australia in my twelfth year.

Twice a week long queues form outside the Embassy. These resigned and yet cross-looking people are seeking visas to enter Australia, to spend a few weeks with relatives they say, but most (according to gossip) hope to merge into the landscape and settle permanently in expectation of a miracle or an amnesty. You are advised to avoid calling at the Embassy on visa days unless you are prepared to wait for your turn in this queue of patient but anxious people.

Even on non-visa days getting into the Embassy is a harrowing business. Its doors are not open in welcome. If you want to be let in, you must press a button on the intercom fixed to the gate, and state your business—provided that someone answers, or that you can hear or make yourself heard above the din of the traffic rushing along this broad, straight roadway, which offers an irresistible invitation for Budapest's manic drivers to indulge their self-destructive urges.

I have an appointment this morning, fortunately not a visa day. As I walk along the street towards the Embassy, I catch sight of a Hungarian gentleman (the briefcase gives him away immediately) angrily pumping the button. I wait patiently for him to do whatever it is he has to do. To my irritation, his business is taking an inordinately long time. He is arguing— as far as it is possible to argue through an intercom in a deafeningly noisy street—with a Hungarian-speaking person who seems to have some official function inside. It concerns some complicated business about importing a motor car—I am not sure into which country—which the person on the other side of the intercom declares to be impossible, absolutely impossible.

After an unconscionable time the gentleman admits defeat, or at least an impasse, and takes his hand off the button, thereby breaking communications with the inside. As I stand there pressing that unresponsive black button, which remains resolutely unacknowledged, probably because the official on the other side of the intercom thinks it is still that tiresome person going on about his motor car, the gentleman launches into a passionate diatribe about these impossible, uncivilised Australians, and advises me to have nothing to do with them. The Canadians, now they are an entirely different story.

CURRIED PRAWNS AND RICE

The Ambassador's residence is on the other side of the river, high in the green hills of Buda. Meetings of an Australian– Hungarian friendship society are held from time to time in a basement rumpus room decorated with posters of Bondi Beach and the outback. These functions are attended by a curious assortment of people. Among them are several more-or-less permanent residents of Hungary. Some are spending a year or two in what is for them a linguistically impenetrable society on various business or technical missions. This evening I chat briefly with the head of the Hungarian branch of an international soft-drink company who—as it turns out—is friendly with some of my Sydney acquaintances. I also meet a computer expert, sent over to set up the Hungarian version of the TAB in this new world of freedom and opportunity. His parodies of the Hungarian language, based on the few words he knows or at least knows how to approximate, provide much hilarity.

Such occasions also serve to mop up those itinerant nationals who do not rate an invitation to an Embassy dinner or reception, but should be shown some hospitality by their country's representative. Among the crowd of people jamming into this smallish room and spilling on to the lawn in the chill autumn night—mostly to have a cigarette since, this being Commonwealth property, the evil weed is of course proscribed—are several Hungarian-speaking people, former residents of Australia who have returned for some reason or another to the country of their birth. One of them, whom I had met once or twice in Sydney, tells me that there are great opportunities for business now, and hands me a bilingual business card, assuring me that he can put me in touch with well-placed people anxious to do business with Australia.

The atmosphere is convivial, reminding me slightly of a meeting of Rotarians I once attended in a large country town. Everyone knows everyone else, and if there should be new faces around, they are welcomed into the group with genuine warmth. There is a strong impression of people clinging together in what must be for many an alien and perplexing culture. Desultory gossip passes around the room about the comings and goings of various Australians; latecomers, some recently returned from a trip to Warsaw, Prague or Vienna, are greeted with enthusiasm. Expatriate life obviously irons out social and political differences. We are all brothers under the skin—for there are, as yet, no women present—no matter what differences might divide us on our native (or adopted) soil.

Someone says that curried prawns and rice are on tonight. Another looks rather concerned: prawns in Hungary, hundreds of kilometres from the sea? Perhaps he remembers that popular myth of the Australia of my childhood—if you are served something curried when you are 'out', it's bound to mean that the stuff's off. No, no, someone else reassures him, it's OK, Joe's had a look at the prawns and they are fine. Joe, I learn later in the evening, is a jovial Hungarian who grew up in Wollongong. He is now employed as some sort of factotum at the Embassy to tide him over the time of the complicated legal proceedings connected with his attempt to gain reparations for his parents' small farm, which had been seized during the 1948 collectivisation of farming land. He is a tower of strength, those in the know acknowledge. He has a wonderful ability, the computer expert tells me, to weave his way through the monstrous and often obstructionist Hungarian bureaucracy—a remnant of the bad old days of only a year ago. And obviously he knows all about frozen prawns.

Joe leaves the small bar—like those you see in advertisements on late-night television—where he has been dispensing cans of Fosters for a modest donation to help with the forging of Australo–Hungarian friendship. He begins ladling portions of a bright pink stew of small curly prawns on to one side of paper plates while a helper plops dollops of steaming rice on the other. In a loud voice throbbing with the accents of Wollongong, bearing no trace of the Hungarian plains on which he was born, Joe summons everyone to come and get some great tucker, curried prawns and rice like your mum useta make, the best you can get this side of the Danube. One of the expatriates inspects, with obvious suspicion, the small curled crustaceans floating in their pink sauce. Where do they come from? Joe is buggered if he knows, but they're beaut, mate, straight from freezer to pot. The doubter dutifully tucks into his portion—it is impossible to question the word of anyone with such natural authority.

The party breaks into small groups. There is nowhere to sit in this sparsely furnished room except for the three or four stools placed around the angled bar. These places are already taken, probably by the canny, who know the routine and have secured them in good time. The rest of us stand around, balancing paper plates, plastic forks and glasses the best we can. I find myself talking to an elderly gentleman of military bearing, one of a number of people here (almost every one of them, it seems, Hungarian) who are wearing small lapel badges in the shape of a gilt kangaroo. These emblems look vaguely familiar, until I realise that Qantas used to—and perhaps still does—hand them out to passengers on the Kangaroo Route.

The appearance of this gentleman evokes certain poignant memories. He stands stiff and erect. His tweed suit looks immaculately brushed and pressed. His shoes are polished to a mirror sheen. He wears a red bow tie with small black dots. His grey hair is closely cropped, almost shaved; his moustache is neatly trimmed. Something about him speaks of a vanished time, and, more particularly, of a person of whom I have only the haziest memories. A close friend, perhaps a distant relative, of my father's mother was a fastidious, almost dandified gentleman of similar bearing, similar hair, similar moustache. He was a retired town clerk who was inordinately proud of the 'Excellency' he had been awarded at the time of his retirement. He struck terror into the family through his self-appointed role as the arbiter of taste, manners and morals. He was also the only person I have ever known who always wore spats.

My companion on this night in the vinyl-floored rumpus room of the Australian Ambassador's residence reminds me of that gentleman, though a quick calculation suggests that he must be a good forty years his junior. This, I realise, is the look of a Hungarian gentleman of former times, with an air of respectable propriety, of a certain pride of bearing, and a faint hint of the military or at least of the regimented. You can no longer see the likes of this formerly quite familiar figure on the streets of Budapest, for even the few well and carefully dressed people in that shuffling crowd have an entirely different appearance—the studied casualness of contemporary fashion with its litany of revered designer labels. Only in Vienna, that theme park dedicated to images of a former life, may you see people resembling this elderly gentleman with the gilt kangaroo pin in his lapel—and it occurs to me that he is, like those people of similar bearing in the old imperial city, one of the last remnants of Kakania to have survived into the new world.

The devious conversation on which we now embark, filled with ambiguity, unspoken implications, innuendo and evasions, confirms that suspicion. He says he is delighted to be talking to someone who has just arrived from Australia. What a marvellous place! He must tell me in all sincerity, and he doesn't mind if I should think he's having me on, that the years he spent there were the happiest of his life. He sketches in a few vague details, leaving as much unsaid as stated. He went out in '38, young foolish fellow that he was, searching for adventure. Of course he got there just before the war, had to spend a bit of time interned, but then they let him out when they discovered how useful he could be. Ah, wonderful years, wonderful country. All that sunshine, those great open spaces, the friendly people . . . He looks around for a moment, obviously searching for another image to complete his litany, and then turns to me and says: 'And all that seafood—prawns, scallops, lobsters; my dear fellow, you don't know how lucky you are!'

While I am reassuring him that I am entirely aware of my good fortune, I realise that this iconography of the wonders of Australia is as limited and consists as much of well-tried clichés as the litanies of the marvels of Budapest and Hungary among my parent's contemporaries as they sat in cafés and espresso bars in Sydney lamenting the awfulness of life in the world of sunshine, empty spaces and plentiful seafood. Their repertoire was just as paltry: the opera, the cafés along the Corso beside the Danube, the bridges spanning the river, the view of the city from the Castle. It seems to me curious that this gentleman who apparently left Australia voluntarily, and who is obviously still in good standing with the Embassy, should be loud in his nostalgia for a world in which he could have stayed. He had not been driven out as those denizens of the Sydney espresso bars felt that they had been driven out by the hate and brutality that tore this world apart half a century ago. And indeed he now launches on a theme which is all too familiar to me in its mirror image. How can anyone live here, he says, in this filth and pollution, among all the corruption and chicanery, all these ruthless and ambitious people? Oh yes, he knows very well that life in Europe offers some delights not available back there. But that's a small price to pay. How I must be looking forward to going back again!

It seems inevitable therefore that I should ask him why he came back to Hungary. Hearing this he suddenly looks very stern, like an old-fashioned schoolmaster. What makes me think he is Hungarian? No, no, he came here to do a most interesting job—now that he's retired he has decided to stay; it's a fascinating time, after all. I ask him where he came from, reminding him that he said he went out in '38. Ah, Transylvania; he's Transylvanian through and through, not Hungarian.

I am about to ask whether being Transylvanian isn't the same as being Hungarian, indeed perhaps the only genuine way of being Hungarian, but something cautions me to hold my peace. There is, as they say nowadays, a subtext here that I don't entirely understand. Transylvania lies in the western part of modern Romania. Much of its population is Hungarian speaking. Many Hungarian patriots insists that a genuine folk culture, unsullied by Slav, Austrian or Jewish influences, is to be found only there, in that world of farmers and shepherds where the authentic Hungarian folk music (not the phoney gypsy stuff) and traditions survive. In the growing nationalism of the new Hungary, it is not unusual to encounter the sentiment that until Transylvania is restored to the Kingdom, Hungary will be neither secure nor stable.

Why then does this dapper gentleman, with his immaculately clipped moustache, insist so strenuously that he is not Hungarian? No amount of devious insinuation on my part provokes him into offering any clarification—he is obviously much more expert at such games of evasion. I begin, nevertheless, to suspect something that, for lack of a more compelling explanation, must lie close to the truth. This gentleman must be in his seventies; he was probably born just after the Great

War, or perhaps even during its closing stages. It is possible, of course, that he is even older—it all depends on what he meant by having been young in 1938. In any event he would have been born at a time when a dedication to Kakania, though that realm was no longer a political reality, still ran strong through the veins of its former subjects. Transylvania was, moreover, not far from the slightly more easterly district known as the Bukovina where Gregor von Rezzori, chronicler and memorialist of the last years of the Empire, began his life as a scion of the Kakanian ruling class among the Ruthenians, Serbs, Jews and Magyars of that ethnographic melting pot. Perhaps this gentleman, in asserting sternly that he is a proud son of Transylvania, is distancing himself from what he, like von Rezzori, would have been trained to regard as vulgar and provincial nationalism. Perhaps his family's gaze also skipped over that parvenu city of Budapest in their attempt to catch sight of the fount and origin of their culture, Vienna, the city of their dreams.

I have noticed that he has held himself aloof throughout this evening from the conviviality, the merry quaffing of cans of Fosters and consumption of curried prawns and rice. Perhaps he regards with absolute contempt the other wearers of gilt kangaroos, in their shiny suits of exaggerated cut which only confirm the sad fact that the creators of contemporary *haute couture* never had short Hungarians in mind when drawing up their sophisticated designs. I can understand such disdain. In this world, especially, the elaborate sign language of clothes still retains some of its former force. The tweed suit, the bow tie, the plain gold links worn with a double-cuffed shirt all signal that this gentleman belongs almost to another order of creation, that he is a product of a network of social standards and preoccupations which those stocky possessors of Armani suits would not understand.

And they do make a ridiculous spectacle. There is something essentially oily in the way they seem to be whispering confidences into the ears of soft-drink tsars and computer wizards decked out in their much less fashionable Australian clothes. They seem to be living parodies of the way Hungarians are supposed to behave according to the popular mythology of the English-speaking nations. Yet one of them, despite his fashionable and expensive suit, gives a very different impression. Taller than his compatriots, thickset in a muscular rather than flabby way, he is sending out complicated signals in which self-confidence and arrogance are equally present. He does not mix with the other occupants of the rumpus room; rather he seems to be holding impromptu audiences with what I can only think of as a peasant-like *hauteur*—reminding me a little of the image Boris Yeltsin's minders cultivated for him during his rise to prominence. There is certainly nothing patrician about this person. He gives, on the contrary, a sense of reined-in aggression, as though he would be more comfortable in battle-fatigues than in the uniform of the successful Budapest man of affairs in 1991. He waves away with an imperious sweep of the hand the paper-plateful of prawns someone offers him. The gesture suggests that he demands more substantial food than an effeminate stew of curly prawns.

Some days later I find out a little about him and his kind, and also about my dapper companion on the night of prawns and rice. The latter, I am told, has been hanging around Embassy functions for years. The consensus seems to be that he would like to go back to Australia but realises that his money will go much farther here. A nice old stick, my informant says.

The other is a very different proposition. He is one of the heroes of '56, people who took advantage of the turmoil and disarray of those terrible days to slip over the border—something my cousin and her husband failed to do. They have been living in Western Europe, in the Americas, in Australia and New Zealand, often prospering in various business ventures where their ingenuity and acumen have reaped considerable benefits. Now that the political system has changed, many of them have come back, claiming that their efforts and their financial contributions have sustained dissident movements through the long years of political repression. Some of them claim to be the true saviours of the country, defenders of the realm who have kept the spirit of Hungarian nationalism alive in exile. They have returned for their reward.

My informant, a wry, sceptical Hungarian who, according to his own confession, is never able to decide whether the political system that happens to be dominant at any particular time is heaven-sent or the work of the devil, is generally scathing about these strutting patriots. They are in the forefront, he says, of a movement to purge the nation of collaborators. An entire university department, he tells me, has been disbanded while its former members are being investigated by the new censors—in the meantime, though, they continue to teach and to draw their salaries because no-one else can be found to do the work. Where will it all stop? he asks. Will bus drivers and street cleaners be condemned as collaborators because they drove the buses and cleaned the streets of a discredited régime? Hungarians will never learn, he sighs, and then grows animated: something must be done to put an end to this culture of blame, to the national obsession with finding scapegoats, on whom all the ills of the world may be blamed before they are driven out or killed.

The clanging door of that Plantagenet prison of the other night at the theatre comes to mind, as I listen to his mild-mannered though deeply pessimistic account. There are aspects of this world which seem never to change. The old cycle of blame and revenge appears destined to continue for ever. Though the streets of the inner city have been renamed in these first years of a new world, they remain the same grimy and chaotic streets they were during the dark years of what everyone in this country now refers to as socialism. This is still the depressing, deeply flawed and probably treacherous world of fierce hatred that I left in my childhood for that land of sunshine and abundant shellfish.

CULTURAL DELEGATION

Australia is very chic in the Central Europe of 1991. Tourist agencies in affluent Vienna carry seductive posters of 'Ayers Rock', koalas and dreamy images of the Sydney Opera House in a misty half-light. While Hungarian universities are gearing up for their first-ever courses in Australian Studies, a prestigious mega-conference on Australian culture is being held in the Swiss city of Bern. Anyone who is anyone seems to be there. One well-placed bomb would probably wipe out of the cream of Australia's cultural gurus. After the conclusion of the conference the delegates disperse. Some head for London, some for New York, at least one hurries to what is still called Leningrad, and a few drift into Hungary—though one visa-less unfortunate, gossip insists, got no farther than the border. On a gloriously sunny weekend, when the soft sunlight already betrays hints of the winter to come, I meet some of these people and become, temporarily, an amateur and somewhat bemused tourist guide.

The weather remains enchanting throughout our rambles around the city. A gentle breeze has blown away the brown murk of the past few days. In the mellow autumn sunshine Budapest looks beguilingly beautiful. The river dances with light as it curves under the graceful bridges linking the hills of Buda and the flat land of Pest. The green dome of the Castle and the stone spire of St Matthew's church are etched against a clear blue sky. Upstream, on the opposite bank, the extravagant fantasy of the Parliament glitters with flashes of gold as the sun touches its walls and turrets. The river is busy with steamers conveying Saturday morning pleasure-seekers to the islands and resorts of the Danube. The seventeenth- and eighteenth-century houses of the Castle district are festive with window boxes and baskets of geraniums. Horse-drawn carriages clatter along the narrow cobbled streets.

My companions are surprised and enchanted. We are standing on a terrace in front of the Castle, the panorama of city and river spread out below us. They had not realised that

Budapest is such a beautiful place, nor that it was so 'European'. I ask them what they had expected. They can't put it into words exactly, but it was something much more grim, much more drab and somehow 'eastern'. But this city, they insist, is like Paris—much more interesting than Vienna, for instance, where they had stayed for a few days on their way here from Bern. Vienna was, they confess, a disappointment—dull, dowdy and rather boring. But this, this is entirely different.

Yet while their excitement and delight grow as we walk along the cobbled streets of the oldest part of the city down to the river bank, and then make our way across the handsome suspension bridge towards the flat, late nineteenth-century city of the opposite side, I am seized by a desire to show them the other city, *my* city, or at least the city that has become the focus of my private mythology about this nation and its people. I want to show them the place on the embankment where hundreds, perhaps thousands of people were machine-gunned by the Germans and their Hungarian henchmen in the terrible winter of 1944. I want to take them to the narrow, over-crowded streets behind this magnificent façade, places where the grim life of the Hungarian *petite bourgeoisie* in poky flats and rented rooms fed the obsessions and neuroses of this world. I want them to realise the implications of those pompous and bombastic monuments and statues that litter the city in praise of brutality and intolerance, some of the ugliest characteristics of humanity masquerading as nobility and patriotism. I want to translate for them the inscriptions on public buildings that commemorate a national pride which borders on paranoia. I want, in short, to make them see what I think of as the cancer of Mitteleuropa, which nothing, not two devastating wars nor forty years of totalitarian repression, could obliterate.

The reasons for that compulsion are deeply buried within my own obsessions. This is the place of origin of the cultural luggage I carry around with me wherever I go, even though it is only here that I become conscious of its weight. I realise that a part of me wishes to respond to the undeniable attractiveness of this place—especially when seen in this sparkling sunshine, as a soothing breeze wafts warm air from the south. If there is some sort of *genius loci* to which we become attached during the first years of our life, something that forms the centre and the navel of all our experiences of the many worlds some of us must inhabit, then this city must provide that location for me. And I have to admit to myself that there is something about my relationship with Budapest which is different from and in a way much more intimate than my attitude to Sydney, a city I know far better, a city where I feel much more safe, comfortable and at ease. Yet, despite the allure of this city of water, hills and monuments, I find myself constantly driven in the opposite direction. For this is the city where most of my family were killed, or else where they started their journey to death. This is the setting for some twelve or fourteen months of panic and fear, of weeks spent in a dark cellar, of many weeks of life masquerading under an assumed name—as an eight-year-old well-drilled in the deceptive tale of a false identity for which my mother had paid with her last piece of jewellery. It was here that I was made to feel that people like me were pariahs, vermin to be exterminated, just because we did not share the physical and cultural characteristics of the high-cheekboned people who are now, in 1991, strolling around in the bright sunshine, enjoying their city in the fond belief that they are now free and masters of their own destinies.

I come to realise more powerfully than ever how much this world has been poisoned for me, that for me the stench of death and hatred still hangs in the air, despite its having been cleansed by the processes of history, or at least that it has been filled with different hatreds and enmities. I also realise that throughout the days and weeks I have spent in this place, more or less on my own, observing yet detached, and even in the course of perfunctory conversations I have had with people (my cousin and her husband, the owners of the small hotel high up in the hills of Buda, the lady at the corner shop, a succession of manic taxi-drivers) I have kept this world suspiciously at arms' length. Now, looking at these sights with people whose cultural preoccupations and obsessions are very different from mine, I find myself forced to admit the possibility that what I take to be an objective and verifiable truth—the indelible corruption and evil of societies such as this—may be no more than a projection of my own particular dilemma generated by history and personal experiences.

I am driven, all the same, to impose that vision on my companions. We visit duly the spot on the embankment— unmarked, forgotten, ignored—where my mother and I narrowly escaped death. The image of that bleak winter day comes back with remarkable vividness. My mother pulls me by the hand as we slip out of the snakelike file into a dark alley, pressing against a doorway as the cortège passes by. Next we look at drab rows of apartment houses, and I speak about the mythology of hierarchy that governed, and probably still governs, these dwellings, the pecking-order based on whether your flat looks onto the street or the courtyard, whether it's on one of the upper floors or closer to street-level, whether it may boast a balcony, and a thousand other snobbish gradations. I show my companions the streets and cafés where, in the days before the queues of people making their way to the river bank, it was fashionable to be seen, and those places which people like my parents would not frequent. I try to impress on them, in short, that the well-known political brutality of this world was merely an extreme manifestation of its stifling and iron-clad social stratification. I tell them about the way servants were treated, even by families who considered themselves humane and considerate, and I also tell them about the strutting arrogance of the gentry and aristocracy, and that if you wanted to attract the attention of the waiter in a restaurant you used to tap loudly on a glass with your knife.

I suspect that I am growing somewhat tedious, as anyone pursuing an obsession is likely to produce tedium. My companions are attentive and thoughtful, however, perhaps because what I am saying has made some impression on them, or perhaps because I am revealing a facet of my personality that they have not met before. It is, nevertheless, when we return to the hills above the river, to the cobbled streets around the Castle that this sour litany seems to engage with something within their consciousness and their experience, something to which they are able to relate more directly than they were when listening to my catalogue of brutality, outrage and small-minded snobbery.

We are standing outside the gothic church of St Matthew, named not merely in honour of the evangelist but also of the fifteenth-century monarch who gave this country a brief 'renaissance', before it was swept away by the marauding Turks. It is a pretty church, a miniature cathedral with a stone spire like that in Vienna. Here is one of the few antiquities in a city which, apart from a handful of modest domestic structures of the late seventeenth and early eighteenth centuries, is fundamentally a nineteenth-century city like Sydney, Melbourne or Adelaide. On this shining autumn day the church draws admiring crowds of tourists. My friends, like most cultivated Australians, are very respectful towards antiquity. They admire the skill that went into the construction of these ancient piles, and they are prone at times to discourse on their aesthetic merits, on the harmony of their design and the wonderful spaces they contain, even though these people are wholly secular in outlook, often contemptuous of what they regard as the mere superstition of religion. Coming from a society bereft of such monuments they are obviously impressed by this imposing church, and I can sense that somehow this increases their regard for this country, seemingly rich in antiquities that speak of a continuity of tradition.

Conscious as I am that they are impressed by this edifice and that they admire the elaborately carved and embellished exterior of the church, I cannot resist telling them that it is by and large a modern reconstruction, a fantasy of what the church, which has stood on this spot for centuries, should look like, rather than what it is or has been. I can sense myself becoming quite harsh and dogmatic as I insist that they recognise the implications of such sentimental reconstructions. I draw analogies between this type of façadeism and the national and political cult of illusions and surfaces. I suggest that there is considerable immaturity about people who find the source of national pride and identity in something so blatantly manufactured, a recreation of their longings and fantasies. They are structures no less phoney than the neo-gothic brick and stone extravaganzas of Australia which my companions regard as the living insignia of our colonial status, of that cultural cringe that worshipped and attempted to emulate the institutions of a distant and arrogant world.

This they are able to appreciate. I am conscious that because this world is alien to them, because they have never felt obliged—understandably enough—to consider deeply its political and cultural confusions and complexity, they had imagined that its appurtenances, its gothic churches, baroque palaces, medieval bastions are natural and 'native' aspects of this society's history. In their own world, our world, such people are very sensitive to the manner in which both the material and spiritual features of Australian society have encoded within them the particular perplexity and ambivalence of life in the antipodes. They are sensitive to the many layers of exploitation, dispossession and fulfillment of wishes in the cityscapes of urban Australia. That Sydney, Melbourne, Brisbane and Adelaide are theme parks does not seem to them an insupportable or offensive notion. They understand the essentially imitative nature of our public architecture, those attempts to reproduce and emulate the social and political structures of a distant and allegedly superior society. The possibility that here in 'Europe' similar emulation, similarly nostalgic instances of trompe l'oeil may be encountered comes to them as a surprise: they had not considered that these apparently self-confident societies, with their histories evident in the testimony of stone, timber and brick, may have sought a spurious respectability as much as the late nineteenth-century edifiers of Australian cities attempted to persuade themselves that they were producing replicas of European culture.

It is possible that their perception of this world may have been altered in the course of these few hours by my hectoring, yet, as we continue our ramble around the city, and as we take up the threads of this topic in the vaulted cellar of a restaurant which does, in all probability, date from the fifteenth century, I am growing aware of the gulf that separates us. In Australia with people like these—as close as our society has been able to get to the nurturing of an urban intelligentsia—I often sense considerable affinity. Though our attitudes and aspirations may differ radically in many respects, we often find a common ground. Our view of life, despite those differences, is far removed from the everyday lives of most of our compatriots— those people who turn their backs on the type of speculation (possibly futile and self-indulgent) which is our habitual pursuit. We experience a certain camaraderie because we stand aloof from what we regard as a hedonistic and material-obsessed society which we think dominates Australian life in the late twentieth century—the entrepreneurs, the grey bureaucrats, the violent crowds at sporting fixtures, and those who spend their lives mesmerised in front of the television.

Here, however, because of my own particular obsessions with this world and its many injustices and dishonesties, I am growing aware of the fundamental difference between myself and people like my companions of the day. They understand now, I suspect, the reasons why I had to delve beneath the surface of their essentially tourist-like enjoyment of this world, to make them see the brutality I see everywhere. A great gap exists between understanding and experience. They cannot, and cannot be expected to, share the distress and anguish that I find hard to disguise in this world; I cannot ask them to be as passionate about it as I find myself becoming, despite my inclinations, despite my better judgement, and my recognition that at any moment I shall become a tiresome bore.

Consequently I come to understand why in Australia I often feel distanced from and not a little scathing about the perplexities, preoccupations and obsessions that frequently torment such pleasant and entirely civilised people. Their responses to my litanies of the terrible things that have happened here, in this world, and to this conducted tour around my private mythology are sympathetic and understanding. Their moral and political sensibilities are obviously stirred by these reminders of a dark and still-recent past. But for them these injustices and atrocities remain merely parts of a universal predicament. They know that societies in every part of the world and at every moment of history are more than liable to exploit and to persecute those who are weaker or defenceless. They know that such is the way of the world, and they might indeed be tempted to identify that condition as the operation of evil, were it not that they are more than aware of the theological implications of that word. So, as they listen to me on this golden sunny day, they are beginning to realise that this world also knew atrocities of the kind they are familiar with—South Africa, Nicaragua, Chile, East Timor. For them this lesson about the darker face of Central European history is, however, no more than another instance of the corrupting influence of power, ambition and hatred. Their passion is reserved for outrages much closer to home.

Inevitably, as we discuss the ubiquity of cruelty and barbarism, the sad plight of the Australian Aborigines creeps into our talk. This is something about which they have very strong opinions, tinged with a considerable emotional charge. They are descended, at least in part, from people who had been directly or indirectly implicated in the dispossession, persecution and slaughter of the original inhabitants of the continent. They feel contaminated by the guilt of their ancestors, even though they know that it is merely a retrospective guilt, or guilt by association. They are also sane and intelligent enough to know that very little may be done to atone for that guilt— short of evacuating the land, leaving it once more to its rightful owners, though inevitably in a depleted and degraded condition. They are, therefore, caught in an emotional dilemma. They know that the cultural and emotional reparations society at large or individuals might make to the Aborigines could easily devolve into tokenism. Yet they also realise that it is impossible to go beyond that probably insufficient attempt at reconciliation. In consequence, this question or problem tends to occupy the centre of their cultural and political consciousness, it forms a preoccupation colouring much of their intellectual life, even though they are aware that they are powerless individually or even communally to act upon that preoccupation. And they become conscious of an impasse, even of frustration as they acknowledge that the guilt must perforce remain merely that—purgation through action cannot become a practical possibility. From such perplexity is obsession born.

I understand and sympathise with their dilemma, but I cannot share it in any immediate or personal way. I cannot participate in these people's sense of personal or national guilt because, for me, the terrible persecution and exploitation of the Aboriginal people of Australia occurred, at least in large part, at a time when Australia had not existed for my family as anything other than an exotic land on the other side of the world. That, I realise, sounds casuistic, and it may well be so: by living in Australia, and by adopting its mores I may well have become just as guilty, or even perhaps more so, than the direct descendants of those squatters, settlers and explorers who slaughtered or enslaved the Aborigines. Yet, much as I understand the terrible perplexity and torment that this consciousness does and should impose on those people, for me it is not something that has entered into the fibres of my being, has not become intrinsic to my emotional life, to the way I look at the society in which I live. It is not a part of my history, it is merely a part of my recognition of the terrible cruelty of humankind. The maltreatment of the Aborigines is, for me, a dark spot in the history of the world, equal to but no more horrible than all the other dark spots in the history of man's inhumanity.

That is precisely how my companions on this day's outing respond to my tale of the terrible events of 1944. For me, though, those events have become a deeply personal and perhaps obsessive mythology. This is something I cannot forget or escape from whenever I am in this world, even though I realise that it happened almost half a century ago, and that many of the people walking the streets of Budapest on this beautiful afternoon were not even alive at the time. All that is beside the point. For me that time has soured this world, making it incapable of redemption, despite my knowing that it is contrary to good sense and to humane principles to think of a world, a nation or a society as being beyond redemption. This is my own particular preoccupation, obsession or secular cross, like the guilt many (though by no means all) Australians experience when they think of the fate of the original inhabitants of their world, or, for that matter, the deep psychic scars that still mark many Australians of Irish ancestry.

For that reason there will always be something of a gulf separating us. Though I have much greater affinity with people like my companions of this sunny autumn day than with the inhabitants of this world of Hungary, I am always conscious of being outside the emotional currents of Australian society. I do not feel the same alarms, or if it comes to that, the same joys that these people experience. For me the Australian landscape, a source of deep consolation for many, is always hostile and threatening. The unremarkable plains of Hungary, which to most Australians seem merely what they are, a pleasant featureless landscape, stir deep sentiments whenever I catch sight of them through the windows of a train or a car. My participation in Australian life, in the fullest sense of the term, must remain provisional, cerebral and necessarily detached, just as my companions are detached emotionally, though not intellectually or politically, from the atrocities that this world has witnessed. It cannot be otherwise. The gulf must be acknowledged despite the inclination to pretend that it is no more than a shallow ditch.

Nevertheless, these people and I have shared a world and a pattern of experiences that make us understand each other with respect and sympathy. And we discover a moment of considerable empathy as, almost at the end of our ramble around the streets of a city that still looks seductively picturesque in the late afternoon sunshine, we return to that gothic church of illusions. The interior is bathed in rich light. My companions almost gasp, as I suspected they would, when they catch sight of its extraordinary embellishments. Every surface of every wall, pillar and arch is covered with gorgeous arabesques of flowers and vines painted in the richest and most glowing hues. This medieval fantasia, the ultimate in kitschy reconstruction perhaps, certainly achieves what its inventors intended: to deliver one of those theatrical surprises that so many of the public monuments of this city strive to achieve. The effect is stunning even though you realise almost immediately that it is contingent and perhaps a little shoddy. If this gothic church had indeed been decorated with rich colours during the middle ages, as all great churches of the time were supposed to have been, it would not have looked like this. This is a modern fantasy, another instance of Central Europe's sad tendency to turn itself into a theme park.

You cannot but be indulgent towards this mixture of naïveté and sophistication; there is something endearing if a little childish about it. I can see my companions smiling with pleasure as they take in the extravagance of the décor. But then they notice something that I too noticed on earlier visits. The pleasant entwining of flowers and vines is interrupted here and there by large frescoes, depicting great moments in the Christian history of the Hungarian people. They realise what I have also realised—several of these paintings depict the subjugation of pagan tribes by a sword-bearing royal saint, his halo clearly visible behind a proud crowned head as he lifts his great weapon to show the might and power of the God of Love.

A GERMAN ON YOUR LAP

The Café Ruszwurm, nestled between seventeenth-century townhouses in the Castle district, is probably the city's most eloquent emblem of Kakania to have survived the political storms of the century. This is not one of the pompous, gilded establishments, football-field sized expanses of marble and mirrored glass which provided the stage-setting for the social rituals of pre-war Budapest. You enter from the street through a modest glass door. The outer room is almost entirely occupied by a large counter and a glass case. As in the smaller cafés of Vienna and Budapest, the cakes displayed in front of mirrored backings have a pleasantly irregular look, as if to suggest that quality rather than appearance were the pastrycook's main concern.

That Kakanian smell is evident the moment you set foot inside. It wafts into the inner room—the café proper—which contains only a handful of tables in front of banquettes ranged along two longish walls. The decoration is simple, homely though stylish. The tiled stove in one corner—a guarantee of comfort and well-being in this world of arctic winters—has been lovingly maintained, its curves and curlicues as fresh as the day it was installed. Everything is, indeed, light and cheery. The cups and saucers, plates and cutlery are made of the finest materials. The carpet, the wallpaper and the chandeliers attest to regular and devoted cleaning. This is one of the few places in the city where the universal grime and decrepitude of present-day Budapest seem somehow to have been avoided. It is as though fifty years of war and misery have bypassed this blessed place. You cannot help wondering how that miracle might have been achieved, what privilege this place enjoyed to allow it to continue so sparkling, so spick and span in a down-at-heel world.

Most days it is impossible to get anywhere near the Ruszwurm. Americans from the nearby Hilton, guidebooks open at the map directing them to this fabled place, loiter outside the entrance hoping to find an unoccupied table. Now and then, a couple of well-dressed Hungarians, members of the new élite in a world where an élite always rises from the ashes of the old, muscle past them, clearing a space with their expensive skin handbags, to assume a position at the head of the expectant queue. The only sensible time to find a table is in that midday lull when no-one in his right mind would abandon the joys of the day's main meal to sit in a café, even the Ruszwurm.

On this early afternoon the café is quiet. Every table is occupied, though there is no queue, no sign of a face peering through the window in hope of encountering the impossible. Most of the customers are in the process of leaving, hurrying no doubt to a hearty luncheon somewhere or other. The neat waitresses in their stiffly starched lacy aprons stand decorously at the back of the room. They have obviously been carefully chosen and well trained; they do not lounge about or gossip like their slatternly 'colleagues' with oversized earrings in the large cafés on the other side of the river. Unfashionable though it probably is to be frequenting the Ruszwurm at this hour, it is one of the most pleasant experiences to be sitting here, surrounded by the wonderful aroma of coffee and vanilla, idly watching the play of light on walls, trees and cobblestones through the large plate glass window. The ticking of an old-fashioned clock marks out the peace and contentment of this quiet haven in a noisy and often neurotic city.

In an imperfect world such peace cannot last. Almost as soon as the young woman at the table adjacent to mine leaves, a group of five noisy Germans occupies the café. They—three men and two women—are very large people. The women wear tight-fitting jeans which do nothing to flatter their flabby middle-aged thighs. Two of the men are sporting loudly checked jackets which used to be fashionable in the seventies—though they were never intended to be worn over knitted summer shirts with broad horizontal stripes describing a series of sine curves over the wearers' bloated bellies. The group looks around the small room for somewhere to sit, discussing the situation in the loud guttural tones of a dialect or provincial accent.

They decide that the table next to mine is the only one able to accommodate their generous bulk. Even so, two spindly chairs and a narrow curved banquette are insufficient space for five large persons. Three try to perch on the banquette, which means that one of the men—the fattest, it seems to me—must squeeze himself beside me with much grunting and sighing. He is almost sitting on my lap. They consult the Hungarian menu with noisy and inaccurate guesses about its contents. My neighbour, I discover, reeks of garlic, the result no doubt of gorging himself on too much spicy Hungarian salami. The discomfort, the noise, the smell of breathy garlic mixed with the subtler aromas of vanilla and coffee prove too much for me. I signal the young waitress who had served me, with the universal sign-language indicating that I wish to pay.

She walks over to my table. She is very young, in her early twenties probably, with wonderfully delicate skin and eyes of the palest blue. There is nothing of the hardness of most of the women of this city about her. She, like the café itself, seems to be a remnant of an older world—she has the appearance of one of those modest young ladies so often depicted by Central European genre painters of the turn of the century. Before she is able to reach my table, however, one of the Germans grabs her by the arm and begins reeling off, in German, a complicated order for coffee and cakes.

I see red. Mustering as much courage and German as I am able, I say (indeed bark) at him: '*Ein Moment, bitte; warten Sie*', wondering what effect this boldness will have. He in turn is flabbergasted long enough for the young woman to escape and to make her way to the other side of my table. As she recites the items I have consumed—two black coffees, a mineral water, a ham and egg sandwich—she looks at me with the wisdom of her twenty years. The Germans are terrible, she says. Rude and pushy. They took over the country in her grandparents' time. Now they are back again, probably for good. And as she gives me my change, I can see her take a deep breath before facing the onslaught of the victorious Teutons.

IN DRACULALAND

SZEGED GOULASH

Szeged goulash is a dish composed of meat, vegetables, onions, spices and the inescapable paprika, all floating in a soup-like sauce. It is like any other goulash except that the diced vegetables are cooked separately and thrown into the pot just before serving. Like Irish stew, Lancashire hot-pot and spaghetti bolognese, Szeged goulash is unknown in the place that gave it its name, though the dish often appears on restaurant menus in other places, notably in cheaper Austrian inns. Yet the town itself is not unlike a stew—a lot of miscellaneous elements thrown into a pot and boiled.

If you travel to Szeged by train, across the great Hungarian plain that used to extend (in happier times) far into what is now Romania and Serbia, the landmark warning you of imminent arrival is a tall white building of recent construction, the salami factory, a source of pride and employment for many of the town's citizens. Salami is, indeed, ubiquitous in a place that knows nothing of Szeged goulash: in the salami factory's immense retail outlet in the centre of the town you may buy all sorts of salamis, some in elaborate gift-packaging contained in satin-lined wooden boxes. Yet as soon as the factory is left behind, the train pulls into the railway station of a very different world. The station itself is surprisingly spacious, though badly in need of repair and painting. It seems somehow much too large and ornate for the drab buildings surrounding it.

Much of Szeged is like its railway station. Once you leave the decaying square in front of the station, busy with the clanging of trams, fouled by the exhaust fumes of decrepit Lada taxis, the buildings become more and more impressive, displaying a certain grandeur and a flamboyance curiously out of keeping with a town tucked into a corner of a small and impoverished country. It is, moreover, vaguely reminiscent of another place—not only of Budapest, two-and-a-half hours away by train, but, you realise as you catch sight of a broad, curving avenue from which equally impressive thoroughfares radiate in an orderly manner, of Vienna, the city that provided the model and the ideal for the towns and cities of Kakania. The buildings of Szeged also display many Habsburg conceits—elaborately moulded decorations, caryatids, muscular titans, their arms folded above their heads to support balconies with heavily-carved balustrades, eyeless classical busts in niches, and, everywhere, the proud double-headed Habsburg eagle.

Elsewhere, though, especially in the cobbled sidestreets, the atmosphere is entirely different. Low single-storey houses with seemingly oversized gateways display a different type of emblem: the rays of the rising sun carved in wood or stone, an ancient image from Hungary's pagan past that was introduced by the Magyar people, descendants of Central Asian nomads. These streets, the mostly elderly people that shuffle along them, the women with kerchiefs tied around their heads, the men in peaked caps, something in the air and in the quality of the light, even the dust that rises with every gust of wind, all tell you that this is the east, even perhaps the Balkans, that world to which no self-respecting Central European, trapped in that dream of Kakania visible in other parts of the city, wishes to belong.

In certain clearly defined sections of Szeged, among the statues and fountains (strutting heroes and demure nymphs) of the large municipal park, or in the open-air café that fills, in good weather, most of a spacious and beautifully proportioned principal square, this seems, by contrast, a city of young people, of jeans-clad students—some of whom have to endure, in the course of the weeks I am to spend here as a guest of two academic institutions, a ramble around some aspects of Australian literature, to the incessant grumbling accompaniment of defective plumbing.

Not far from the square and the gardens there are other

symbols and icons of urban ambitions. An enormous, hideously impressive neo-romanesque cathedral in liver-coloured brick (Patrick White's suburbia blown up to gigantic scale) dominates a vast open space, filled with rising tiers of seats, a grandstand for spectators at a summer arts festival modelled on Salzburg. Opposite, an archway, also in liver-brick, is flanked by two monstrous statues of armed men carved in the simplified and brutal style that symbolises the moral and political decline of Europe through its flirtation with Fascism. A few steps in the other direction takes you to a shopping complex, constructed this time in terracotta-textured brick, that conjures immediately other images of an Australian suburb—a shopping mall with its characteristic mixture of the tawdry and the utilitarian. Outside the broken telephone booths near these shops (including the one displaying cellophane-wrapped salami in satin-lined boxes), dark-skinned youths lounge, argue, eye and whistle at the attractive girls hurrying about their business. They are Romanian refugees, gypsies, according to the locals, (watch out for your wallet!) though they look harmless enough, only poor, bored and dispossessed.

A mixture such as this should be heady and exhilarating. Yet during these weeks of a wonderfully mellow autumn the town comes to strike me as curiously sleepy, boring and very provincial. It is, somehow, all show, none of it quite right or hanging together, a dead place, despite the bustle, despite the crowd of young people enjoying the soft sunshine. It would not surprise me if the handsome buildings were nothing but façades, empty behind their imposing exteriors. The grandeur and scope seem not merely inappropriate but, in some indefinable way, alien and imported. And there is, besides, a vaguely familiar sense which, in the course of these weeks, leads to two realisations. The first and more obvious, confirmed by guide-books and histories of the city, is that this is in many ways a little Vienna. The other is much more personal, even perhaps idiosyncratic: Szeged, planted in that world where Europe begins to become the despised 'east', is an invented city, as most Australian cities were invented from a mixture of nostalgia and hard-headed politics, therefore providing a contrast with, or even perhaps an affront to, the physical and spiritual environment in which they were constructed.

In the days before the Treaty of Versailles, which robbed Hungary of what are the western parts of Romania and a considerable portion of Serbia, Szeged, now a border town, was the commercial and administrative centre of a large and prosperous agricultural district. It was also an important bishopric, though it could not at that time boast of the many fine seats of higher learning which distinguish it today. They settled here when Hungary lost more than half of its territory in the aftermath of the Great War, and several Hungarian-language institutions, such as the university of what is now the Romanian city of Cluj, were obliged to seek shelter in the remaining parts of the nation. In the nineteenth century Szeged was also the hotbed of Hungarian—that is to say Magyar—nationalism. The abortive revolution of 1848 against the Habsburgs was directed from this city, just as almost a century-and-a-half later the movement to free Hungary from Soviet domination began here. Szeged was always, if its proud citizens are to be believed, a thorn in the side of those foreign bullies who have oppressed the gallant Hungarian people throughout the many centuries of their turbulent history.

The city is situated on the river Tisza (after the Danube the country's most important waterway) a capricious and danger-ous stream given to sudden and difficult-to-control flooding. One of these inundations, in 1879, destroyed most of the city, with disastrous effect on the morale and the economy of the town. In what must have been an act of extreme political cunning and cynicism, Franz Josef, the Emperor and also King of Hungary, directed from Vienna—the stronghold of the hated Habsburgs—the reconstruction of the devastated city along the most modern lines. This instance of the care and love shown by the benevolent monarch for his Hungarian subjects turned out to contain an unmistakable political message. Whereas the old Szeged had been a Hungarian town that had grown with its people and their way of life over the centuries, the new city was to replicate the grandeur of Vienna here, in a different world on the banks of the Tisza.

The focus of the city is a curved boulevard, running from river bank to river bank, a diminutive and provincial replica of the Ring, that arterial emblem of Viennese imperial pride. Lined by substantial buildings, all flaunting the insignia of Habsburg power, the atmosphere of these boulevards is studiedly Viennese. The layout of the city contains an echo of the physical and cultural polarity of the imperial capital. At one end of the inner town, as in Vienna, stands a splendid theatre, surprisingly large, solid and ornate for a city of two hundred thousand souls. At the other, in the vast space filled with tiers of seats, the Votive Church, the cathedral of Szeged (not finished until 1930), dominates everything within sight, glaringly self-important in its liver-brick bombast. Religion and art, Catholicism and the cult of the opera embrace a Szeged rebuilt at the dictates of the King-Emperor, in the same way as identical shrines of Central European political and cultural life mark out the polarities of imperial Vienna. Everything seems to have been replicated here—under a different sky, it is true, and perhaps on a smaller scale, but Szeged, away from those cobbled sidestreets and their kerchiefed women, is nevertheless a dream or fantasy of Vienna set in the middle of the great Hungarian plain, where the unruly east encroaches on the confidence of Europe.

The city is imposing in a pleasantly sleepy way. Perhaps it even represents a model of town planning, providing a near-ideal urban environment, large enough to offer the civilised amenities of life yet sufficiently small to avoid the evils of big cities. Yet the sense that Szeged is, in some hard-to-define way, not quite right, that there is something inappropriate about it, far from diminishing, grows stronger the more familiar the city becomes. At first, during these weeks of a faintly absurd endeavour to teach Australian literature to a group of young people who know very little about that distant land and lack almost all curiosity about it, I suspect that the atmosphere of the place is the result of its (and indeed of the whole country's) having languished under communism for many decades, a vague feeling that these sleepers had only just woken. There is, however, more to it than that; the inappropriateness, the sense that things do not quite fit together appear to be much more deeply ingrained than the effects of nearly half a century of totalitarian rule could explain. There must be, it comes to me from time to time as the curiously unsettling atmosphere of the city descends on me, some other explanation, something more particular to account for the inescapable sense that here is another theme park—not as self-conscious or efficient as that of Vienna, yet a sentimental construct, for all that.

The municipal museum and art gallery is housed in a self-important neo-classical building bristling with columns and heroic statues. The paintings it displays are commonplace enough, theatrical nineteenth-century genre pieces of the kind that Hungarian artists seemed able to turn out in their thousands. In another wing of the building there is an historical and ethnographic museum filled with metal and stone tools, peasant costumes and examples of folk art. One of the rooms displays an engraved panorama of eighteenth-century, antediluvian Szeged. The orientation of the city, as far as you can tell from the engraver's rather feeble attempt at composition and perspective, was different from that of the modern city. It seemed to run parallel to the bank of the river, rather than radiating from the semicircular Ring that now marks the limits of the inner town. Old Szeged obviously lived with its river, its lifeblood and *raison d'être*. The engraver showed wharves and jetties, the busy commerce of a town on an important waterway. The new city turned its back on the river, perhaps to forget the terrible devastation that necessitated its birth. It is now protected by sturdy dykes and massive embankments, arranging its own shapes and contours as though it were an inland city, ignoring that terrible stream which now flows placidly through the autumn drought.

Looking at that old engraving, the implication of the new

city's being a replica of Vienna, the distant place from which its rebuilding was planned and directed, becomes clear and poignant. Szeged was deliberately conceived as a dream of Vienna transplanted into an alien and possibly hostile soil. It is no accident that one encounters a succession of neo-baroque public buildings with their emblems and insignia of Habsburg power, parks and tree-lined boulevards, and that most revealing antiphony of theatre and cathedral—culture and religion— that lies at the heart of Vienna's urban symbolism, where the Stephansdom and the Opera House frame the cityscape of the inner town. The new Szeged is a colonial city. It did not, in its present form, grow naturally out of a place, a people and a way of life. It shows, rather, the essentially parodic nature of those cities where the architecture, the planning of the streets, the images, symbols and emblems displayed on build- ings and monuments enforce a lesson of dependence and nostalgic memories of a distant place. Reality, such places seem to say, is elsewhere: the local and indigenous are, almost by definition, beyond contempt. They must be tamed and transformed precisely in the way that the old riverside town of Szeged, that haphazard collection of streets, wharves and warehouses, was transformed into a little Vienna after the great flood.

That is why there is something essentially unsettling about such a transformation, such mirroring of a different, and in the context of the 1880s, distant society—just as Australian cities mirror and emulate, in the wrong hemisphere as it were, the cities and towns of England. Colonial cities always retain some sense of artificiality—inevitably so, since they did not grow as a matter of necessity or as a consequence of people's attempting to create a space in which to pursue their way of life. They are in essence always nostalgic, and their nostalgia is fundamental to the colonial mentality, which invariably looks elsewhere for models to emulate.

Szeged, like other colonial cities—Sydney or Melbourne or Adelaide or Brisbane—was built and moulded in accordance with standards and aspirations appropriate to a very different place. It replicates the townscape of Vienna in a dream-like fashion, it represents a mixture of diverse elements all derived from the city that provided its inspiration, yet it fails to achieve whatever unity or appropriateness such elements had achieved in their natural habitat. On the Hungarian plains, under a sun that tells you that you are far away from Vienna, the proud eagles, shields and heroic pediments embellishing the principal buildings, the way these buildings themselves are laid out along admittedly well-planned thoroughfares produce a clashing that is very like the oddity of most Australian cities which strikes so forcefully many European visitors.

Sydney also displays several buildings where such inappropriateness is particularly evident: the proud campanile of Central Railway towering over a space without any civic or ceremonial function, or the old Department of Lands building, designed with a memory of broad tree-lined avenues and rows of imposing monumental buildings. In such places the jarring sense of displacement produces odd, occasionally weird effects. Szeged provides therefore an appropriate location for me to attempt to bring together, briefly and provisionally, two cultures, Australian and Hungarian, both victims of the curious effects of nostalgia and make-believe. Szeged, this improbable dream of Kakania, is in many ways an ideal place to attempt to define a culture and a society which had also looked, at least until very recently, towards a distant land for its inspiration, its life-blood and its justification. Such places always betray an often incompatible mixture of elements of a kind that compose both this city and the dish named after it.

In the main shopping street, closed to traffic and lined by boutiques which also echo faintly the glitz and gloss of distant Vienna, a banner slung across the middle of the thoroughfare proudly announces the opening of Szeged's first Chinese restaurant. Beneath its ideograms, fire-breathing dragons and crossed chopsticks, a group of Peruvian musicians entertains the city's bemused citizens. They sing and dance, play their flutes and beckon passers-by to throw coins into something that looks suspiciously like an ancient Arnott's biscuit tin. But, on the days that I walk along this memory of the Graben, the tin is usually empty.

Big Teachers' Room

Late afternoon in front of an open window in the decrepit building which houses the English Department of one of Szeged's many learned institutions. Sunlight streams past the double casements, revealing how much they are in need of a good scrub. It picks up the dust floating in the air and lying on top of the piles of books and magazines on the desks and shelves of 'The Big Teachers' Room'. The adjective does not refer to the size of the instructors; it differentiates this room from that next door, which contains a desk and a photocopying machine. In this room the various lowly personages connected with this institution, part-time instructors, people on secondment from Britain and America and the odd visitor like myself, are housed. The 'heavies' have rooms of their own.

I have been given the use of a desk in the middle of the room—its owner is spending a few weeks in Graz attending a course on the teaching of English as a second language. It is piled high with brightly coloured manuals, cheerful pictures intended to convey images of the privileged life of those who are lucky enough to live in a world where English is spoken, as much as instruction in the intricacies of the language itself. The permanent occupants of the room are rather puzzled and, I suspect, not a little suspicious of me. I probably represent a vague threat, one they can't articulate, yet one that makes them apprehensive and edgy. The difference in age doesn't help either—these people are, I realise, not much older than my sons.

The two Americans are friendly enough, but the three or four young Hungarians who are lucky enough to have found jobs in this institution are sneeringly unfriendly. I sense that as far as they are concerned Australia is beyond the pale, the

very sticks—their beady and hungry eyes are obviously firmly
set on America, their land of heart's desire, the Ultima Thule
of immense salaries and prestige. I avoid the room as much
as possible, spending my free time in the ample and sunny
visitors' flat across the courtyard—probably another bone of
contention and envy. The only occasion on which the Hungarians drop their undisguised hostility is when I come in search
of a printer to hook up to the small word processor on which
I had written my lectures for my course on Australian literature.
They stand around, admiring this most desirable of icons—
they only have the departmental desktop, for which there seems
to be much ill-tempered rivalry. They ask all sorts of technical
questions which I cannot, I have to admit with shame, answer.
One of them asks whether he could have a go, and as he slips
a disk into the drive and begins to type onto the small LCD
screen, he turns to me, saying with an obvious mixture of
delight and contempt that this is stone-age technology, surely
I could afford something better. Now when he was in America
last year . . .

The Big Teachers' Room also serves as a meeting place. In one
corner a coffee machine is permanently on the boil—by this
time of the day the contents of the glass bowl have assumed
an unpleasantly glutinous appearance. An Englishwoman and
I are the only occupants at the moment: we are wondering
whether the coffee's worth drinking. She has been in Szeged
for almost six months now, as an English-language instructor.
She says that it's not ideal—especially since she cannot
understand Hungarian and has to rely therefore entirely on SKY
television for news and entertainment—but she thinks that
she's lucky to have a job at all. Things are very difficult in
Britain, she says with resignation.

Her one great worry, she goes on to say (as we decide that
perhaps it's not wise to drink the dregs in the glass container),
is what she will do when her contract runs out. There are no
jobs in Hungary as far as she can tell, because as a consequence
of the change in the political system most of the formerly state-

supported teaching positions are being discontinued. What she would really like to do is to go back to Australia. What are things like there; is it difficult to get a teaching-post in a college or a university? I am unable to give her much comfort. Things are just as difficult there as in England, perhaps worse, I tell her, and she replies by saying that it's a pity, that she'd like to go back there very much.

When was she in Australia? I ask. She gets a dreamy look in her eyes. Oh four years ago, visiting some friends near Armidale. She'd also been to Sydney and Melbourne, loved every moment of it. She thought Sydney was stunning; she'd had a couple of ferry trips on the Harbour—it must be wonderful living near the water. She says that she would, nevertheless, prefer to live in the country. She is not a city person even though she'd lived in Manchester most of her life. What she would love to do would be to settle in one of those towns like Armidale or Tamworth, that would be wonderful. And she would also love to got to the outback, to look at Ayers Rock and those rainforests. Yes, that would be marvellous: to see those great empty spaces—they are so strange, so forbidding, yet somehow much more exciting than Europe. Europe's too crowded, too neatly arranged. Out there, she'd imagine, you would be thrown on your own resources, you'd be tested—and yes, she'd read *Voss*, thought it was terrific. She is sure that it would be quite creepy out there in that great emptiness, but she would love to experience that thrill. Anything to get away from Europe or England. They're dead, trapped under the weight of all that history, hate, cruelty.

I confess to her that I've never been to the outback, that I fear empty spaces, and I begin to tell her about the panic that seizes me every time I fly out of Australia. I tell her how, from that great height, you realise how fragile and provisional our 'civilising' of the continent has been, how the patchwork of fields and farms soon gives way to a lunar landscape beneath you, stretching to eternity it seems. I tell her how that sense increases as you fly, hour upon hour, over that nothingness until, finally, even that void peters out and tumbles into that other nothingness, the sea.

A few days later I am chatting with one of the senior people of this institution during the afternoon lull. The glass urn is filled with freshly brewed coffee—the last of a batch, she tells me, that someone brought back from Vienna a couple of weeks ago. Next week, she says with a grimace, it'll be the revolting local stuff again, until someone goes out and remembers to bring some back.

That phrase—going out—has a curious and disturbing resonance in this world. For forty years or more it meant crossing the Iron Curtain, entering Austria and therefore the fabulous world beyond its border, or else boarding a great gleaming plane and heading for the cities of Western Europe or America. You did not 'go out' when you went to Prague, Moscow or Bucharest. To go out was to leave behind the repression, privations, the drabness of these peoples' republics to experience at first hand (though always under the strictest surveillance) the decadent delights of the west.

By now, the autumn of 1991, those restrictions no longer apply. Hungarians are free to travel anywhere—indeed, I point out to my temporary colleague, she may enter France without a visa which I, with my Australian passport, am no longer able to do. Yet the old habits and casts of mind linger. People still speak of going out, and going out provides considerable problems for people living in a soft-currency economy where all except the very rich find it almost impossible to afford a night's accommodation in a down-at-heel Viennese pension. And there is, besides, for people like this middle-aged woman, the effects of nearly a lifetime of conditioning.

She begins to tell me of a time in the seventies when she was allowed to go to West Berlin to attend an intensive language-training course. She was frightened, she says, by the possibility of freedom, of slipping off the leash. The person in charge of the group could be easily evaded. One night she went to a party given by some expatriate Hungarians, people who had escaped in '56. They talked politics all night, but not in the carefully guarded terms they used at home, when they always made sure that there were no strangers, potential informers, around. The talk was open, dangerous—thrilling of course, but terrifying. Afterwards they went off to a nightclub.

During those weeks someone she had met offered to take her to Paris for the weekend, reminding her that all she needed was her passport—neither the West Berlin nor the French officials would stamp it, he assured her, so no-one would find out that she had broken the rules. Looking through the open window, into the late afternoon sunshine, she describes for me the terror that filled her when she tried to contemplate the limitless freedom of a world where it was possible to hop on a plane at a whim and travel as far as you wished—provided that you had enough money. It was a relief to her when the course came to an end and she could return to the drab world of restrictions and surveillance, where she had little control over her life, where someone else always made decisions for her. She couldn't, she realised, deal with unlimited freedom—the great expanses of the world still fill her with fear and alarm. And no, she didn't go to Paris—it wouldn't have been proper, anyway.

GUIDED TOUR

Visitors arrive, an historian from Melbourne who is spending a year establishing courses in Australian Studies in Budapest, and her friend, a Greek-born linguist. They have come to look over Szeged. As a result of Byzantine rivalries in Hungarian academic circles and also (I suspect) because of similar rivalries and enmities in Australian academic and bureaucratic quarters, Szeged, an important university town, has missed out on the programme to establish Australian Studies in Hungary which has been funded by the Commonwealth government. Bad blood everywhere. The university people of Szeged, it seems to me, have no particular desire for Australian Studies in their institutions, but once they discovered that they had been snubbed they immediately felt aggrieved and suspicious. The historian's visit has been arranged to build bridges, or to smooth ruffled feathers.

A meeting has been set up for the afternoon, just before one of the series of two-hour classes I am giving here as some sort of rival Australian Studies course. The historian and her friend will stay for the first hour of the class, and in the break when the students and I stop for a few minutes, someone will drive them to the station for the 6.15 express to Budapest. Meanwhile they have the morning to look around. One of the students, who earns her living as a tourist guide, is detailed to show them around. Out of courtesy and curiosity, I join the tour. In her flat, American-inspired English, betraying the characteristic difficulties Hungarian-speakers experience with the diphthongs and stresses of English, our guide treats us to a sing-song account of the history of Szeged.

She tells us about the flood and points out an impressive monument—waves of stainless steel fastened with sturdy bolts to a stone plinth—symbolising the might of the river and the ingenuity of Hungarian engineers in taming it. I wonder, as she reels off a string of technical details, whether five years earlier her counterpart would have been required to say 'socialist' instead of 'Hungarian'. Next we admire the river and the nearby bridge, its arch not unlike a bonsai version of Sydney's. We are led to inspect the Bishops' Palace near the Votive Church, built of the same liver-brick and in the same ghastly 'simplified Romanesque' style as the church. The guide delivers an account of Szeged's history, and mentions that after the partition of Hungary the great university of what is now the Romanian city of Cluj established itself in Szeged. It is a consequence of that, she tells us, that Szeged is one of the leading academic centres in the country.

At this point a minor dispute breaks out. Our guide, descanting on the scientific achievements of that uprooted seat of learning, mentions that it was here that a famous scientist—

indeed, Hungary's first Nobel laureate in science—discovered the wonders of vitamin C. The historian's friend is sceptical. Surely, he insists, vitamin C was discovered in Britain or America; he can't remember at the moment where but he's sure it wasn't in Hungary. The guide is equally insistent. No, no, it was Albert Szent-Györgyi who won the Nobel prize in 1937 for biochemistry for the discovery of vitamin C.

A long-buried memory from my childhood suddenly rises to my consciousness. I am three or four years old. There is a terrible fuss because I am refusing to eat the red capsicum my mother (or more likely my nanny) has cut into long strips. My parents are very enlightened people. You don't coerce children; you reason with them. My mother tells me therefore that capsicums are full of a wonderful substance called vitamin C which helps to make me strong and healthy, especially in wintertime. She goes on to say that it was a clever Hungarian scientist who discovered that these capsicums, which grow so abundantly near a place called Szeged, are packed with vitamin C. And that was such a wonderful discovery, it helped so many little boys and girls to stay healthy and well throughout winter that some people in Sweden gave him a big prize for it. And that is something we Hungarians can be very proud of. The ruse did not work. My mother's attempt to make me see reason ended in anger, threats and tears.

The guide and the historian's friend are disputing the point with some heat, though without any rancour. I, nevertheless, see the danger that the situation might get out of hand. I offer therefore the peacemaking formula: perhaps Szent-Györgyi discovered that capsicums and peppers were a rich source of vitamin C, thereby making the substance available to the inhabitants of Continental Europe much more conveniently than from its other rich source, citrus fruit. My companions accept the compromise, the emotional atmosphere cools, and we continue on our tour of the wonders of Szeged.

We enter the Votive Church. The interior is, if anything, even more depressing. It is filled with devotional images and nationalistic emblems of a particularly offensive stridency. Our guide embarks on a long and rambling account of the construction of the church, how the people of Szeged made a solemn vow to Our Lady that if she would help the city recover from the terrible effects of the flood they would build a splendid church in her honour. She tells us that the money needed for the construction was raised by public subscription and that construction commenced soon after, though the building was not completed until 1930. She reminds us that some of the great cathedrals of medieval Europe took centuries, not decades, to complete, so that it should not be surprising that the pride of Szeged took so long to finish, given that the First World War set back the plans of the city's devout citizens for many years. And then she returns to the topic of the bishopric and recounts how, after the consecration of the building, the bishop returned with the treasures and relics. We could now see these beautiful devotional objects around us in this church, faithfully restored a few months ago, following years of neglect, after Hungary had regained her freedom.

The historian's friend is champing at the bit. He doesn't like being inside a church; he thinks that people should be discouraged from all that superstition, which is, after all, only a way of keeping them in control, under subjection. The guide is beginning to show signs of distress: she has probably never encountered a western left-wing intellectual who seems to espouse the doctrines that had been, during her adolescence, the unquestionably correct point of view, but are now, as the cross around her neck declares, as much in disfavour as religion had been not too many years ago. I cannot but feel some sympathy for her, understanding, as I think I do, the complex inhibitions and insecurities she must be experiencing. For our guide, the young historian and her friend, who live on what I would regard as a fairly small income and face the prospect of unemployment once the historian's one-year appointment comes to an end, represent the glittering world of the west, a world of unbounded opportunities, of salaries undreamt of in Hungary, of travel and experiences which she, in this impoverished little country, will never achieve. Despite my ambivalent attitude towards the growing nationalism in the 'new' Hungary, accompanied by many obvious signs of xenophobia—'Watch out for the gypsies!'—and supported, just as it happened half a century ago, by a narrow-minded, retrograde church (which seems to have been almost wholly untouched by Vatican II), my sympathy goes out for this young woman, who is now showing signs of a troubling confusion and perplexity. I should, it seems to me, do something to get her out of her embarrassment.

As she guides us to a carved crucifix in a side-chapel, and launches into an account of its sculptor, and how he had given the crucified Christ his own face, I draw the historian aside and ask her to tell her friend to stop needling our guide. The historian turns on me quite sharply: 'Oh, he's not doing any harm, she can look after herself!'—and in a way she is quite right, yet I am conscious that somehow, in an uncomfortable way, I am caught between two currents, two loyalties. As always I feel much greater affinity with my Australian colleague, and decide that she's probably correct—or is it, I ask myself straight away, cowardice?—and therefore let the matter drop, for I too am troubled by this young woman's unquestioning acceptance of ambiguous national and cultural myths.

And so we continue our way around the huge interior, admiring a painting here, a reliquary there, a gilded inscription inside the dome, and mosaic in the floor. At length the glories of the Votive Church are exhausted. Over lunch in a cellar restaurant the atmosphere relaxes a little, my young companions find common concerns—the difficulties of student life in particular—despite the whiff of brimstone that still hangs in the air.

The guide asks what else would we like to do, assuming her professional manner once more. The historian's friend jumps in—he has obviously done his homework. He would like to see what he believes is a splendid art-deco building with an equally renowned café on the ground floor. He produces a piece of paper with the address on it, but we can't find it on the map—it is a socialist street name and our guide doesn't know which holy or imperial name has replaced it. The young man tries to explain what he is talking about, perhaps she knows the building, but the term 'art-deco' means nothing to our guide. So I break the inflexible convention I had imposed on myself throughout this tour—which has been conducted entirely in English—and try to explain to the puzzled guide in Hungarian, with the awkwardness of someone who has not spoken the language for many years, about 'art-deco'. The attempt proves futile; she doesn't know the place—there are so many cafés in town, she says. The historian's friend has two other items on his list: the synagogue and, he believes, a Serbian Orthodox church with a celebrated iconostasis. He would like to see both, in spite of, it would seem, his ideological qualms about superstition.

Our guide seems reluctant, she wonders whether there's enough time, whether either place will be open. But we prevail on her and finally she resigns herself to the inevitable and leads us into a sidestreet where we come upon a substantial iron railing behind which stands a nondescript building obviously much in need of repair. Here is a remnant of an aspect of the city's history that no-one seems keen to remember.

Szeged's thriving Jewish population was almost entirely wiped out in the course of the war, all that remained was this vast and crumbling synagogue, a memorial to a lost time and tradition. Recently the interior of the building has been subjected to a vigorous programme of restoration. This 'eclectic' interior (the word comes from the official descriptions of the edifice) is once again resplendent with gilt and sky-blue, with inspirational texts painted on the walls in Hebrew and in Hungarian—in the latter case in elaborate gothic lettering. Chandeliers hang above the ample space of this imposing building, used nowadays mostly for concerts and cultural activities.

A handful of practising Jews remains in the town, far too few to be anything other than lost souls in this huge building. They receive visitors with undisguised enthusiasm, immediately extracting an entrance-fee of ten Hungarian forints (the equivalent of twenty cents) for which they will give you a ticket with the quip that it's the cheapest movie ticket in town. They usher you into the synagogue, and before you have had time to take in all the gilt and blue, all the brass and marble, they will begin to enumerate, in a singsong voice, the cost of restoring the building to its former magnificence. So many millions for the roof, so many for the floor; so much for the gold lettering and for the hangings, and we haven't even started yet—we need many millions for the glass, and many more to make the structure sound. It is all very realistic and practical. But as the bent little man who has taken charge of us continues his fiscal litany, you cannot but begin to entertain disturbing suspicions about racial stereotypes—perhaps Jews are as obsessed with wealth and money as their detractors claim them to be.

Whatever the reason, this litany of restoration produces embarrassment in all of us, except in our guide, on whose lips I see the faintest of smiles as she translates some of the old man's monologue. Then something extraordinary occurs. The old man breaks off his account of the vast sums spent on the refurbishment of this place of worship and breaks into a long sinuous chant. His voice is unsteady and cracked, yet for all its imperfections, his chant pulses with echoes of a world none of us has experienced—a world of worship, belief, a sense of community with a people in its joys as well as in its sufferings, a world richer and perhaps more satisfying than our humdrum existence. And I begin to sense that despite the shabbiness of this old man, despite his unattractive singsong accounts of vast sums of money, his life may be fuller, more worthwhile and certainly closer to God than mine.

We are mercifully saved from further exposure to the glories of the synagogue of Szeged by the clock. It is time to leave. There will be no opportunity to search for the Serbian Orthodox church. Our guide seems to realise this, and looks not a little pleased.

FLOWERCOFFEE

When he was a young man in the 1920s, my father lived for a time in Aachen, Charlemagne's city. He boarded *en pension* with the family of a lawyer, an upright and inordinately proud gentleman who was mortified because the economic chaos Germany experienced in those postwar years obliged him to take in a lodger. The lawyer's teenage daughter was turned out of her pink-and-white room—she was made to sleep on a trundle in her parents' bedchamber—to accommodate the young student from Budapest.

My father's year or eighteen months in Aachen supplied him with a fund of anecdotes about life in those hectic times. He used to tell the tale of his career as a smuggler. He would slip over the Dutch border with a friend, to return with a couple of blocks of cheese for use as currency in the complicated barter economy that emerged in that world of galactic inflation. That was also the time when his fascination with opera led him to travel all night to a distant city—Dresden or Leipzig, even Munich on one or two occasions—to stand through a long performance, returning to Aachen by another endless night journey in third class. He also had a mild flirtation with the lawyer's daughter, the refugee from the pink-and-white room, which her parents condoned because it was kept well within the rigid bounds of propriety.

He often spoke about the shortages and privations—the lack of fuel and food but especially of coffee, Central Europe's essential drug of addiction. All sorts of substitutes for those unobtainable beans were tried by the ingenious Germans, but they were, according to his account, uniformly vile. From time to time you could get hold of some real coffee, or something approximating to it at any rate. Those were red-letter days. So precious was the substance, however, that it was made into a very watery, weak brew, so weak indeed that you could clearly see the flower painted on the bottom of your cup. It was called *Blümchenkaffee*—flowercoffee—as a sardonic commemoration of its weakness.

The history of Central Europe in the last two hundred years or more is marked by wild fluctuations in the consumption of coffee—vast quantities of thickly glutinous 'espresso' in good times, *Blümchenkaffee* in the bad. In 1942 and 1943, when the war was beginning to encroach on Hungary, my parents spent more and more time scouring Budapest in search of a few hundred grammes of the precious beans. The last batch they were able to purchase consisted of unroasted green beans—our flat was filled for days with the pungent aroma of coffee roasted in a pan on the kitchen stove.

Now, almost fifty years later, the citizens of Hungary are still conscious of their deprivation. Coffee is plentiful, but it is mostly poor stuff. To have real coffee, people tell you, you must go to Austria. And, of course, every visitor brings some back, even though the cost is crippling. But then coffee is the spiritual staple of Central European life. Though café-life involves much more than eating or the consumption of coffee, coffee is nevertheless the vital ritual object in its ceremonies. It lubricates the conversation and the gears with which social relationships are made to work. You cannot sit in a café without a cup of coffee in front of you, for it establishes and validates your membership of a privileged society. A foreigner ordering tea in a Hungarian café commits a faux pas of considerable gravity.

Szeged's chief café is called *Virág*, The Flower. The coffee served under crystal lights in its ample, flock-papered rooms is probably a far cry from the watery flowercoffee of my father's youth. It is, nevertheless, dreadful stuff—you suspect that finely ground, powdery coffee has had steam forced through it any number of times in the café's porcelain-clad (and, of course, flower-embellished) espresso machine. Gossip insists that if you go to the café shortly after it opens in the morning you might, if lucky, get a cup out of the first or second infusion. As the day wears on, so the quality of the coffee served in the café's faded rooms, or on the ample terrace in fine weather, deteriorates.

Like so much else in this city, the place seems too large for the patrons it is able to attract, or indeed for a town of this size. Like the vast Votive Church, or the blue-and-gold synagogue, or indeed the National Theatre with its tiers of boxes rising to a domed ceiling, the scale of this café speaks of Szeged's former pride as an important outpost of Kakanian pomp. When the city commanded the rich agricultural and pastoral lands that now lie in Serbia and Romania, the café, the cathedral, the theatre and perhaps even the synagogue must have played essential roles in the public rituals, embracings and exclusions that gave substance to that world. The complex reticulations of a heterogeneous society no doubt met and diverged, to refashion themselves into other meetings and divergences, in places such as this.

Sitting in the nearly empty front 'salon' at that hour of the afternoon when the cafés of Budapest are buzzing and crowded, I cannot help trying to visualise the clientele for which this place had been designed. They must have been very different from the few people here this afternoon—jeans-clad students, a harassed mother with two tots whose faces are covered with custard, an elderly couple, ethnic Hungarians on a visit from Serbia, converting their worthless dinars into somewhat less worthless forints, and at the table next to mine two squat middle-aged men in loud shirts displaying quantities of gold in the shape of chains, bracelets and signet-rings.

I try to imagine how this place would have looked around the turn of the century, at the time when this café together with the rest of the flood-devastated city was rebuilt, refurbished and converted into an embodiment of the Kakanian good life. No doubt its patrons would have been more elegantly and appropriately dressed, observing with provincial dedication the elaborate sartorial rules that governed so many aspects of life in this part of the world. Landowners and their wives, in town for business or pleasure, would have displayed the insignia of their caste—the women in clothes purchased perhaps in Budapest, but more likely in Vienna, the men decked out in the carefully chosen rusticity of tweed and loden-cloth.

There would have been members of the city's bourgeois upper-crust—magistrates and lawyers, highly placed medical specialists, perhaps even a respected writer or two. Their manners would have been more refined than those of the landowners and their wives, yet lacking that aristocratic panache and nonchalance the rural gentry sought so hard to emulate with their precisely calculated coarseness of manner. There would have been children of course, demure schoolgirls and well-behaved boys (their hair neatly brushed, parted and glued) dressed in their sailor suits. There might also have been one or two raffish characters, the local merry widow and the odd rake, whom the well-bred and caste-conscious patrons would have assiduously ignored in the rituals of greeting and acknowledgment that characterised the mysteries of social life.

Would the Jews of Szeged have set foot inside this place, or was Szeged one of those places where the sporadic antisemitism of Kakania—at times fierce, as in Vienna, but mostly benign, as in Budapest at the height of its prosperity—established impenetrable barriers? That question is unanswerable, for an answer would depend on an intimate knowledge of the social networks of the city's past. It would be nice to imagine that this large provincial café at what was then the geographic and perhaps spiritual heart of Kakania, the meeting place of many of the peoples, races, faiths and languages that populated that complicated realm, would have been a focus where rivalries and enmities came together to be neutralised and reconciled, even if only within its elaborately papered walls. I would like to believe that here, in my grandparents' time, Hungarians and Austrians, Jews, Catholics and Protestants, even perhaps the bourgeoisie and the gentry might have discovered something of that social harmony that the rulers of Kakania sought to inculcate among their often unruly subjects.

That harmony was more a matter of dreams and aspirations than of substantial reality. Kakania may never have been anything other than a pious dream, as its nickname, a scurrilous comment, clearly suggests. Its ideals were supported by hypocrisy, pretence and snobbery, a self-satisfied smugness that contaminated most elements of social life. Nevertheless, the image I have conjured (or manufactured) of this café of the Habsburg world at the turn of the century—the discreet clinking of good china and heavy silver, the buzz of conversation, the greetings, smiles and nods—is alluring, even irresistible. I want to believe that such a golden world did exist, that it did contain a possibility of achieving at least a partial reconciliation of its tensions and rivalries. I would like to imagine that its destruction came from forces outside its cosy and comfortable ordinariness, that the beguiling aroma of coffee and vanilla carried no trace of the noxious fumes that spread over this continent. Yet I know that the symbol or exemplar of that evil grew up in the pleasant city of Linz, another site, some five hundred kilometers to the west, of the Kakanian dream which also had, no doubt, its own characteristic Habsburg café. And I also know that these places in Linz and Szeged, and in the other towns and cities of the realm, overheard terrible sentiments and hatreds expressed over cups of thick rich coffee, or the weaker brew of the days of hardship.

My neighbours, the gold-embellished citizens of Szeged, are loud in their complaint about the revolting quality of the coffee these days. What is happening to the world? they ask. OK, so socialism's dead, but are things any better? Both are convinced that life is harder than it used to be. Under the old régime you could make a bit of money out of all sorts of things—but now, well now prices are going up and up, it's almost impossible to do business and show a profit. Look at the price of petrol, it's disgraceful! And besides, there are all those Romanian refugees to house and feed. Neither knows where it will all end.

The younger of the two, resplendent in a cerise shirt, lifts a nicotine-stained finger and tells his companion that he knows why Hungary is in such a sorry state. It's simple, he says, Hungary's been betrayed once again, just as she has been in the past. It was all very well for the Americans to promise the earth once it seemed likely that the Russians would leave. But did they do anything? Of course they didn't. And why? Well, he tells the other, it's simple—it's all those crooks in Budapest, especially the Jews: they're creaming off all the benefits for themselves. Of course there's money there. Why only last week he had to go up for the day—he couldn't believe his eyes: the wealth, the ostentation. Here in Szeged, he continues, Hungarians, the truest of true Hungarians, are deprived, struggling to make ends meet, exploited and, yes, betrayed again. And then he begins to tell his friend about a café in Budapest—full of Jews of course—where you can get coffee the likes of which he hadn't seen for years and years. Rich, thick, smelling like real coffee, not the muck that the gallant and plucky Hungarians of Szeged are forced to endure.

THE VAMPIRE'S TEETH

A few kilometres to the south of Szeged lies Yugoslavia, or more accurately perhaps Serbia, the most aggressive or the most exploited (depending on your point of view and allegiances) member of what is still in 1991, a federation. The Romanian border is a short distance to the east—the citizens of that other troubled country often spill across the Hungarian frontier looking for shelter, food and employment. This is an unlikely place for a discovery about Australian literature, yet it happens precisely here, where three countries meet, where (people will tell you) Europe comes to an end, merging with the lands of the Slavs and other denizens of the east.

This is not a major discovery; it is more like a footnote or a gloss on a minor text. It may indeed be the case that it had already been noticed, that the critic who had picked up the allusion had not thought it worthwhile to record such a trivial observation—or else had buried it somewhere in an essay or a critical book I have not read. The discovery provides, nevertheless, a moment of curious poignancy, tinged with irony. It would seem that the fates had decreed that I must come back to the country of my birth, though to a city I had never visited before, to understand a conceit in a minor *jeu d'esprit* of a great writer.

We are in a seminar room on a late afternoon in October. Though it is supposed to be autumn, the weather is still warm, the students are still clad in their international summer uniform—jeans, tee-shirts, sneakers. Sunlight slants through the open windows; a butterfly, surely the last of the season, flutters past, lifted by a surge of warm air. Even the grey institutional buildings across the courtyard manage to look pleasant in the golden light of evening. There is an atmosphere of somnolence—not at all unusual in such circumstances—a furtive watching of the clock by teacher and taught alike. And I, half choking from the dust of eastern-bloc chalk that crumbles between your fingers and sends clouds of white powder everywhere, grow increasingly conscious of the neat symmetry and irony of things.

It is a curious, somewhat unsettling feeling to be negotiating two cultures, two languages, two very different countries: a landlocked bit of Central or Eastern Europe (again it depends on which point of view you opt for) and that vast arid continent in the southern hemisphere where you are obliged to fly for hours on end over desert and ocean whenever you set out for a place like Szeged. I am a juggler, an illusionist. Most of the proceedings have to be conducted in English, for my rudimentary command of Hungarian does not extend to conceptual or literary terminology. Yet occasionally, with the showmanship that's an essential though often unacknowledged part of the art of teaching, it proves very effective to introduce the odd word in Hungarian, ostensibly to elucidate the meaning of an expression, or to offer an analogy, but fundamentally to provide a moment of surprise, a little nudge to make people pay attention, to stop them sinking into late-afternoon lassitude.

On this sunny afternoon, about half-way through a three-week course on Australian literature for students whose knowledge of Australia does not extend beyond Kylie Minogue, AC/DC, koalas and kangaroos (and one of them had seen

Crocodile Dundee), we are reading Patrick White's 'Miss Slattery and her Demon Lover'—hardly an adequate introduction to White, but a nice way of bringing Australia and Hungary together, even if only contingently, through White's venomous settling of scores with a couple of expatriate Hungarians he had known in Sydney. Miss Slattery, ('Pete', which is short, according to her, for Dimity) a full-blooded no-nonsense Australian girl falls into the clutches of Tibby Szabo, a squat, hirsute Hungarian inhabitant of a good Sydney address with a stunning view of the Harbour, the proud owner of deeply piled wall-to-wall, and (most importantly perhaps) of an obscene mirror fastened to the ceiling above his ample double bed.

One of White's jokes raises more of a laugh from these students than it would from readers of almost any other nationality. Why, Miss Slattery asks, is the gentleman (who will presently become her lover) called Mr Szabo and not Mr Tibor since the name above the bell says clearly 'Szabo Tibor'. These students know why—because, as Tibby tells the long-limbed market-researcher, 'In Hoongary ze nimes are beck to front'. That moment of mediation, when my audience and I have privileged access to two modes of nomenclature, achieves little epiphanies, explanations, clarifications. It is a way of bringing them to a very small understanding of an alien society through this comedy of the meeting of 'old' and 'new' Australia at the front door of an expensive home unit. I tell them about the social topography of Sydney in the sixties, about the conspicuous way of life led by many wealthy Hungarians in the Eastern Suburbs, about the espresso-bars of Double Bay and Bondi Junction ('Please, what does junction mean?'), and of the way these people often spoke broken English with an overlay of broad Australian—unlike the students in Szeged (I am careful not to add) whose excellent English is delivered in an American monotone only slightly tarnished by the characteristic open vowels and the absence of accentuation of Hungarian-speaking people. I also tell them about the social and financial *éclat* of a splendid water view.

181

And then follows my own tiny discovery which, for me, could not have occurred elsewhere. Tibby Szabo, who grows more than a little interested in the self-confident market-researcher who has fetched up on his doorstep, has short, pointed teeth. White draws our attention to Tibby's vampire-fangs very early in the story, and returns to them towards the end when Miss Slattery, disenchanted ('pissed off' would probably be a more accurate though less acceptable way of saying it) with her 'demon lover', notices that those short teeth are markedly discoloured and blunted. I had not noticed that detail before, or if I had, I had paid no attention to it. Now, with that alertness most of us experience when teaching—a slight nervousness that we might dry up or even (worst of all fates) be found out—I become very conscious of it. Once again I am filled with admiration for the cleverness and wit of a writer like White, who puts us teachers and critics, barnacles on the great craft of literature, very properly in our place.

Until the wise statesmen meeting at Versailles in the aftermath of the Great War redrew the boundaries of Central and Eastern Europe, Szeged sat in the middle of the great granary of Hungary that stretched a long way to the south and, of more particular interest in the case of Miss Slattery and Mr Szabo, to the east. There beyond what is now the Romanian border lies a land rich in Hungarian folklore and traditions. It is where, according to some present-day ultra-nationalists who are beginning to mutter in an alarming way about regaining the 'homeland', the true Hungary is to be found—more so than in the pathetic rump that remains, and certainly much more so than in a cosmopolitan, polyglot Budapest—a place, according to some citizens of Szeged, such as the pot-bellied patrons of The Flower, still unaccountably full of Jews. In that world of a lost heritage, where Bartók collected the true Hungarian folk music (not that dreadful gypsy stuff that passes for Hungarian music everywhere else, including of course Budapest), the spiritual and national characteristics of the Magyars (the only true Hungarians) are preserved, even though the towns and villages, streams and forests now bear Romanian names.

In the south-east of that countryside rich in Magyar nostalgia and national pride rise the Transylvanian Alps, homeland of my companion on the night of curried prawns and rice. There arose the dark legends of the blood-sucking vampire, of the living dead, the terrible and insatiable lord of a remote castle, protected by mighty chasms and cataracts, whose razorsharp fangs constantly searched for the blood of nubile maidens. Ethnologists have, of course, offered rational explications for these wild stories: local history tells of a haemophiliac nobleman and of clumsy attempts at blood-transfusion. But the legend of the vampire—Dracula or Nosferatu—is of far greater imaginative strength. It speaks of fears and longing, of desires that are best not acknowledged yet are shared by most nations and cultures. The story of Dracula is one of the few great European myths to have emerged since classical times, yet Dracula speaks with a pronounced Hungarian accent—as did the actor Bela Lugosi, with his irresistible mixture of monster and courtly aristocrat.

I point to the open classroom window on my right into the gathering dusk, in what I hope is the direction of Transylvania, and remind the young people of Szeged about Count Dracula—as much a part of their cultural heritage as those patriotic heroes who are this year gradually thawing out of the deep-freeze into which socialist ideology had placed them many years before these people were born. Their reaction, though, is curious: they seem not to know much about Dracula. I try Nosferatu and one of them, no doubt a film buff, says he remembers the silent film . . . was that set in Hungary? I cannot remember whether the setting in those flickering images I have only seen on SBS was at all specified, but I say yes, probably it was meant to be Hungary, or nearby, anyway. Nevertheless, they seem not very interested in Dracula, and I realise that perhaps the Count had been banished by the healthy ideology of the previous half-century or so, together with all those nationalist agitators who, despite all their

bluster, failed to represent the noble ideals of the dictatorship
of the proletariat. And the thought also strikes me that, while
the memory of those nineteenth-century swashbucklers was
kept alive in the imagination of most Hungarians through
the long years of what everybody still refers to as socialism,
poor Dracula had a stake driven through his heart, at least
as far as this part of the country is concerned.

That moment, I realise later in the evening, as I am heating
some rather suspicious-looking packet soup on the stove in the
spacious kitchen of the visitors' flat, meant more to me than
to my students. They, as things turned out, were much more
interested in other elements in the Patrick White story, those
which I take to be fairly predictable and unremarkable. They
were fascinated by my description of a baked dinner with three
veg which Miss Slattery cooks for her demon lover (and he
ungallantly chucks out of the window). The manufacture of
gravy seemed to them a magical process. Shelling prawns on
the Esplanade in Manly led to a lively discussion of the
nomenclature of crustaceans—of which there are several
interesting varieties to be found in the Tisza, the river that flows
through the city. The young grazier with the stockwhip and
the suspiciously new elastic-sided boots who turns up at the
'bohemian' party which forms one of the climaxes of the tale
proved to be someone they could understand: the Hungarian
plains around Szeged have their own stockwhip-cracking
cattlemen. But when Miss Slattery appropriates the stockwhip
and begins plying the delighted Tibby's naked thighs with it,
their attitude changed. They became almost prim, embarrassed—they are, after all, still products (probably the last) of
socialist educational attitudes of the sort that seem remarkably
similar to the prudishness of the Australian moral right. Sexual
perversions, bread-and-butter stuff to most Australian undergraduates, are still somewhat tricky topics in contemporary
Hungary. That will probably change soon: the Hungarian
edition of *Playboy*, concocted in Budapest and printed in
Austria on high quality art-paper, is likely to see to that. At

present, though, Pete and Tibby are still able to bring a blush to the cheeks of young Hungarians.

And yet for me the centre of that late afternoon seminar remains Tibby and his vampire teeth. It seems to me entirely fitting and perhaps altogether inevitable that I should have learnt something about Patrick White in Hungary, a country almost wholly unfamiliar to me, yet one not without some influence on my life. The extent of what I learnt that afternoon was not very large. Tibby's teeth will not add greatly to the sum of human knowledge about White's art, even if they had remained undiscovered until my sojourn in Draculaland. Yet it was, personally, a discovery of considerable importance. It brought together, momentarily and provisionally, the two societies and countries that have formed me, and provided a brief integration of their opposed and contrary claims.

A Little Tea, A Little Chat

The French lady, as everyone calls her, lives in the flat behind mine. She, too, is one of the lucky ones, enjoying visitor status, even though she has been in Szeged for years. I met her shortly after my arrival, as she was attempting to manoeuvre her Hungarian-registered Peugeot through the building's vaulted gateway. We introduced ourselves and shook hands. Later in the day, I asked one of the academics about her. I learnt that she has been living in Hungary for many years and has worked as a French *instructrice* here for at least a decade. She teaches at the university, at one of the colleges and also takes classes in one of the city's excellent secondary schools. A few days later, in the same gateway, we fell into conversation once more, and she invited me to visit her the following evening for a little tea and a little chat (as the English translation of her staccato French phrase would run).

The day turns out to be hectic. There are calls to be made on vice-chancellors, on heads of departments. I am taken on an inspection tour of a multilingual secondary school. I also give a particularly gruelling class on Australian literary culture—the students (I begin to suspect) have had just about as much as they can take of photocopied examples of the literature of a distant and peculiar place. By six-thirty any notion of squeezing in an evening meal has long been abandoned, and in any event last night's fat-rich dinner is still a particularly vivid memory. I wonder though what 'a little tea' implies and, more worryingly, how we will manage to conduct a little chat. Madame claims neither to speak nor to understand Hungarian or English. My French is, to say the least, rusty. It is one thing to be able to read a newspaper or even a novel, quite another to follow the machine-gun speech of most French people, let alone trying to frame some appropriate form of reply.

I am not therefore in the best of spirits as I ring the bell on her door. Perhaps she has forgotten the invitation and has gone out for the evening, I tell myself. That, however, does not seem very likely, for I can hear the sound of a television set. Madame opens the door, we shake hands once more, and I am immediately conscious of my first faux pas: I have come empty-handed. She is, however, all graciousness. She ushers me into a large, spotlessly clean though rather spartan living room, turning down the sound of the French satellite television channel which will continue to emit its soundless spectral dance of images throughout the evening—voluptuously enticing visions of a consumers' paradise alternating with icons of brutality and terror. She invites me to sit in one of the sand-coloured armchairs placed around a low table, and thus we embark on several hours of halting, and for me exhausting, conversation.

Very soon I begin to suspect that Madame is putting one over me, that she has me firmly trapped in a linguistic vice. She assumes that French is the only language we have in common. No, she never learnt English, and as far as Hungarian is concerned, well, it's impossible—though I have been told that she understands and speaks more of the language than she is willing to let on. It is, therefore, up to me. I must, for the next two hours or so, attempt to make civilised conversation in a language I am able to read with some confidence but I am unable to speak with any ease or assurance. Madame offers me a drink, a glass of the glutinous Tokay everyone around here consumes with relish, and I am relieved to see that there is some food on an elegant glass platter—a few savoury *bouchées* purchased, no doubt, at the 'Little Flower', the café's take-away annexe where, at most times of the day, long queues wait patiently to buy cakes, savouries and aspic-covered sandwiches.

Then our little chat begins. It soon transpires that Madame had heard some gossip around the place that there would be someone staying for a few weeks in the front flat, someone to teach in the English Department. Am I from England or America? she asks. So far, at least linguistically, so good. I understand perfectly what she has said, and I am able to answer (with colloquial aplomb, I hope) '*Non, non, l'Australie*'. This provokes a torrent of sounds in which I am able, I think, to distinguish the words 'surprise' and 'Australian'. I assume therefore that I need a) to reassure her that I have indeed come from Australia, b) to make it clear that I am here to teach Australian literature, and c) to explain why I have come to Szeged to do so. The demands of this exceed my command of French: from now until the end of the evening I shall be obliged to fall back on the cowardly phrase '*Je ne sais pas comment dire*', which is probably incorrect yet comprehensible, as well as on extraordinarily complicated periphrases to get around the terrible gaps in my vocabulary and grammar.

Madame's interest is aroused by this intelligence. She is a woman of indeterminate age with sparkling eyes, an inquisitive aquiline nose, and possessing a style and elegance (despite the unfashionable clothes she is wearing) that contrast wonderfully with the utilitarian drabness of the people of Szeged. As she offers me one of the *bouchées*, it becomes clear that I am now required to deliver a disquisition on Australia. If I have understood her correctly, she has just told me that I am the first Australian she has ever met, that she knows nothing about the place, but has always been fascinated by exotic countries. After a brief excursus on—I think—her impressions of Marrakesh, she sits back in her comfortable armchair, takes a sip of sickly-sweet Tokay and indicates with unmistakable body-language that it is up to me now—I must sing for my supper, or at least tell her about *Australie*.

The problem exercising me over the last few weeks, how to describe Australia for people who aren't wildly anxious to find out about the place, now takes on a particularly pressing urgency. I must achieve that feat in the simplest terms possible, not because my hostess is incapable of dealing with sophisticated concepts, but because of my own linguistic shortcomings. I must offer her an account of Australia (whatever 'Australia' might be) in a primitive vocabulary, without nuances, with the constant possibility of being misunderstood, and without the command of grammar and idiom seemingly necessary for such a task. Remembering a phrase of one of Madame's compatriots, I embark on a 'degree zero account' of Australia— simplicities, the bare bones of something complex and contradictory and something moreover about which I have my own complicating ambivalences. Added to those difficulties is the difficulty of perspective. In Australia, when generalising or pontificating about the world in which I have spent the greater part of my life, I am always conscious that no matter what authority (spurious or otherwise) I might have, I must always acknowledge that my roots or origins are not of that place, that my views and judgments are likely to be coloured by those early and formative years of my life which I spent here, in Hungary. Similarly, in Szeged, as I was standing earlier today in front of a class of undergraduates and tried to tell them something about Australian life and literature, I was very conscious of a possible confusion of perspective: that I, the 'Australian', belonged in some indefinable sense to this world, even though I had left it many years ago, and even though I was almost entirely ignorant about it, having only superficial impressions, forty-five-year-old memories and the remnants of a family mythology to represent it.

In Madame's living room I find yet another perspective, one that has its own ironies and possibilities of confusion. Knowing nothing about Australia except that it is very far away, somewhere down there at the bottom of the globe, she has no preconceptions about it or about the people inhabiting it. She knows, I think, that English is the common language, but that to her is no more surprising than the fact that French is spoken in Algeria. She obviously has no preconceptions of the sort that British people have whenever I am incautious enough to say to them that I am an Australian.

As I begin my discourse on Australia in a language of adverbs and adjectives—it is arid, very large, very empty, very warm, an ancient continent—I become aware that she takes me for a 'native' inhabitant of the land. She probably thinks, I tell myself, that I come from a family that has lived there for centuries, perhaps millennia, for it is quite obvious that she knows nothing about the history of the South Pacific—even though I try to remind her about Tahiti and Nouméa, and the nuclear testing her government carries out (but I decide to say nothing about the *Rainbow Warrior*). La Pérouse, she remarks, is the name of a street and a famous restaurant in Paris—she didn't realise they were named after an explorer. Should I tell her, I ask myself, that I am not what she calls an *autochtone* in any sense of the word? The opportunity passes because I have to spend some time figuring out the meaning of that word.

The conversation becomes even more difficult as I have to pass from the physical world, where my repertoire of adverbs and adjectives with an occasional noun proves reasonably adequate, to an attempt to describe the social and political complexion of Australia. As I begin to tell her about Cook's voyages, a glimmer of recognition plays across her eyes. *Mais oui*, she remembers now, she has read something about that—wasn't he eaten by cannibals? As for the rest, surprise follows on surprise. Settled by the British in 1788? A penal colony? (Initially there was much difficulty with that—Devil's Island became the way of overcoming that hurdle.) Was there really a gold rush? There are cities? How many, how large? As large as that? How interesting! At about that point my ability to communicate these bare facts, this skeleton of a description of Australia, breaks down. We are now talking about universities. She is mildly surprised that there should be so many, and that people from those institutions should travel to other parts of the world to teach courses in literature—though I do sense in her voice some contempt for the academic standards of the country in which we are conducting this curious conversation.

And then we reach an insurmountable obstacle. I am unable to say in my pidgin-French that our universities have lost in recent decades much of the autonomy they once possessed, and that they have passed into the control of a rigid central bureaucracy. That is too much for me: I try the shameful expedient of saying it loudly in English, but my hostess still fails to comprehend. Then I use the Hungarian equivalent of the phrase 'centralised bureaucracy' (very much in the air these days as the political and administrative structures of the country are in the process of being redrawn) and my hostess understands immediately and indeed speaks a few appropriate words in a broken, heavily-accented but nonetheless comprehensible Hungarian. Fatigue, frustration and hunger (for there is plenty of Tokay but precious few of the *bouchées*) have made me desperate. I pounce on this to express my surprise and delight that she speaks Hungarian, and begin elaborately to compliment her on her command of the language, hoping thereby to switch the conversation to a tongue much easier for me to manage than French, even though it too presents many hurdles and pitfalls.

I have not reckoned, however, with Madame's casuistic skill. No, no, she insists, she only knows a few words, she couldn't possibly conduct any sort of conversation in that outrageous language. And besides, she must compliment me on my linguistic ability. I must be very gifted indeed to speak French as well as I do (but I notice a slight curving of the lips) and to be able to speak Hungarian as well! How extraordinary! And then the trap shuts. Not at all, I tell her, I was born here.

What follows next is almost impossible to comprehend—
a torrent of animated French, a click-clacking out of which
I am able to glean only the barest essentials. Madame's eyes
sparkle, she smiles, wags an admonitory finger, refills my glass
and expresses her delight at understanding everything. Of
course, it's all clear now. I am a European, that's why I speak
French, that's why I seem a very cultivated person who has
been asked to teach English literature here—she seems not to
have taken in my laborious attempts to tell her about one or
two Australian writers and Patrick White's Nobel prize. Of
course, of course. How interesting it must be to live in that
primitive world, to attempt to civilise the *autochtones*. It must
be a real mission; I must tell her what it's like to introduce
a complex culture to people who must have little conception
of it. The challenge must be wonderful, but oh, she understands
what a relief it must be to come home—twenty-four hours,
is that how long it takes?

No matter how much I protest, I cannot impress on her that
she has got it all wrong, that it's not like that at all. I try to
tell her as patiently as possible, and with as much linguistic
complexity as I am able to muster, that Australians are among
the most urbanised people in the world, that until recently at
any rate Australia was a carbon-copy of European societies,
that we are not any longer colonists in the true sense of the
word, for we have shamefully but effectively all but got rid
of the *autochtones*, or at least robbed them of their way of
life. I try to say something about the nature of cultural and
academic life in a country which she might, if she ever visited
it, find unusual but not all that strange. I tell her that Sydney
is not of course as grand or as sophisticated as Paris, yet that
it has its opera house, its theatres, restaurants, public buildings
and art galleries. We may not have many old masters in our
galleries, I tell her, but there are some very interesting
Australian painters. None of this makes any impression on her;
she is firmly fixed in the conviction that *Australie* must be like
those African countries that were once under French domination, an exotic, picturesque place of curious customs and

traditions on which people like myself have attempted to impose a simplified version of European high culture.

It strikes me, as I come to realise from my very imperfect understanding of her monologue, and as I am grateful to discover that she disappears momentarily into the kitchen to produce a trayful of little quiches, that this curious and off-beat image of Australia—a faraway place, a cultural desert—is not at all unlike the attitude of those people who had fled to Australia to escape the upheavals of Europe, people who lamented that they were forced to live in a crass, primitive and unsophisticated world. They saw themselves as a cultural and social élite exiled in a curious land—and some indeed aspired to a type of missionary zeal in their attempt to bring European high-culture (music and Kakanian cream-cakes) to that be-nighted land.

Madame has obviously set me aside as unrepresentative of that world because of my European sophistication, as she sees that quality from the perspective of a small corner of an insignificant European country. This is not substantially different from the setting-aside that people of my parents' generation practised in Australia in the years immediately after the end of the Second World War, or, for that matter, the sense of isolation I still experience in a place where I have spent by far the greater part of my life. I am intent on not falling into that trap or being guilty of that abuse, that is of consenting to such a blanket denigration of the world in which I live. I discover once again something that is no part of my conscious life 'at home', a fairly simple patriotism that inevitably forces me to exaggerate my country's achievements. And I can see, as Madame places a quiche on my plate with a delicate silver implement, that she doesn't believe a word I've said.

Here, in this pleasant sitting room, the confusions and ambivalences of the past weeks come to a particular head. I know that Australia is not at all like the place she imagines it to be, but I also begin to wonder whether it would not perhaps be a more interesting and satisfying place if it were. I also know that I am drawn, as I have always been, to her world, whether it be this obscure corner of a little country, or that glittering world of Paris she left, she tells me, many years ago because she found it impossible to make a living there, and also because it was so noisy, messy and violent. I realise that we are fellow exiles, and I realise too that she is probably exaggerating the extent of her attachment to Szeged. She tells me what a pleasant place it is, how nice the people are, how high the academic standards. And culture? Oh, she says, there's the opera. But when I ask what it's like, all she says is 'What can you expect?' At that moment I catch a glimpse of those people who used to sit around the tables of cafés and espresso-bars in the Sydney of the fifties loudly lamenting the 'natives' ' laughable attempts to mount opera performances that they were obliged to endure.

I am also conscious of the confusions of identity our little chat has provoked. Anyone who has crossed nations, languages and cultures must suffer, to a greater or lesser extent, from ambivalence and perplexity. I suffered it on the first occasion I stood before my class of Hungarian undergraduates, introduced myself, spoke a few words in Hungarian, and then slipped into English, the only language I am able to command with any measure of competence. Yet as I began to speak about life in Australia, devoting the first session to the physical characteristics of the continent, its early history before the coming of the British—topics that I had also attempted to convey in a shower of adjectives and adverbs in this living room—I found myself slipping into Hungarian whenever it became obvious that my students' excellent English did not extend as far as some of the facts and ideas to which I wanted to introduce them. There I straddled cultures and languages, finding miraculously that all sorts of long-forgotten Hungarian words rose to the surface of my consciousness when I was attempting to explain to these people concepts, objects and experiences which they could not understand in English.

Here, as the evening at last seems to be coming to an end, I am perhaps in an even more confusing environment. The polarity of Hungary–Australia, evident in so much that I do or that happens to me here, has an additional and quite piquant element: the French lady herself, her almost wistful words about France and especially Paris, the city where she cannot any longer afford to live. With her my confusions of identity are even more pronounced, for she cannot 'place' me in the way that Australians, British people and Hungarians are capable of placing me—even if I should disagree violently with the way in which they have done it. With her the confusions exist on many levels and in several dimensions, not the least of which is my constant sense of the terrible barriers of language.

We shake hands again as I am about to leave. Madame tells me how enchanted she has been to have made my acquaintance. She wishes me every success in my endeavours, and expresses the hope that we shall meet again. She says that she would like to thank me most cordially for having found time to visit her, and she would also like to assure me how instructive the evening has been for her. And also very diverting.

Back in the front flat, as I am waiting for the kettle on the stove to boil, I muse on the confusions and difficulties of the evening. I am so tired that I haven't even the energy to get undressed and go to bed, but I know that I must teach again in the morning and that I must contrive to arouse some interest in Australia among those young people, whose understanding of it is as limited as Madame's—though I do not, it is true, have to restrict myself to the utter simplicities that my poor command of French made necessary. In bed, having shuttered the windows tightly to keep out the noise of the traffic, I find that I am unable to sleep. Floating images of the past few hours swim around in the darkness. My mind is playing over those linguistic tricks I tried so unsuccessfully to play. An odd assortment of French phrases—prohibiting smoking, leaning out of windows or affixing bills to walls—insists on going round and round in my head, waking me every time I am about to fall asleep. In this half-waking nightmare, even more alarming than a full-blown *cauchemar* (a word that suddenly comes to me apparently out of nowhere), I realise that I do not even know the Hungarian word for nightmare. I am still awake when the first light of dawn creeps through the shutters.

REMEMBRANCE OF THINGS PAST

Unfinished Business

The earliest of my consecutive memories are centred on a house—or villa as we called it—on the outskirts of Budapest. I think I can remember one or two scraps of my life from the time before my parents moved to that house late in 1938, when I was almost three years old. I suspect that those very vivid memories belong to that strange no-man's-land between the remembered and tales transmitted by a cherished family mythology.

One occasion is, nevertheless, firmly etched in my memory: my mother is holding me, swaddled in blankets, in front of the glass door that leads from the living room of our Budapest flat to the entrance hall. On the other side of the door, crowded in the narrow hall, are my Budapest grandmother (as I distinguished in later years, the owner of the Ferris wheel), my uncle and aunt, and possibly the spats-wearing Excellency who was resurrected for me a few weeks ago on the night of curried prawns and rice. I can still see, though I am unable to distinguish the features of those onlookers, my family staring at me through the panel of glass that occupies most of the door. I can also see quite clearly the door's narrow wooden frame, painted a glossy, brilliant white.

It seems unlikely that this could be a precise memory. The occasion is my second birthday. The family had been invited to my parents' flat to celebrate the great event. They had travelled across the city to pay homage to the infant prince. When the maid opened the front door to let them in, the myth insisted, she noticed that my aunt had a heavy cold. Hearing this, my mother refused to allow the deputation to pass beyond the entrance hall—they had to be content with a ceremonial viewing through the glass panel. The family rift took months to heal.

Is that my earliest memory? It seems to me improbable that I should have retained such a precise, clearly etched vision of a very early time of my life. When I found the street where that block of flats used to stand—a couple of days ago, after my return to Budapest from the stint at Szeged—it evoked nothing familiar, nothing that stirred any memory, no matter how faint. But then, it occurred to me, perhaps the street had lost all resemblance to the way it had looked fifty-three years ago. It had certainly lost its name for many years. I could not find it on any map of the city until, rounding a corner on the way to the university to deliver yet again my party-piece on Miss Slattery and Tibby Szabo, I noticed a fresh, brightly painted street sign above a battered plate bearing a now discredited socialist name, and realised that I had stumbled onto a mythological site.

I hurried back to that street as soon as the business of Tibby and Pete Slattery was finished. It was a long, drab thoroughfare, but it revealed here and there echoes of former glories. Everything was wholly unfamiliar, I could remember nothing about it until one more scrap of memory (or myth) rose to my consciousness. At one end, near the park, not far from the block of flats where we had lived, there used to be a water tower, a large cylinder on massive brick pillars. The tower had clearly been pulled down years ago—if indeed it ever existed. At the top of the street I did find, though, a large semicircular space, the terminus of several trolley-bus routes, which could have formerly contained such a structure.

That night in my hotel room I watched an ancient Hungarian film on television. It was a romantic comedy made in 1936, very much in imitation of those sparkling Hollywood films which my mother, suitably hatted and furred, used to enjoy in some of the city's fashionable cinemas. The plot revolved around a bored, spoilt young woman—her father, a monocled and bespatted aristocrat, tried unsuccessfully to keep her in proper maidenly subjection. Her amorous escapades led to many witty and diverting situations.

The actress playing the part of this unconventional young

woman was dressed and made up to resemble Katharine Hepburn. The romantic lead—a sophisticated, perhaps slightly dissolute portrait-painter who lived in a modern, airy apartment with glass-panelled doors—could never persuade the young woman to allow him to come to her house; indeed she refused to reveal her name or give him her address. She insisted that all their meetings should take place in front of the water tower at the top of the street where he lived—a large cylindrical container on four massive, arched brick pillars, surrounded by what looked like the trees of a municipal park on the scratched, flickering and slightly out-of-focus images of that ancient black-and-white film.

My memories of the villa to which we moved a few months after that disastrous second-birthday party are much more precise and continuous. Yet no photograph had survived from those years, or so I had thought, until I found, on first meeting my cousin, the single image which had been preserved, showing a summer idyll, the two of us splashing in a wooden tub filled with water. Nothing of the villa is visible in the photograph apart from a small portion of the back porch. Our sandals are neatly lined up on its edge; folded deckchairs lean against the wall. I asked my cousin whether she'd been back to that place, whether she knew if the house still existed. No, she didn't know, she's never been that way, why should she? And it struck me, indeed, that there was no reason why she should have gone to that outer suburb to find a house where she had spent some happy times as a young girl. It was possible, after all, almost at any time in the last fifty years for her to catch a suburban train and travel to that outlying district of the city. I, on the other hand, who have been cut off from that past for so many years, and who will, moreover, leave this world again in a few weeks' time, found myself consumed by curiosity to know what had become of that house where I had known the only relatively peaceful and secure days I ever enjoyed in this country.

My cousin tried to dissuade me from finding the place. It's bound to have been pulled down ages ago, she said, all I was likely to find was row upon row of apartment blocks. Besides, it's a business getting there: the trains no longer run into town: you have to go to the end of a Metro line and change, I was sure to get lost, she added. Her husband produced a large fold-out map of the city. We found the suburb easily enough—it is no longer on the edge of the city of course—but we could not recognise any of the street names. My cousin said that she didn't remember the name of the street, but the odd thing is that the name had come back to me a few days earlier, and also the number: 3 Tátra Street. They looked at me with astonishment: how could I have remembered that?

I could not, of course, offer any cogent explanation. I have come to realise in the course of these weeks, that I have retained all sorts of odd facts and details about my early life—about places and about people—probably because those fragmented memories are parts of a myth world, not of everyday reality, as they are for my cousin who has spent her life surrounded by these places and images. Precisely because these mundane things—addresses, dates, the relationship among long-dead people—have been fixed in the fluid but always consistent world of my mythology, they have stayed with me in a way that many details of my 'real' life in Australia, that distant place, have been consigned to oblivion. Nevertheless, a careful scrutiny of the street names printed in minuscule type on that large map failed to reveal any street approximating that memory.

So it came about that I heeded my cousin's advice, and didn't try to find that house in a suburb of Budapest, but went off to Szeged to further the cause of Australian Studies in Central Europe. Yet in the course of those weeks, perhaps because the unaccomplished sentimental journey became a nagging piece of unfinished business, I thought from time to time about the house and the part it had played in my earliest consecutive or at least sharply etched memories.

Those memories have the particular clarity of early child-hood; many are shining, brightly coloured images, all the more vivid because they are surrounded by blankness. Our maid

Rosie is sitting astride a squawking, flapping goose, forcing corn down its protesting gullet. The dull swoosh as the caretaker-handyman shovels away the snow piled high on the flat roof. A row of tiny cactus plants, each in its small terracotta pot with matching saucer, on the low windowsill under the picture window of the living room. Rosie and the caretaker hanging a Persian rug at the foot of the stairs to prevent the heat of the tiled stove from escaping. Standing in front of my mother as she peels off me layer after layer of cardigans after our afternoon walk in winter. The dark-hued painting, a nude with her arm twined around her neck, hanging by the stairs. Picking redcurrants in summer. Being told to stay indoors while several men thwack at the walnut trees to dislodge the hard, white-shelled nuts still nestling in their dark green husks. The red stripe that runs around the perimeter of the black rubber floor-covering in the hall. The hiss of the bottled gas burner, on which all the cooking was done in summer, after the solid-fuel kitchen stove had been shut down at the end of spring.

Some of these memories are connected with events, with the structures of cause and effect, with stories rather than with static, shining images. They are, moreover, much more darkly coloured. The house is filled with long-faced people. A hearse drawn by two jet-black cockaded horses stops in front of the house. Then the house is empty. 'Don't worry,' the maid who is looking after me (we are probably between nannies) says. 'They'll be back soon, they've only gone out for a little while.' But I know what is going on: great-grandmother has died. They're going to put her in a hole in the ground and she'll never be able to get out again. Then everybody comes back and I am carted off for supper and bath.

Another time I wake up in the morning. I ask for my mother. She had to go into town early, before I was awake, my grandmother tells me. Will she be back by evening? Of course, my grandmother says without much conviction. Next morning, and for many mornings after that, I am told the same tale. Mummy has a lot of things to do in town, she goes in early and gets back after I've gone to bed, but she comes and looks at me every night and hopes that I've been a good boy. I know of course that my grandmother is lying. My mother is dead. My father is with the army, somewhere far away. I weep uncontrollably, for days on end it seems. But I will not speak those terrible words 'Mummy is dead'; there are certain things you mustn't ever say. Then, one morning, she is back, smiling at me over the side of my bed.

Explanations of a sort were probably given; no doubt there were presents and treats, at least as far as it was possible to indulge in treats in a world rapidly heading towards destruction. It was, however, only much later that I came to understand the combination of courage and folly—so characteristic of much of my mother's behaviour in those years—that generated that inexplicable absence. My father had been called up for one of his periodic stints of army service—though in truth it was more forced labour than military duty. It was autumn, still warm, like high summer, just as this autumn almost fifty years later is still indistinguishable from summer. My parents assumed that my father would spend four or five weeks in a camp in a little town not far from Budapest, as he had done on every other occasion. He left in his summer uniform, though I have no memory whatever of saying goodbye to him.

On this occasion, though, he found himself going much farther afield, into Transylvania, where the Hungarian army, supported of course by our gallant German allies, was engaged in the heroic struggle to recapture our homeland. The deeper they penetrated that land of mountains the colder it became. Frostbite, chilblains and even worse afflictions threatened. Somehow my father was able to get word to my mother asking for his winter clothes to be sent to him—though for security reasons he was not allowed to reveal the locality.

The message arrived late in the evening. My mother hurriedly packed my father's winter uniform, reeking of mothballs, as much warm underwear as she could find in haste, and set off, carrying her own heavy topcoat (from which she had prudently removed the fur collar), for Transylvania and the unknown.

She had no idea where she might find my father. She had not imagined what risks she took in travelling through that turbulent world, on her way towards a raging and particularly bloody conflict—as all conflicts in that unhappy land always are. She was almost arrested as a spy, a haggard and chain-smoking Mata Hari. She had to contend with the sullen and murderous hostility of the many warring races that inhabit Transylvania. Even the Hungarians, whom this military action was supposed to bring back into the bosom of the homeland, looked on her with suspicion—who was this Hungarian-speaking woman who was clearly not one of us?

She travelled from village to village, sometimes on foot, sometimes in a farmer's cart and even in an army truck. She went from place to place where people, sometimes with gleefully malicious intent to mislead her, told her that units of the Hungarian army might be found. At last, after two or three days of wandering around that mountainous, bitterly cold terrain, she came upon yet another large camp surrounded by barbed wire. As she had done time and time again she called out to the groups of hunched, shivering men standing behind the wire. On that occasion one of them went away and returned, a moment or two later, with my father. All my mother could do was to hurl the suitcase of clothes over the wire before my father hurried off. There was no time for talk, no time for love. She returned to Budapest by the same difficult and hazardous route.

That was the first time in my life that I had been betrayed—that is to say, the first occasion on which I was forced to realise that I was not the sole centre of my parents' world, that my mother had to exercise a choice when she was called upon to rescue my father from the bone-freezing cold of Transylvania. For that reason, too, that house occupies a position of absolute centrality within my memories. It was there that my life was somehow formed by influences that I could understand, where I was able to say, time and time again with the insistence of a five-year-old: 'You could have told me, you could have told me; I thought you were dead.' It was in that place, in other words, that I began to enter into the world of experience, where I came to the recognition that people—even those close to you, those that formed the centre of your life—were, in the final analysis, untrustworthy and fickle.

The last time I saw that house was three or four years later, in 1944. By then the war was raging around the city. Our situation was desperate. We needed false identity papers, for which the price was high and rising each day. The house had been abandoned a year or so earlier, but a small metal box remained buried beside the sour-cherry tree in the garden. My mother and I left the city at dusk—the trains were, miraculously, still running. As we approached the village the boom of not-too-distant guns grew louder, bright flashes illuminated larger and larger patches of the night sky. We picked our way through darkened streets, past many abandoned houses. Our house stood in darkness. With the light of a small torch, around which she had wrapped a handkerchief to soften its glow, my mother found a spade in the toolshed. She dug beside the cherry tree, where an innocuous looking stone marker had been carefully placed. She took out the small metal box, containing the last bits and pieces of gold. She didn't even bother to fill in the hole.

The railway station was deserted by the time we had made our way back there. No more trains would run that night, perhaps no more trains would run at all. We started walking the nine or ten kilometres to town along the road that ran beside the track. Occasionally an army vehicle roared past, its shielded headlights casting small pools of light on the surface of the road. One of them stopped. The door was thrown open by a Hungarian-speaking person in German uniform. We were ordered to get in. The officer—whose Hungarian was now revealed to be heavily accented—began quizzing my mother. Who were we, what were we up to so close to the war zone? My mother embarked on her well-prepared story. She gave her name, a suitably Magyar surname. Her husband had been killed fighting for the fatherland in Transylvania. Her mother—and here she named our former caretaker's elderly mother, who had always lived in that village—was mortally ill. She had to visit her, and allow the old lady to say goodbye to her only grandson.

The soldier then turned to me. I was sitting in the back of the armoured car, staring at my mother's back. What was my name? Where did I live? Who was my father? I answered as I had been drilled. The inquisition continued throughout the half-hour trip to town. He seemed satisfied with our performance, for he dropped us off at the carefully selected false address my mother had given him—a district of the city where wives of soldiers fighting on the eastern front had been settled—and, reaching into a compartment of his vehicle, he handed me a bar of army-issue chocolate. I have often wondered whether our transparent performance had taken him in, or whether we had been on that night recipients of a small spark of compassion and humanity in an infernal world.

An idle Saturday morning seems a good opportunity to embark on a sentimental journey in search of that house, to finish that piece of unfinished business. I am aware, as I squeeze into an overcrowded carriage on the Metro, that the search will probably prove futile. No amount of poring over maps of the city has revealed a street of the right name anywhere near that suburb. We arrive at the terminus. I follow the signs leading to the suburban trains. Coming out of the subway, I find myself in front of a huge concrete barn, some sort of a marketplace. Short, mostly elderly people are hurrying around with shopping bags filled with limp cabbages, pale carrots, black potatoes. Elderly women, black scarves around their heads, sit beside plastic buckets of autumn flowers—there must be a cemetery nearby.

I find the train I must take without any trouble, but another problem immediately presents itself. There are three stops bearing the name of the village or suburb where we used to live. Where to get off? An answer of sorts presents itself: the middle one of the three stations is also identified as an airport stop. There had indeed been a small airfield near that villa;

we left the place largely because of the increasing severity of
the air-raids against that military installation. That, logic
suggests, is where the search should begin.

The train pulls into the station and I recognise immediately
a familiar world—unless each of those stations presents the
same aspect. A row of shops lines the roadway running along
the left side of the track. On the right, luxuriant trees shield
ornate nineteenth-century villas, each of them a miniature
Versailles, a tiny Belvedere. I remember how we used to cross
the line to reach the shops where ice cream could be bought,
or where the primitive flea-pit cinema was situated. But I also
remember that there was a place where you could purchase fruit
and vegetables on 'our' side of the line—and there indeed I
see a small weatherboard shop with a prominent Marlboro sign
in its window.

Beyond that, memory fails. I zigzag through the leafy streets,
still green in the late autumn sunshine, though piles of brown
leaves lie in the gutters everywhere. I wander past rows of
ornate villas, stucco garlands and medallions over deep bay
windows or beneath cantilevered balconies. Here and there a
more modest timber house interrupts the uniformity, and even
one or two small, obviously recently constructed blocks of
apartments. In one street I find a man burning leaves in the
gutter—something I have not seen in pollution-conscious
Sydney for many years. I ask him whether he could direct me
to the street, but he assures me that there is no such street
around here. I walk a little farther and come upon a young
woman pushing a child in a stroller. No, she's only lived here
a couple of months; doesn't know the place at all—and hurries
on nervously.

There seems little point in persisting. I turn back towards
the station. At the next corner I see an elderly lady shutting
the gate of a small garden. Why yes, of course she knows the
street. It's back there, where I've come from: first left after
the church. She tells me what it is now called. Memory comes
flooding back. The steeple of the church had been visible all
along; why had I forgotten that you could see it from our back

garden? Why had I not made for that beacon? I now know exactly what to do. Walking briskly along the wide avenue, I turn left into a short, much narrower street, and there, in a garden surrounded by a high wire fence, stands—familiar and yet totally strange—my parents' pride and joy, an art-deco villa constructed in 1937 which had been extensively featured in the architectural journals of the time.

I stand on the opposite side of the street, lost in the past. The house looks as though it had fallen on hard times. The handsome walnut trees that used to screen it from the street are gone; the green wire fence seems a recent installation. The cement-rendered façade, sparkling white in my memory, is browny-grey. An external staircase runs up one side, ending in a small porch covered in coloured fibreglass, which is obviously a recent addition. On the other side, where the garden furniture used to be placed under another handsome walnut tree on sunny summer days, there now stands an ill-constructed garden shed. I take my camera out of its case to record these images of a lost world.

I have not noticed that I have aroused the suspicion of a middle-aged man who is raking the grass behind the wire fence. I am embarrassed: I would feel similar alarm and hostility if I found someone photographing our house in Sydney on a quiet Saturday morning. I cross the road and call out to him. He comes over to the fence, even more suspiciously. I apologise, telling him that I don't want to make a nuisance of myself— I've only come to look at the place where I spent some of my childhood. His reaction to that is even more hostile: that's impossible, he says. His family has lived here since 1945, and the people who were here before emigrated to Australia. They were called Riemer. But they're all dead now, he adds, obviously bringing the interview to an end.

What follows is, in a curious way, touching. Hostility and suspicion are converted into amity. The alarm experienced by this middle-aged man in a sweatshirt and baggy tracksuit pants visibly increases when I tell him of the miracle of my survival. It is, however, tempered by his curiosity. He comes closer to the wire, asking all the inevitable questions. He shakes his head in disbelief as I give a brief account of how I happen to have fetched up, out of the past, seemingly out of death, on this sunny autumn day. How did I find the street? I tell him about the old lady. Ah, yes—and he mentions a name.

Then his mood changes, becoming almost violent. What am I after? Nothing, I assure him, I've only come to look at the place, to fill in one of the blanks. He looks half convinced, but launches into something that sounds like self-justification. His parents, he tells me, bought the house from mine, he can't remember when, '42 or '43, when he was a baby, and before his brother was born. They didn't come here until '45, after the siege ended, because (he says) there was an airfield here—it's still there, he adds—and the district was always being bombed. Pointing to one corner of the house, he shows me where it was hit, not by a bomb but by a large piece of shrapnel: there was quite a bit of damage. At any rate, he goes on to say with some vehemence, they were here before '48.

I now realise the reason for his hostility. In the weeks that I have spent in this country one topic has dominated the many contentious issues examined by a society trying to sort out the social and political priorities of a brand-new order. The government is to make restitution for property seized by the state in 1948. Daily on the radio, on television or in the press some official or other stresses that this restitution is to be in terms of cash payments, not in terms of real estate. No-one living in houses or flats, on farms or small holdings purchased from the state in the course of the more liberal 1970s and 1980s need fear dispossession. Yet few believe those soothing assurances. The crowds gathering for curried prawns and rice at meetings of the Australian Hungarian Friendship Association include several expatriates who have returned in an attempt to repossess ancestral estates. Even my cousin and her husband, who purchased their flat in a block built in the 1950s on the site of a bombed-out pre-war building, are worried about the security of their title.

I try to reassure the man behind the fence that I have no

ambition whatever to repossess this fragment of the past. He seems somewhat mollified, or at least his curiosity gets the better of him. Would I like to have a look around? I make the usual apologies about not wanting to be a nuisance and so on, but he opens a gate in the wire fence, and I cross over a curious threshold into a segment of my past. We walk around the garden. The back is covered in long grass. One or two low and gnarled trees seem desperately in need of pruning. I remember where the sour-cherry tree used to stand. The borers finally got to it, I am told. And the walnuts trees? He doesn't know what became of them, probably chopped up for firewood in '45.

As we walk slowly around this unkempt garden, his hostility is converted into an almost benign friendliness. I must come inside, he says, to meet his wife, and his brother who lives in the downstairs flat. Indeed, he becomes importunate: it would be unthinkable for me to go away without having a look inside, there must be so many memories. It would be churlish to refuse. His wife and brother are summoned, and, after general amazement, we climb the external staircase leading to the upper floor, and enter by a door which has been cut, I realise, through what had been the outside wall of my bedroom. The place is unrecognisable; yet as I am ushered into a hideously over-decorated living room—crimson cushions everywhere—I see that this is what used to be my parents' white bedroom, which had been sparsely furnished with angular salmon-pink and grey pieces, the ultimate in sophistication in 1938.

We chat over a cup of strong coffee. The brothers tell me that they lived in this house with their mother and father. When property was to be nationalised in 1948, their father subdivided the house and installed his widowed sister-in-law and her two sons in the downstairs flat. That way, I am told, the family could retain the property, which otherwise would have been seized by the state. Now their parents are dead; the brothers find it convenient living here, a bit cramped, a bit too far from town, but very pleasant and quiet—and suddenly, from my childhood, I can see my mother, gesturing with her crimson-painted nails, assuring a visitor that there were so many advantages to living in the country, despite the distance from town.

The conversation passes to the present. As always, the account I give of the reasons that have brought me back to Hungary produce mild disbelief. The younger brother is, however, anxious to know more about Australia—what are things like there? As I give an inevitably foreshortened account of the benefits and inconveniences of living in that strange place, he interrupts me to say that he has been thinking of emigrating there. He used to be a systems manager in a state-run institution. Now he has set up in business as a management consultant. It's very difficult, however, given the circum-stances—he has thought once or twice that he ought to take his family to somewhere like Australia, where there must be a great shortage of skilled managers. I try to tell him as gently as I can about the queue of unemployed management consul-tants that seems to stretch from one end of the country to the other. He looks downcast and I, in turn, experience a sense of mild guilt for having shattered yet another illusion.

It is time to leave. We say goodbye without any sense of that awkwardness and hostility with which the encounter had begun. Yet as I am about to leave, having taken a couple of photographs of the interior, the elder brother asks me whether I could wait for one moment. He dives into another room and returns a few minutes later with a sheet of yellowing paper. It is some sort of document covered with elaborate official stamps. The faded typescript declares that in 1943 the brothers' parents purchased from mine this property for an undisclosed sum. Beneath are the four signatures of the vendors and the purchasers.

I cannot understand why it should have been important for me to inspect this document. I try to make a suitable comment, agreeing that their title to the property seems beyond question, when once again I am interrupted. No, I do not understand, I am told. Not a penny had changed hands; the undisclosed sum was a legal fiction—the property had been 'sold' because my parents were (and he finds it almost impossible to pronounce the word) Jews. Do I not see, he continues with a curious mixture of embarrassment and bitterness, that anything might happen; at present there is no talk of restitution for property seized before 1948, but who knows what retrospective legislation will be passed in the future. And then, to my considerable distress, both brothers begin to plead with me: they have lived here all their lives; their father had rebuilt the house after half of it had caved in; it's the only security either of them has.

I interrupt them with more vehemence than politeness tolerates. I tell them that I have not the slightest wish to reclaim this house, or indeed to have anything to do with Hungary after I leave for home in a couple of weeks' time. I grow agitated too. I stress and stress again that this world means nothing to me, that when my parents and I left it forty-five years ago, we severed whatever connection there had been between us and this place where so many of my relatives had met a terrible death. I tell them that my home, the world where I belong, is there, in Australia, a place where we had discovered safe harbour after leaving this contaminated world. I assure them that I came here merely out of perhaps misplaced sentimentality, to finish a piece of emotional business, but certainly not one connected with real estate. I hear myself thanking them for their hospitality, assuring them once more of my good intentions. Yet, as I set out for the station and as they are standing in the garden, safe behind their fence, waving, I begin to wonder guiltily what future fears and alarms I have sown in the minds of these people who have lived for a very long time in a house where I spent no more than three or four years of childhood.

ICONOSTASIS

We are standing before a screen of icons in a small Serbian Orthodox church; in front of us prophets and saints are frozen in eternal mystery. My cousin's daughter, a currently unemployed teacher of English, looks around at the decrepit late eighteenth-century building, a typical example of Austrian baroque, which had been constructed, in all probability, on a shoestring budget. She fixes her gaze on the cracks in the elaborately plastered dome. She wonders, she says, whether the authorities will manage to get around to fixing the building before it collapses. The saints and prophets look on unconcerned, their minds set on more important matters. Outside in the bright autumn sunshine, after exchanging a few words with the elderly woman seated by the church door who is selling postcards and devotional objects, my young cousin remarks on how few antiquities there are in Hungary.

On our way to this small town called Szentendre, an artists' village and tourist trap on the outskirts of Budapest, we drove past a few Roman columns and brick foundations beside the busy road, remnants of the Roman settlement of Aquincum. Behind us rose a vista of identical-looking multi-storey blocks of flats—'socialist flats' as they are called by the inhabitants of the city. Those depressing buildings, a source of anger and contempt for the citizens of a newly 'liberated' Hungary, are nevertheless not much different from the architectural standards achieved here in former times. You would not come to Hungary to admire the architectural excellence of its antiquities. There are, admittedly, a few medieval castles (or in most cases their ruins) scattered around the country. There is also a handful of old churches, most of them 'modernised' during the eighteenth century. Here and there you may come upon remnants of the Turkish occupation five hundred years ago. But mostly this is a country with only paltry monuments of the past.

In Budapest, where my young cousin lives in what is the only old part of the town—a series of medieval streets around the fortifications of the long-since demolished fortress, composed mostly of eighteenth- and early nineteenth-century houses—most of the buildings date from the turn of the century, a period when many large cities, Sydney and Melbourne for instance, received their present-day aspect. The two cathedrals in Sydney are older than the pompous neo-baroque basilica in Budapest. Most people in this city live in houses or apartment blocks built since the 1880s. Budapest is, in other words, a relatively new place.

My cousin is fully aware of this. When she remarked that even the iconostasis in the church we had visited wasn't particularly old, she began to speak about the sense of deprivation she felt in Hungary. There is, she said not for the first time, so little that is old, so few things to put you in touch with real civilisation, to give you a sense of being in contact with the past, with continuity and with things that really mattered. She spoke wistfully of the fortnight in the early 1980s, it was still 'socialism' then, of course, when she and her husband, an economist, managed to obtain permission to 'go out'. They went to Italy; they didn't get as far as Rome, but were able at least to drive around Tuscany and Lombardy. Her eyes began to sparkle as she recalled that wonderful time. Now, of course, they were free to go anywhere, but they didn't have enough money—and besides the girls were growing up, costing a great deal to keep. The most they can manage to do is to go to Vienna for the weekend to stay with friends and stand through a performance at the opera on the Saturday night. Vienna is much better than Budapest, she remarked, it has, after all, something of a past, but really she felt that she would have to get to Italy or Greece or the south of France soon, otherwise she would dry up.

The three of us—her husband, who had gone off to look at leather jackets in one of the craft shops that line the main square, has by this time joined us—pick our way down a steep flight of stone steps into a flagged courtyard where a particularly grubby individual is selling the Hungarian version of damper. As we stand around a rickety counter, trying not to get garlicky grease on our clothes, both my cousin and her husband point out that the courtyard and the steps were probably laid out in the fifteenth century. They tell me that the Catholic church above the courtyard is also a very old foundation, but it was reconstructed in about 1810. Why couldn't it have been left as it was? they ask. There's precious little gothic left in Hungary. It's the fault of those wretched Austrians, of course, imposing their showy baroque on every land they conquered.

Then my cousin's daughter turns to me and begins to say what I had been expecting her to say all day. How can I live in Australia? How can I do without the past? Doesn't such a life lead to spiritual desiccation? Not that she is religious, she hastens to add, almost embarrassed, but there are things of the spirit . . . She must admit that there is a spiritual dimension to life; she had always thought so, even at school when, naturally, she was taught that there was no such thing as the soul, only chemistry and electricity running round your body. I could call that sense whatever I liked, but how is it possible to live without those spiritual things in such a *new* place, such a raw place, as Australia must be?

An autumn afternoon in a crowded tourist resort filled with noisy Germans loudly converting Hungarian forints into marks or schillings is not an ideal place to conduct a typically intense Central-European conversation about culture. Nevertheless, on the short drive back to Budapest in an efficient little Fiat which had recently replaced (I was told) a rattling socialist death-trap, my relatives come back to that question. How can I bear to live in Australia? How could anyone who has made culture and literature his occupation do without the past, without that contact with continuity, all those things capable of enriching life, that you can't find in Hungary, admittedly, but are not far away, in Italy, in Greece, in the south of France? Don't I feel spiritually deprived, denied those things which sustain the only real life there is?

In the back of the Fiat I begin to consider what reply I might make. I mention the ancient and complex culture of the original Australians, their art, their rich store of myth, legend and belief. But no, my relatives cannot accept that—no doubt it is a rich culture, they wouldn't deny that, they had indeed seen photographs somewhere. But it isn't *our* culture, is it?—and they begin to rattle off the familiar string of names in Europe's pantheon of high culture. They too, I realise, have their own iconostasis, their saints, heroes and prophets in front of whom they worship and whose shrines—in Florence, Athens, Nîmes and Avignon—they hope to visit for spiritual replenishment. I am about to say something about the way that culture is internal, how it doesn't ultimately depend on secular pilgrimages, and I am also going to raise the possibility that we in Australia may be more fortunate because we are assisting in the birth of a culture, rather than observing one already formed, as a series of exhibits in a museum, inside a mausoleum or on a screen of icons. The opportunity does not, however, arise. The first of the phalanx of socialist apartment blocks comes into sight. The traffic increases and my young cousin and her husband settle down to a noisy argument about the best way of avoiding the weekend congestion, and whether it is wise for him to be doing 100 in an 80 kph zone.

HUNTING PARTY

Upstream from the town of icons stands the fortress of Visegrád. This is the Danube Bend where the river, as in the famous Wachau region of Austria, passes through a gorge flanked by high hills. In times past the hills and promontories around here controlled the fate of nations and kingdoms. Today Visegrád looks over towards Czechoslovakia, until recently a sister socialist republic, otherwise a Soviet puppet-state (depending, as always in this world, on your point of view). Boatloads of sightseers from Budapest arrive every Sunday to marvel at ancient stones and fortifications, and also to consume rich food at the restaurant conveniently situated adjacent to the wharf. The climb to the fortress is strenuous; corpulent elderly women puff and wheeze their way along the cobbled path to a rough-hewn, square keep where they pay a token admission fee for the privilege of climbing more steps to inspect this monument of Hungary's ancient glory.

The ancient glory, as it turns out and as I might have

217

suspected, is a trifle contingent. Visegrád was the court of a great monarchy until the vicissitudes of history swept it away. For centuries the fortress was a little more than heap of rubble—the few houses of the small village nestled around it are said to have been built from its stones and timbers. The keep rose again early this century, in the wake of that nostalgic search for a national past that swept across this country after the disintegration of the Habsburg world. Here is, in other words, another theme park, another sentimental reconstruction of a fantasy, a past both picturesque and stirring, like the 'medieval' castle in the municipal gardens of Budapest built from scraps of ruined buildings brought to the capital from all over the country. The puffed visitors marvelling at the splendid interior of this ancient monument are lost in admiration of the theatrical skill of twentieth-century architects.

The interior reveals, surprisingly and not a little disconcertingly, an entirely different essay in nostalgia. Having walked respectfully past the few bits and pieces of the original fortress embedded in the walls of the new construction, you come upon a well-lit chamber on one of the upper levels of the keep. This great space contains a number of large boards displaying a series of much magnified photographs. A photographic exhibition is itself enough of an incongruity in a place dedicated to (and reconstructed for the celebration of) an ancient glory of the long distant past, before the age of technology which produced both the photograph and those political and mechanical structures that saw to the extinction of Hungarian independence. Its subject matter is even more curious. Visegrád is a nostalgic monument to a time of independence, a time when the kings of Hungary could hold their heads high and survey, from this hilltop, their proud domains. The photographs represent, on the other hand, a collateral branch of the House of Habsburg, that hated tribe of Austrian overlords, inventors and maintainers of the dream of Kakania, who kept the gallant Hungarian race in utter subjection—or at least did so according to the propaganda of the age of revolution in the nineteenth century.

218

These photographs depict intimate scenes of family life among the 'Hungarian' Habsburgs. Many were taken by the Archduchess Isabella, the wife of the Archduke Friedrich, nephew of the Emperor Franz Josef, on the family's estate near Pozsony, the Slovakian city of Bratislava which Friedrich and Isabella would have known by its Kakanian name of Pressburg. They show the archducal family at rest and at play. A cosy family scene depicts someone playing a cornet, accompanied by a demure lady at the piano, while other members of the family pursue various pastimes. Another series depicts the young Albrecht, Friedrich's heir, now standing on the back of a pony, now dressed in miniature imperial uniform. Other photographs are concerned with those enormous gatherings of European royalty which show only too clearly the dangers of inbreeding—everyone is obviously everyone else's cousin. In some the Archduchess poses with embarrassed members of the local peasantry dressed in their embroidered national costumes, while pigs and pig troughs are clearly visible in the background. The photograph was intended no doubt to indicate Isabella's dedication to the well-being of her consort's people.

The exhibition room is crowded. These large black-and-white images obviously appeal to the sense of longing for a lost and glamorous past evident throughout Hungary. The people crowding around them point with approbation at details of the ladies' elaborate clothing, at the gilt chairs and ormolu clocks of imperial apartments, at the splendid furs worn by both men and women on those stiff archducal picnics where official photographers were always in attendance. Here is a welcome contrast to the drab present. Ah, those were the days, they seem to be saying. Wasn't life gracious then? And look at the jewellery! Now isn't that something!

One part of the exhibition draws particularly animated responses. It consists of a series of photographs taken on various hunting expeditions. In the foreground of most of these pictures a heap of slain animals is artistically displayed, somewhat in the manner of those mounds of fruit and vegetables indicating nature's bounty in the produce hall of the Royal Easter Show in Sydney. Behind the slain deer, chamois and winged creatures of all kinds stand the victors. The men are carefully dressed in the correct hunting costume of the time: breeches, loden capes and feathered hats. But it is the women who attract the greatest attention. There they stand, staring fiercely into the camera, with their hunting rifles held firmly and displayed with obvious pride. They are Amazons or Valkyries, but they always wear full-skirted hunting suits, greatcoats or furs and, of course, large hats, which sometimes cover much of the upper parts of their faces, layered with baroque decorations of feathers, birds and fruit. One aristocratic lady points the toe of her fastidiously polished boot towards the heap of game; another seems to be raising her gun to pot yet another bird. In several of these photographs menials of various kinds may be seen hovering around their masters and mistresses, tending to the needs of these great hunters.

These images are nauseating largely because of the grating incongruity between the formal elaboration of the hunt and its pathetic objects—heaps of limp-necked two- and four-footed creatures. The visitors in Visegrád do not, however, seem to find these scenes of carnage at all distasteful. Observing their interest and admiration, I recall the many shops in Vienna and Budapest which are dedicated to the art of venery. Unlike the grim and shabby gun shops to be found in the less salubrious parts of Sydney and Melbourne, they are very tasteful and dignified affairs. Their display windows are usually arranged in the manner of nineteenth-century stage sets with painted backdrops depicting mountain crags or reedy marshes. Wax dummies of the hunter and the hunted are artistically disposed in picturesque configurations reminiscent of tableaux on the stages of the opera theatres in Vienna and Budapest. These charming perspectives form a beguiling setting for the display of various implements of slaughter—in one establishment in Vienna pride of place is occupied by a horrendous crossbow of shiny metal with telescopic sight and its fan of terrible steel-tipped arrows. This, I conclude perhaps unfairly, is a culture dedicated to death and killing.

For the people crowding around these images of death in the keep at Visegrád, there seems to be no obscenity in the celebration of the noble art of the hunt. For them these are obviously emblems of a glorious past, remembered in a shabby present. It strikes me, therefore, how odd the effects of nostalgia usually are. These people frozen in seventy- or eighty-year-old black-and-white images are the oppressors, the over-lords, the cruel tyrants of a nationalistic mythology. They, and their forebears, were regarded as the blood-sucking exploiters, the suppressors of the Hungarian nation. Yet here they are being remembered fondly by drab day-trippers as the representatives of a better life, just as their statues and monuments are being replaced and lovingly restored all over the capital, after the overthrow of a more recent tyrant and oppressor. I begin to wonder whether they too, like the Habsburgs before them, will one day be fondly recalled.

As you leave the 'medieval' keep by the exit door, having followed one-way passages and staircases to the roof and down again, you come upon a small bookstall guarded by an intense, chain-smoking lady of advanced years. Among various pub-lications on display I notice a blue-covered book containing reproductions of the Habsburg photographs. I enquire about the price—given the rate of exchange in this country for even a currency as dicey as the Australian dollar, the book represents a remarkable bargain. I tell the lady that I would like to purchase one, with an English text if possible. She rummages through a pile in a box which (I notice) once contained bananas from the Caribbean, and produces what she claims to be the last English-language copy—she has some Hungarian and German copies, and of course several in Russian, but nobody wants those now, she can't imagine what would have possessed them to produce it in the first place.

We fall into conversation. She congratulates me for having decided to purchase the book. Isn't it wonderful? Aren't we lucky to have had these photographs so well preserved? Ah, those were the days! I have not the heart to tell her that I've decided to buy the book because the photographs seem hilarious

in a macabre sort of way, but I do ask her why they were
exhibited here, of all places. She looks at me with surprise.
Where else? she asks; the family used to love coming here. A
moment's reflection tells me that by the family she means those
Hungarian Habsburgs, oppressors of a gallant nation, who used
to be thought of as the exploiters of the greatest people on
earth, of a nation which has never been wholly vanquished.
And she launches on a complicated account of the opening of
this exhibition a couple of months earlier by some daughter,
granddaughter, great-niece or some such relative of Friedrich
and Isabella, who came here from Switzerland to officiate.
Wasn't that wonderful? My informant drops her voice and
whispers confidentially to me: 'And she told me—mind you
she wouldn't tell anyone else—that she's going to come home,
to live here, and what's more she's going to get back some of
the family land. Now what do you think of that?'

I do not know what to think, but I am spared the
embarrassment. My informant's monologue now takes a fresh
and unexpected turn. She can't imagine why anyone would
want to live here. That is a sentiment I happen to share, but
probably for entirely different reasons. It soon becomes clear
why she thinks anyone would be crazy to want to live in
Hungary—this is a story I have heard many times and in many
places: in the streets of Budapest, from my cousin, from wildly
gesticulating taxi-drivers as they negotiated Budapest's chaotic
traffic. Things are infinitely worse than they were under
socialism, the lady tells me. She has to live on a pension—
oh yes, she ekes it out with a job like this, but it's only
commission work, and nobody has money to spend on books.
It was bad enough trying to make ends meet before; now it's
impossible. Her rent has tripled; food costs an arm and a leg
and God only knows what the heating charges are likely to
be this winter. Yes, certainly, there's freedom, but does that,
she would ask, fill your stomach, or pay the rent, or heat your
room? Under socialism everyone had enough, not too much—
and of course people grumbled, but then that's what people
are like. But there was enough; nobody was rich, nobody was

poor. Then, looking at the illustration on the dustjacket of my book, she sighs. Perhaps those were the best days; perhaps people didn't know when they were well off. And it was a graceful time. People speak a lot of rubbish about exploitation, but surely these people—pointing vaguely towards the bull-necked Habsburgs—knew what their responsibilities were. Nowadays all you get is thugs and confidence men.

Nostalgia is a powerful drug. As the old lady drones on and on in the autumn sunshine about the hardships she is forced to endure, she is conjuring for herself a powerful fantasy of a happy world, sometime in the past, sometime before she was born perhaps. I begin to wonder about the world that had bred her—which also bred me—about the injustices and even perhaps atrocities she has had to endure, and it occurs to me that perhaps the present always seems worse than the past, that we tend to romanticise an unsatisfactory former world because it seems more glamorous than our drab present. I think of my cousin's daughter aching for old things, and I think of all those elderly people who used to sit in cafés and espresso-bars in Sydney, lamenting this world, a world they had not only lost but had been driven from by hate, brutality and persecution.

The lady's monologue drones on and on. We are now in the thick of family history, of her difficulties with her daughter and son-in-law, of some obscure dispute about the ownership of the small house she rents in a village a couple of minutes' by bus from this tourist site. I begin to grow weary of her, indeed of Hungary and its obsession with its glorious and infamous past, of the political and social immaturity of its complaining citizens. Beneath us, on the river sparkling in the late afternoon sunlight, I catch sight of the white tourist boat making for the jetty. I murmur hasty apologies and hurry down the steps towards the wharf, while behind me I can hear the lady's voice wishing me all the best, a safe journey back to town—and also, of course, to Australia.

A Place on the Map

The proprietors of the small hotel high in the Buda hills are hard-working people, anxious to please. Nothing seems too much trouble; at the height of the tourist season, when all rooms are occupied and booked months ahead, when guests spill over into rooms rented from the occupants of nearby houses and apartments, they deal with a constant stream of questions and requests in a remarkable variety of languages. They arrange excursions and opera tickets, procure taxis and hire cars, advise on shopping and sightseeing while attending to the chores required to keep the establishment in tip-top shape. They are shining examples—as several American guests remark—of the virtues of a free-enterprise economy. Their energy and professionalism certainly provide a marked contrast to the lassitude of functionaries in those enterprises which are still controlled by the state—the bored woman issuing tickets at snail's pace from the single booth at a busy railway station, the spivvy youth in charge of the advance booking office for Budapest's major theatres. If Hungary is to make a successful transition from the somnolence of a command economy to the brave new world of capitalism, it will be people like the owners of this hotel who will deserve the credit.

There seems to me, nevertheless, something alarming and at the same time sad about their energy and assiduousness. By breakfast time—7.00 a.m.—the wife already looks tired. For the next three hours she will supervise the two waitresses and the distribution of an ample (in truth too ample) meal. Her husband is installed in one of the booths of this dining room decorated with nostalgic emblems of Hungarian folklore— wooden platters ranged around the walls, embroidered hangings, garish paintings and watercolours depicting scenes of rural and village life. That booth serves both as an office and an observation post; there accounts are made up, books kept, reservations made, and the staff supervised with eagle-eyed concentration. Both husband and wife are vigilant, indeed tense; each seems to think that the least delay in serving food, or the least sign of dissatisfaction in a guest implies instant ruin.

They are probably in their mid-thirties—perhaps even older. It seems as though they are obsessed with the need to make up for lost opportunities, for all those years when their energy, business acumen and desire to succeed were thwarted by an oppressive economic system. They seem very conscious of those wasted years and are also obviously aware that their new-found prosperity may be shortlived. It is imperative to succeed now, to seize every opportunity that presents itself, before age or one of those violent changes in the political climate which this world knows only too well renders them powerless.

From his office-booth, in between making up bills, changing money and taking bookings, the husband conducts complicated deals on the telephone—the purchase of a vacant lot here, an apartment there, an Austrian-registered Mercedes someone wants to sell or a consignment of prime-grade salami from Szeged. He bargains, flatters, cajoles, telephone tucked between between neck and shoulder, while he punches figures into a pocket calculator and transfers the calculation to a well-covered sheet of paper. Meanwhile his small green eyes, set in a chubby, pig-like face, dart around the restaurant, trying to read his guests' assessment of the morning meal. His wife, a short blonde who is sure to become, in a few years, yet another overweight Budapest matron, stands in front of the small bar, her eyes fixed intently on the swing-door that leads to the kitchen, indicating to the waitresses what their next move in this well-orchestrated dispensing of food should be. They are models, as I have been forced to acknowledge throughout these weeks of commuting between this hotel and my flat in Szeged, of energy and dedication, despite the faintly ridiculous zeal with which they pursue their commendable ambitions.

The small entrance hall of their hotel is decorated with an elaborately framed and much embellished map. This carto-graphic fantasy is also to be seen in many places in every part of the city. It is another emblem of deep desires, of a belief that icons and rituals are capable of giving life and substance to longings bred out of nostalgia and the fulfilment of wishes. Many guests, certainly those from America, Britain or Australia, would not recognise the significance of the map, even if they happened to notice it in the ill-lit foyer. For anyone at all familiar with the intense mythologies that have emerged from this world, it speaks eloquently, however, of deeply ingrained dreams and aspirations.

It represents Hungary as it used to be—or better to say, perhaps, as it should have been—before it was slashed to pieces by the victors of Versailles. It is an accurate enough representation of what used to be the Kingdom of Hungary. A bulbous piece in the south-western corner ends in a strip of the Adriatic coast around the city of Fiume (now called Rijeka). That is the reason why, in my childhood, this landlocked country was ruled by a dictator—masquerading as the regent of the kingdom—who gloried in the rank of admiral. To the north and the east the country represented on the map bulges out to embrace not only modern Hungary but those lost lands which provide such a potent mythology of regret for latter-day patriots—in the east the land of vampires, in the north and to the south the rich farmlands of what is now Slovakia and the Serbian Banat. The cities, towns and streams marked on that map cannot be found in any modern atlas, for they are the names these places bore when they were possessions of the proud and unconquerable Magyar race.

At some time during the history of this unstable part of the world, when national and regional boundaries changed in accordance with the varying fortunes of great powers and ambitious princes, the rulers of Hungary may have indeed commanded the extensive tract of land depicted on this map embellished with the emblems and devices of proud cities and fertile plains. In the fifteenth century, before the coming of the Turks, the kings of Hungary may have enjoyed empery over precisely such a substantial portion of Central Europe. Nevertheless, this map depicting a Hungary stretching from the Adriatic to Transylvania is in essence a construction of

Kakania, representing the lands and territories over which the Habsburgs gave a limited autonomy to the unruly Hungarians after the political accommodation of 1867. Habsburg power and Habsburg political cunning decreed those boundaries within which Hungarians believed that they were masters, as animals in a zoo might imagine that they rule the cages in which they are confined.

I do not know what prompted the owners to decorate their entrance hall with that fantasy map. It is most unlikely that they are fiery nationalists urging—as some people are—the exploitation of political instability in Romania and Serbia for Hungary to regain its lost homeland. Political instability is the last thing these people would want: it would be bad for business. That does not mean, however, that they would not welcome the return of lost territory, for they are well informed people, and they know that Hungary in its present geographic state is much less viable economically than that extensive kingdom of former times. It may be that they had been driven by an essentially irrational though by no means insignificant compulsion. Perhaps they told themselves that if a representation of a Hungary great in territories and resources is displayed in sufficient hotels, restaurants, shops and private homes it will, in some mysterious way, attract reality to itself, become actual, not merely an idealised fantasy.

A conversation in the breakfast room a few days before my departure provides a glimpse into the complex network of fantasy and hard-headed realism that characterises these people. The hotel has emptied; the season is over. The weather has changed: a cooler wind from the north-east has blown away the lingering Indian summer and has brought with it the acrid fumes of heavy industry. The proprietors say that now they will be able to relax a little—the hotel will close for two weeks in mid-November for a thorough cleaning, for painting some of the rooms, and repairing the central heating that's been giving trouble on the top floor. They'll probably go to Vienna for a few days' holiday while the work is carried out. They have some very reliable workmen who can be left to themselves for a couple of days.

As I am dutifully consuming the ham and eggs they insist on pressing on me each morning, and as I comfort myself with the thought that I have a little anti-cholesterol pill to take each night, they stand beside my table chatting desultorily. I have just finished telephoning Sydney, timed with a stopwatch by the husband so that the appropriate amount may be added to my bill. They ask about my family, how many children we have, whether my wife has to work, what life is like in Australia. They are surprised to learn that summer is about to begin and that my wife has just told me that there has been an early burst of heat which caused several serious fires on the outskirts of Sydney. But this is the end of October, they say in disbelief, autumn, almost winter—until I remind them, as I had to remind the students I have been teaching during these weeks, about the reversal of seasons in the two hemispheres.

Our talk soon switches to their hopes and aspirations— Australia is obviously too far away, much too hypothetical in a way, to engage their interests for long. They both express their fear that the present economic liberalism won't last— already they're being taxed out of existence. It's most unfair, they complain with passion, that those who are prepared to work and help the country find its feet are made to carry the burden of all those layabouts, good-for-nothings who aren't interested in doing an honest day's work but prefer to live on generous handouts. I haven't the heart to tell them that this is an all too familiar tale, that they do not have a purchase on the miseries of the *rentier* class, for they have launched into a loud and heartfelt litany of complaints, an eloquent lament for the way Hungary has again been betrayed and exploited.

What emerges in the next quarter of an hour or so, after they have accepted my invitation to join me at table and to share the generous pot of coffee they've provided, is a tale of woe I have heard many times, with minor variations, through-out these weeks in Budapest and Szeged. It amounts to a national paranoia, an essentially immature—and therefore alarming—view of economic and political structures and processes. The basis of these tales is always the same. They reside in the undoubted genius, inventiveness and skill of the Hungarian people, the true representatives of Central European civilisation. My hosts are too sophisticated to speak of Hungary's great destiny as a leader of nations, in the way that some political hotheads have been doing, but such sentiments are clearly implicit in their complaints. They do speak, however, of the great potential Hungary enjoys: plentiful food, considerable technological and commercial skill and, mercifully, freedom from the ethnic and racial tensions of Yugoslavia and Czechoslovakia. It would be unwise, I think, to point out to them that the last of those blessings is almost entirely due to the efficient ethnic cleansing of the country during the forties.

All those advantages, they go on to say, have been compromised because Hungary has been betrayed. The husband, after speaking those portentous words, pauses significantly, drawing on his cigarette, to emphasise the gravity (and in a way the finality) of his pronouncement. It's up to me to make the next move, to ask how Hungary has been betrayed, even though I know more or less what the answer will be. It is always the same. This gallant, long-suffering, hardworking and ingenious nation has once more fallen victim to foreign guile and chicanery. Hungarians are too trusting, too ready to believe that the promises of support and encouragement when they were fighting to throw off the Soviet yoke would be honoured by the powerful nations of the west. Well, they risked all and won. And what has happened? Betrayal. The Americans promised the earth, and what did they do? Nothing! Absolutely nothing except to offer loans at impossible rates of interest. The Germans are just as bad—they were driven out in '45, but they're back again plundering the country, buying up everything with their marks.

The complaints grow even more strident and animated. If all this weren't bad enough, there are traitors at home, too. Look around you, the husband gestures around the empty

restaurant, and you'll find the same time-servers and oppor-
tunists in government, in the press and the media as before.
They're very good at looking after themselves, of course, but
the country—well, the poor country suffers while they grow
rich. It's Hungary's fate to be the underdog, to be betrayed
by the unscrupulous: it will never change.

He is about to begin, it seems to me, to reel off the customary
roll call of traitors: former communists, gypsies, Romanians
and—as always, inevitably and sickeningly—the Jews, that
cancer in this world which nothing is able to eradicate. I have
heard this from excited taxi drivers prophesying civil war
tomorrow or at the latest the day after. I have overheard it
in crowded buses, in cafés, and among the expensively dressed
patrons of the State Opera. It is, moreover, a complaint that
has always been heard in this world—except that my host, who
is of course conscious that he must provide hospitality to all
and sundry, wisely refrains from specifying the identity of these
villains and exploiters, preferring to leave it all to innuendo
and implication.

No doubt much of what they say has some justification—
no one would deny the difficulties experienced by a society
attempting to change economic, political and social direction
in a troubled world of uncertainty and severe economic problems. There is, nevertheless, more than a suspicion of immaturity, of a failure to recognise the sad fact of the real world
in these complaints. The fundamental problem has always been
a reluctance to realise that in the cold hard world of political
brutality, nations must stand on their own, must try to work
out their destinies without sentimental expectations of justice,
fairness and benevolence. Australia, it occurs to me, has not yet
learnt that lesson fully, though it has gone farther towards that
goal than Hungary, which is still trapped within its romantic
belief that a gallant people should be treated with gallantry. For
this reason, political debate in Hungary, both formal and spontaneous, almost always devolves into a hunt for the scapegoat,
someone to blame for all the ills, difficulties and misfortunes
of a small country trying to survive in the 'real' world.

Such an attitude is, of course, yet another manifestation of a basically colonial mentality, of a people and a nation who have for hundreds of years been the subjects or clients of foreign powers. Ever since the victory of the Turks at the battle of Mohács in 1526, Hungary has been a subject nation—first the Turks, followed by the Habsburgs, then, after the brief flurry of independence in 1919, the growing reliance on Germany, to be replaced, at the end of the Second World War, by the long years of Soviet rule. Whatever has happened in this country, whatever it has suffered or whatever glories its people have achieved have always flowed out of policies formulated elsewhere, decisions made by powerful men in a distant city or fortress. Naturally enough, therefore, reality is always imposed, never endemic, always a consequence of what they—whoever they may be—have decreed.

That sad realisation is confirmed by my host's peroration. Lighting another excessively long ('luxury length') American cigarette—for no-one of his standing would smoke the terrible locally manufactured muck—he leans forward and says, in gravely confidential tones, that he is about to tell me what the solution should be. I have heard a number of these solutions in the past weeks: they are usually violent, ranging from public hangings to the dropping of a few nuclear devices on selected targets. I am, however, entirely unprepared for what I am about to hear: the solution to Hungary's problems, he says, is union with Austria.

I am unable to disguise my astonishment. I could have expected such sentiments, perhaps, from my grandmother, the owner of the silver Ferris wheel, or even from my mother, who never lost her sentimental attachment to the dream of Kakania. But I had never imagined that a true son of Hungary, a gallant Magyar whose national mythology had long rested on the terrible exploitation of his people by the hated Habsburgs, should, on this cool morning in a little hotel on one of the hills of Buda, seriously advocate a turning back of the clock, a return to Hungary's shameful state of subjection. Yet even as I am seized by astonishment and disbelief, I realise that I have been noticing all over the city in the course of these weeks signs and emblems of a nostalgia for that Kakanian past. Several bookshops, for instance, display Hungarian versions of those little books recounting the sad tales of Sissy, of Rudolf and his Marie, of Maximilian and Franz Ferdinand that grace the shelves of similar brightly lit establishments in Vienna.

My host has all the answers; he says that he's thought a great deal about this, and he is convinced that his is the only viable solution. Hungarian energy, capacity for hard work and ingenuity need bolstering. The country would benefit from Austria's wealth and present influence. Of course at first Austria would be dominant—that's only to be expected given that Hungary has been retarded by all those years of socialism. But Austria's day is past; it is decadent, and of course they all realise this in Austria, even though no-one will own up to it. That's why they need Hungarian energy and ingenuity. In a few years, he'll wager, the tables will be turned. Then Hungary will be on top, the most vital political and economic force in Central Europe. And now he says what he had been reluctant, it would seem, to say earlier. 'That will confirm our destiny, put us on the map once and for all.'

SÉANCE

Half a century of war, occupation and communism have not diminished the exuberance of Budapest's pastrycooks. At Gerbeaud's, once the city's most fashionable café, they still serve the baroque extravaganzas I remember from my child-hood—towering cream slices, rich slabs of chocolate cake, sculptured petits fours and huge mounds of worm-like chestnut purée layered with sweetened cream. Even the room is much as I remember it. Perhaps the brocaded wallpaper has faded, the large mirrors are now spotted with flaws, and the chandeliers do not sparkle as they used to. Only the clientele has changed. Most of the customers are corpulent Germans spilling over their small gilt chairs or else members of the jeans-clad international back-packing society anxiously counting their money. The few natives of Budapest who feel that it is safe once more to appear in a place like this in furs, jewels and expensive clothes are lost in that polyglot crowd.

To see a more vital remnant of the café life of old Central Europe, it is necessary to visit a smaller though equally richly decorated establishment a kilometre or so away. This is the Artists' Café, much patronised by singers, musicians, designers and directors from the Opera House across the road, on the other side of a broad avenue. Only one or two of the seething throng of tourists crowding into the square kilometre of the inner city penetrate this far. Here echoes of a former world may still be heard.

The best time to go is, once again, mid afternoon, before the fashionable early evening rush. The atmosphere is relaxed, even slightly somnolent. There are not many customers at this time, the waitresses are able to relax, leaning on the brightly polished counters, thinking no doubt about their aching feet. The room is almost empty; it is possible on most afternoons to find a table at the back, in front of the large mirror that covers almost the entire wall. In these cafés you should avoid, if at all possible, sitting at one of the tables in the middle of the room because from those tables you cannot survey the other customers with the required aplomb.

Most of the people are elderly or middle-aged; several are obviously regulars. The buzz of talk is subdued, discreet, not the babel of the other café—and the language is Hungarian. These people are the remnants of that fabled café-society which flourished in Central Europe during the early years of the century, and managed to hang on, in a significantly diminished form, until coming of Nazism. In those establishments many of the epoch-making ideas of that world were born. At a lesser level of cultural intensity, these cafés became the literary and artistic salons of the bourgeoisie, places where people could absorb the outlines or the surface of the world of ideas, of the intellect and of the arts. Here you could at least learn the names of up-and-coming painters, writers and composers, and get to know something about the works they were creating, even though you yourself might have found their books, paintings and string quartets entirely strange and daunting.

One couple, seated at the only table with a RESERVED sign on it, and placed in the most advantageous position to survey the room, has fascinated me each time I have come here. They are both elderly; they may or may not be married; they may, it strikes me, be brother and sister. She is intense, angular and chain-smoking. He seems more relaxed but also a trifle melancholy. She fidgets most of the time with the glass of water that is always served with coffee in these establishments. He spends time fussily adjusting his black beret. As with most members of this world, his attaché case, that great distinguisher of the professional classes, is placed on the floor beside him. From time to time, without any signal or bidding, a waitress brings them fresh coffee. They never seem to order any food.

From where I am sitting I cannot catch any of their conversation, for their talk, as of the other customers, is subdued—unlike the mega-decibel uproar at Gerbeaud's. I begin, therefore, to spin fantasies about this elderly pair, whose appearance, demeanour, clothes and gestures evoke long-buried memories. How old are they? They seem to be in their late seventies; that would make them the same age as my mother if she were still alive. Had they known my parents? That question is not as absurd as it sounds; Budapest café-society was a small, self-contained community in which most people within an age group knew or at least knew about each other. It was always, and seems to remain, set apart. For much of the population of Hungary, such as the two pot-bellied entrepreneurs whose lamenting conversation I overheard in that café in Szeged, metropolitan and cosmopolitan people have always seemed somewhat alien, and often undesirable. They do not stand for that myth world of courage, manliness and intense national pride that the true Hungarian clings to. The broader horizons of the people who used to haunt such cafés, and still do so judging by the appearance of the pair at the reserved table, have always been seen as a threat by those suspicious of anything smacking of 'internationalism'. You often hear people saying (with pride or with scathing anger, depending on their point of view) that cultural, artistic and political life in Budapest is still in the hands of the Jews.

It is not impossible that my parents would have known these people. Looking at the lady I begin to fancy that I recognise something familiar in her, something fleeting, hidden and overlaid by the years. This is all absurd, I remind myself, yet somehow the conviction grows on me that there is something ineffably familiar about her appearance, or more precisely about her gestures. It strikes me that her hands, nervously fiddling with her glass of water or with the chain of cigarettes she lights one from the other, are those of an artist, a sculptor perhaps. I am seized by the conviction—absurd and fantastic though it probably is—that this is the sculptor, whose name I have long forgotten, who played an extraordinarily intense part in my mother's life for a few months in 1944.

By that time my father had been taken off to a labour camp and my mother and I were living—hiding would be a more appropriate term—in one of those gloomy blocks of flats that were constructed everywhere in this city in the last years of the nineteenth century. Almost every night we hurried down to the cellar, carrying rugs, pillows, water and bandages, as the air-raid sirens screamed their warning. In between raids we stayed indoors, making hurried forays into the street to pick up what little food remained in a world about to collapse into ruin.

One of the people living in that block of flats was a sculptor, a widow, an intense, chain-smoking woman whose hands, my mother said, were those of a true artist. I was told that she was very famous. Had it not been for this terrible war, her works would have been exhibited in New York—the ultimate accolade according to my mother's cultural horizons. She possessed, besides, other gifts. She was psychic. She could summon spirits from the dead who would, at her command, answer the hushed questions on everyone's lips: 'When will it end? Will we survive?' As the days of that terrible year grew shorter and shorter, as there were more and more hours of darkness before the inevitable 10.00 p.m. air raid, several women gathered around a spindly-legged table, hands spread out and touching each other, as the sculptor entered into her trance.

After a while the muscles of her face would stiffen. Soon her body seemed wholly rigid. She would begin to sway slightly, back and forth, back and forth, and in a voice that seemed to echo with the chill of the grave (or so my mother insisted), she would summon spirits to come to her. And mostly they came. Very soon the table would begin to move and shake, and then to obey her command to tap once if any spirit were present, twice if there were none. Crouched on the floor in a corner of the darkened room, both enthralled and terrified, it did not occur to me to question how absence could tap at all, let alone twice.

She had a varied menagerie of shades, who obligingly tapped once, spelt out their names, and conversed with her (in Hungarian) by means of the tapping alphabet—one tap was A, two taps B, three C . . . Marie Antoinette was the most troublesome, refusing after a while to tap nicely, often flying into tantrums, hurling the table about and, on one spectacular occasion, shattering several of the legs. Fra Angelico was much more serene and gave the dates of his birth and death correctly—someone had an encyclopaedia that confirmed this. The most helpful of the spirits was someone called Claudius, not the Emperor, but an official, according to his account, of the Roman colony of Aquincum on the outskirts of modern Budapest. He proved a useful source of information, though his answers were in almost every instance riddling, like those of the Sphinx.

In later years, during our life in Australia, my mother spoke scathingly about those wartime séances. The sculptor was probably a fraud, she would say—well, if not a fraud she was probably pushing the table subconsciously, and you'd expect her to know Fra Angelico's dates, wouldn't you? But that was in Australia, a dry and matter-of-fact world. In Hungary during those terrible and hectic days of death and fear she was eager for those nightly séances, for gleaning whatever illumination she might gain from Claudius' cryptic taps, or for that matter from Marie Antoinette's tantrums. Ghosts and revenants are somehow appropriate to Europe; they seem faintly absurd in the harsh glare of the southern sun. I cannot imagine middle-class Australian women sitting intently around a slender table asking agonised question—if séances are held in Australia, the questions are most likely to be concerned with the domestic arrangements of the other place. Perhaps you need to have experienced terrible atrocities and outrages before ghosts will come. The Aborigines, who have had their own share of atrocities to endure, are perhaps the only Australians to live in the world of the spirits.

As I look at the elderly couple at the table reserved for them in a strategic corner of this quiet café, I am both amused and slightly embarrassed. Yet I cannot put out of my mind that sculptor of a half a century ago, or those séances, or yet the differences between the two worlds in which I have lived. It is absurd to imagine that this elderly lady, lighting another cigarette from a dying butt—an unladylike but appropriately bohemian habit, surely—might be that psychic sculptor, yet there are many absurdities in our everyday lives. Reason and the intellect are the enemies, at times, of truth, no matter how much we might wish to put our trust in them. And then I am amazed to see the lady place her hands on the marble top of the table and spread out her fingers, with thumbs touching each other, as she is explaining something to her companion. Both laugh and she lifts her right hand to retrieve the cigarette hanging from her lips. I remember, simultaneously, that the sculptor was much older than my mother, and that if this lady were indeed she, she would probably be very close to her hundredth birthday.

MUSEUM

The Museum of Jewish History is housed in an annexe of the main synagogue in Budapest. While the synagogue itself is largely empty, the museum is filled with people. The exhibits are commonplace enough, reminding me, disconcertingly, of those museums of colonial life you come across in places like Berrima and Beechworth. The reason for that seems to be the faint air of incongruity hovering over the objects exhibited in the glass cases scattered around several rooms of the museum. They reveal a crossing of two traditions and societies. Here is a Meissen plate, all gilt and decorative curlicues, redolent of the prim proprieties of the Central-European bourgeoisie of the nineteenth century. Yet the figures depicted on it, crinolined ladies and frock-coated gentlemen, are seated around the Friday night *Seder* table. It is an odd *objet d'art*, as odd as those pieces of English china manufactured for rich ladies and gentlemen in the colony of New South Wales with representations of emus and kangaroos, and of idealised scenes of life in Australia Felix. Many of the other exhibits are equally curious objects. Groups of visitors, mostly elderly, inspect them with a mixture of reverence and boredom. At one end of the large central room a noisy guide hectors his charges in a guttural language which is probably Hebrew.

Tucked away almost apologetically at one end of the museum is a small room illuminated by several spotlights trained on a series of large, unframed photographs fixed to austere black walls. They present, as a demonic iconostasis, the story of the persecution of the Jews of Budapest. You notice odd things: that the official decree of 1944 establishing, for the first time in the history of the city, a ghetto—a quadrangle of streets within which all Jews had to live—was poorly, almost amateurishly typed on a machine very much in need of a fresh ribbon. It looks quaint, an almost harmless document, despite its sinister message. The grainy photographs also reveal curious paradoxes: a jaunty, dandified man, hat worn at a rakish angle, stands beside an advertisement for salami; the yellow star is prominent on the lapel of his well-cut topcoat. A group of men, some little more than children, others elderly, almost decrepit, pose for a photograph at a forced labour camp. Who took the photograph? you begin to wonder as you notice that on the whole the group looks cheerful enough. Was it one of their number who had somehow contrived to bring a camera with him, or was it (as is much more likely) one of their captors, recording for eternity this example of the racial cleansing of gallant Hungary?

Other photographs present more terrible images. One depicts a large group of women, suitcases and bundles beside them, massed in a railway yard, on their way to Auschwitz no doubt. Did they know what was in store for them? Scanning the picture for any sign of alarm or fear on these faces proves futile; their features are hardly to be distinguished, let alone any sign of emotion. Were they told that they were on their way to some pleasant, healthy place where they might make a new life for themselves? In one image, an elderly lady, a country-woman judging by the kerchief tied round her head—a poignant contrast to the befurred matriarch in a nearby photograph—stares at the camera in apparent panic. Was that expression habitual? Was that the way she always looked at a perplexing world? Or did she know that she was looking at death?

The last image, as you leave this little room saturated with the atmosphere of cruelty and death, is the most terrible. It shows a mass of people pressing against a lone, impassive figure. His hands are tied in front of him as he is being fastened to a stake. The photograph was taken during the last moments in the life of a man called Szálasi, the leader of the puppet régime established by the Germans in 1944, who was largely responsible for the mass extermination of Hungarian Jews in the last months of that terrible year. I do not know why this image of a brutal and degenerate man about to face the firing squad should be even more disturbing than the other images of death placed around the walls of this blackened room. If anyone deserved to die, it was surely this man, not the yellow-

starred boulevardier with his rakish hat, nor the kerchiefed
countrywoman with her expression of fear and puzzlement. But
that, of course, is the point. The cancer of this world is the
seemingly inescapable and endemic cycle of outrage and
revenge, which has continued unabated since the day that that
bully and henchman, whom the rest of the world and perhaps
even Hungarians themselves have long ago forgotten, was tied
to a stake and shot to death.

I, however, cannot forget him, for his name entered into
a diabolic mythology that was carried over the seas, to the other
side of the world, by people like my parents, who had been
brushed by his brutal insanity. Here in Hungary I cannot forget
his days of power and greatness, even though I was only a child
at the time, and only partially aware of the peril in which we
stood—and from which we mercifully escaped. For me the
history of that time is written into every stone, every paving
block of this city. It may be unreasonable to be so conscious
of events I had rarely thought about during half a century of
life in another part of the world. Yet they colour my every
perception, perhaps because, unlike those who stayed here—
my cousin for instance—I am encountering them afresh, and
with particular force this afternoon in this little black museum.

The city to which I have returned is for me still the city
of 1945, the city in which people spoke proudly that they had
been present when Szálasi faced the firing squad. And for that
reason the final image in this museum proves to be the most
deeply distressing. I cannot say to the people standing around
me with that reverential mien one might encounter in front
of holy objects or a screen of icons, that it would have been
better to have spared this man's life—not because he didn't
deserve to die, but because it is always better not to kill. To
say so would no doubt offend these people and even perhaps
cause them to misinterpret my sentiments and aspirations.
They might even mistake me for one of those people who daub
antisemitic slogans on statues and monuments in squares,
avenues and parks all over the city. Nevertheless, this place
which records images of a twentieth-century martyrdom should

not display images of vengeance as well—even if, possibly, such vengeance should be sanctioned by divine will.

It also occurs to me that in this room, an infernal camera obscura, images and experiences that have followed my movements around this small country (nominally my homeland, yet one towards which I am able to feel little warmth or love) coalesce in strange and disturbing ways. We tend always to to be moved deeply by memories of the suffering or the persecuted. The puzzled, insouciant or terrified faces displayed around these walls are united by one common and entirely inescapable bond. They were all about to die, and, more importantly, they were all aware—the boulevardier as much as the henchman—that death was near, just behind the camera or just around the corner. Martyrs and monsters, saints and vampires, become indistinguishable in the presence of that obscenity.

For me, though possibly not for others, Australia is innocent of such obscenity. And that is the answer that I should have given my young cousin when she asked me how I could continue living there. The very absence of the patina that age imposes on the great cultures of Europe is also the absence of those nightmarish images that are represented on the walls of this blackened room. Living in such a vacuum, in a land of innocence for people of my kind, might imply life at lower intensity, an existence cut off from the life-sustaining forces of the culture and art celebrated in Europe's nostalgic pantheon. It may even reduce potentially dangerous creatures, the fabled vampire of Transylvania, into the risible figure of Tibby Szabo, the podgy sensualist with sharp teeth and a vulgar taste in interior decoration. It may mean, therefore, that the culture in which I live is, and must continue to be, second rate, one incapable of producing resplendent images of saints because it lacks monsters. So it may indeed be cowardice of a kind not to take the risk and plunge myself once more into the world of vampires. Yet all I seem able to do during these seemingly endless weeks in my 'homeland' is to count the days until I can board the train for Vienna, on the first leg of my journey home.

THE LAST CAFÉ

Change of Programme

A hastily scrawled notice on a large sheet of cardboard propped up against a gilt chair in the foyer of the Budapest Opera House announces a last-minute change of programme. The performance of *La Fiamma* scheduled for this evening has been cancelled because of illness; it is to be replaced by the Hungarian State Opera's contribution to the Mozart bicentenary year, *The Clemency of Titus*. For me at least that piece of news is by no means unwelcome. I had been warned by an acquaintance that *La Fiamma* is, to put it kindly, undistinguished. If opera tickets in this city were not ridiculously cheap, and if I had not been at a loose end for the last three or four days, I would no doubt have heeded that advice. As things turned out, I am to be spared Respighi's no doubt dismally unsatisfactory opera. It seems entirely fitting that my last visit to the opera in Budapest should be to attend a performance of one of Mozart's last major works, written, a few months before his death, for the coronation of Leopold II in the imperial city of Prague.

My own change of programme came about as a result of a telephone call from the Australian Embassy three days before I was due to leave Budapest for Vienna, intending to spend a few days there before embarking on the long flight to Singapore and Sydney. I was asked whether I would consider saying a few words at a reception for a group of people—engineers, economists, computer experts, teachers—who were about to leave for three months' study in Australia. The Embassy would appreciate it if I could see my way to staying on for the function: after all, I had a foot in both camps, so to speak, being both Hungarian and Australian. Vanity and curiosity made me accept the invitation, as long as I succeeded (I told them) in altering my travel arrangements—a complicated business in a country which, until recently, did its best to discourage people from making last minute changes of this sort. A telephone call to the airline's offices in Vienna obtained a changed reservation easily enough. Another informed the proprietor of the small hotel in the building where Mozart composed *The Abduction from the Seraglio* that, unfortunately, I would be prevented from returning for the few nights they had reserved for me. Only one hurdle, and that the most terrible, remained: to change the booking for the two-and-a-half-hour train journey to Vienna. Securing the existing booking took almost as long as the journey itself: I dreaded having to endure that ordeal again.

It seemed, however, that I was meant to stay on for that function. Just as I was about to devote the best part of the day to queuing at the reservations desk of the principal railway station, waiting once more while the official behind the counter dealt with her customers in a maddeningly lackadaisical, enervated manner, in between prolonged telephone conversations discussing the state of her nerves, health and finances, a message from one of my acquaintances in Szeged arrived, saying that her husband would be driving to Vienna, and would be happy to give me a lift. I rang the Embassy to confirm my acceptance, and bought a ticket for *La Fiamma*. 'You'll hate it,' my knowledgeable acquaintance said, 'it's frightful.' I didn't have the courage to tell him that having paid the equivalent of five dollars for a good seat in the stalls, leaving at interval would not be an irresponsible act. And anyway it was better than spending the evening watching satellite television in my hotel room.

And now I am greeted by a pleasant surprise: the prospect of attending a performance of *The Clemency of Titus*, an opera I have never seen, one that is said to be among the least satisfactory of Mozart's mature works, yet one surely worth 'collecting' in this bicentenary year. The performance is about to start by the time I find my seat—except that here everything seems to start about ten minutes after the advertised time. For that reason the theatre is still half-empty, though it is filling rapidly as people at last begin to heed the hortatory bells that have been shrilling in the foyers for the last minute or two. There is the usual flurry as the confusing method of numbering rows and seats in Hungarian theatres defeats the endeavours of a large number of foreign visitors to find their places.

My seat, at least, is secure—I have made sure that I am in the right place, remembering the embarrassment that led to my introduction to the pharmacist of Glebe. I suspect that the well dressed Americans who have just sat down beside me are in the wrong place, judging by the tentative and puzzled way they matched the directions on their limp pink tickets with the seats they are now occupying. That suspicion is confirmed as soon as the houselights begin to go down. Two dumpy ladies, their white hair neatly arranged in buns, wearing dark dresses and silk stoles, arrive and begin, with great politeness, to claim their seats. For an instant I entertain the fear that I shall have to act again as an impromptu interpreter. I am, however, saved when it turns out that one of the ladies is able to resolve the confusion in surprisingly confident English. The Americans scurry off in search of their seats on the other side of the auditorium. With some shuffling and arranging of handbags and stoles, the two ladies settle into their rightful seats just as the orchestra strikes up the first notes of Mozart's overture. My neighbour, seemingly the elder of the two, gives a little start and, after a hurried consultation with her companion, leans over to me and asks whether I know what opera is being performed this evening.

She turns to me again as soon as the curtain falls on the first act. Would I be kind enough to tell her how I knew about the change of programme? I mention the sheet of cardboard in the foyer. Ah, they didn't notice it—they were running terribly late, the buses are so unrealiable these days. So I didn't receive notification either? I look blankly at her. Well, she reminds me, they usually notify subscribers if the programme has to be changed. I explain that I am not a subscriber, at which she seems greatly surprised. Surely I was sitting here last time, and the time before that—she and her cousin have changed subscriptions this year, and she would swear that they had sat beside me on the other occasions. This is the moment for me to produce the line I have been obliged to produce time after time during the previous few weeks: I am a visitor; I've lived most of my life in Australia; I am indeed about to return home.

Thus we fall into conversation during the long interval separating the two acts of Mozart's homage to imperial (Roman and Austrian) clemency. There is something very pleasant about the behaviour of these elderly ladies sitting beside me in the plush-padded stalls of the Budapest Opera House. Their appearance is neat, with a modest and under-stated style quite unlike the highly-coloured glitz of Budapest's very nouveaux riches in this, the second year of freedom and liberty. My neighbour is wearing a black dress covered in white dots. Her feet are shod in sensible lace-up shoes. A small silver ornament is pinned to her breast. It strikes me that, but for the shoes, this lady resembles my grandmother, the owner of the Ferris wheel. She wore every day of her life—at least in the years I knew her—such a dress, in warm wool during the long winter months, cotton in the summer and silk for the few occasions that she left her small, overfurnished apartment in an unfashionable part of town to spend an evening with relatives or close friends. As for shoes—though she must have owned some during the course of her life, had worn them no doubt when dancing with my grandfather during the years of their engagement and married life (before he defected to enter a scandalous liaison with a woman in Prague)—when I knew her (before she vanished from the face of the earth, together with most of my father's family, in 1944) she always wore calf-length boots which were ceremoniously laced up with a silver-handled hook.

I continue chatting with these ladies in the empty auditorium where only a few people remain through this long interval. In the orchestra pit a lone oboist is practising an elaborate semiquaver run. The odd thump behind the curtain indicates that some adjustment is being made to the minimal scenery in front of which Mozart's opera is being performed. I tell my companions about the purpose of my visit; I mention the weeks I have spent in Szeged, the lectures I have given here in Budapest. They are fascinated, delighted. The lady sitting next to me says that she used to teach French, while her cousin is a teacher of English—well, she has actually retired, but still works part time to make ends meet in these difficult times.

Perhaps it is the gilt-and-plush surroundings of this elaborately decorated theatre—tiers of boxes rising to the domed, frescoed ceiling, couchant sphinxes everywhere—that make these ladies, who are intoning the by now familiar litany of hardships, seem less crass or less obsessed than those people who had spoken similar words to me in the past few weeks: my cousin, eyes ablaze as she worked herself into a lather of distress; the custodian of the keep at Visegrád; the green-eyed proprietor of the little hotel in the Buda hills. Whatever the reason, these women seem less intense, much more civilised. They show a nicely ironic detachment from the ills and confusions of this society. They had seen it all before, their demeanour seems to suggest, and, given that both must be well into their seventies, it is obvious that they have experienced several changes of régime, several brave new worlds come into being in this unstable country.

I find to my surprise that this polite, desultory conversation in a near-empty theatre is a very pleasant experience. Trying to understand why that should be so, the thought occurs to me that (through some sort of regression into childhood) the fleeting resemblance of these ladies to my long-dead grandmother, whom I can only remember as a featureless image in a polka-dot dress, has brought me to a partial and probably temporary reconciliation with this world. Other forces must also be operating here; the civilising influence of art—even if it should be something as fundamentally trivial as opera is in the opinion of many people—may have converted something that would seem, outside the privileged confines of the golden enclosure of this theatre, crass and even neurotic. Or is it, I ask myself, that in these weeks of moving around the country, listening, observing, heeding chance encounters, I have been isolated from the better, more refined, at any event less hectic, elements of this society, ones which one may encounter only on an occasion like this?

This sense of ease, of not being on one's guard, helps me to face with reasonable equanimity the question I knew was coming, a question that cannot be avoided in such conversations. What is it like being back in Hungary? my neighbour asks—and I realise, as I am about to launch into my well-prepared standard reply, that she has not used the word 'home'. Both nod knowingly when I say that it's nice to be back, even though it is strange to visit a place you hadn't lived in for almost fifty years. I am about to proceed to the platitudes I consider fitting in such circumstances—how hospitable everyone seems to be, how this may be a better world than the one I left etcetera—when my neighbour's cousin leans across her companion and touches my sleeve. It must be very painful, she says, to have to come face to face with memories, to remember all sorts of things that I had forgotten or hadn't wanted to remember. There must be great distress in such recognitions. And then she says something that has occurred to me several times during these weeks and, of course, even more poignantly, a year ago, when I returned to this world for the first time after all those years of absence. The past, she says, with a faint smile of self-consciousness, is another country—she knows it's a banal thing to say, yet it's true.

The moment marks something strange, inexplicable but—or so I am convinced—very significant. The barriers of suspicion and reticence are lifting. Why is it, I ask myself with some bitterness, that I am able to experience some sense of community, of a shared understanding, with total strangers, to whom I would probably not have spoken had there not been a last-minute change of programme at the opera, when with others, even with my cousin, I keep myself aloof, reluctant to allow them to come too close? I cannot, I realise (as I notice that the audience is beginning to trickle back into the auditorium) account for this curious change of attitude, and perhaps I should not seek explanations—perhaps these moments of insight and even reconciliation must come like this, unexpected, mysterious and fleeting.

I think that my companions have also recognised that something significant has occurred—something which they are probably as incapable of putting a name to as I am, yet something which (judging by our silence) has touched them too. Then, since such moments cannot and perhaps should not last, my neighbour begins to chat about tonight's performance. What do I think of it? Of course the standard is not very high, she knows that. What can you expect, though? The singers are paid next to nothing, so it stands to reason that if they get the offer of an engagement abroad they're off like a shot. Didn't I know, she asks with a smile, that that is why so many performances are cancelled because of indisposition? Some years ago the authorities relaxed the rule that all operas must be performed in Hungarian. Singers are now able to learn the more popular works in their original languages—German, Italian, French. So that if a singer suddenly cancels a performance in Graz or Linz, or even in Vienna, someone gets on the telephone and—pouff! the opera in Budapest is off. You can't blame them, she remarks; poor things, they work so hard, yet they scarcely know where the next meal will come from. And, of course, some never come back.

I tell them, again with greater candour than usual, that my visits to the opera throughout these months have been more sentimental and mythological than musical. Pointing to one of the boxes on our left, now occupied by a pair of extremely bored-looking people, I begin to speak about those months in 1946 when, as a gesture of farewell to the world we were about to leave, my parents brought me to this theatre most Wednesday nights, to sit in that box and witness spectacles which have come to stand, throughout the many intervening years, as shining images of the old life, the life that had been poisoned for us by hatred and barbarity, yet a life we yearned after in our exile. I describe for them some of my memories of those nights long ago; I speak about the way those probably pedestrian performances enchanted an impressionable and undiscriminating child. But the lady in the spotted dress interrupts me: no, she remembers that year, some of the performances were surprisingly accomplished, given the appalling circumstances. Had I, she asks, ever heard of Otto Klemperer?—and I tell her that I do indeed remember him conducting performances in this theatre, and that furthermore, many years later, when I was living in London, I used to attend concerts given by the then famous and practically crippled musician, and that I used always to remember how my parents would mention his name whenever he took his post at the podium here in 1946.

Reminiscence, sentiment and nostalgia are interrupted by the polite applause greeting the conductor of tonight's performance. The houselights dim. The second act, in which Titus' magnanimity will be confirmed, begins. The performance is, to say the least, mediocre. The person sitting directly behind me, who resolutely refuses to cover her sneezes, proves to be a distracting nuisance. Yet I experience a sense of strange contentment as I watch this tedious opera weave its way through a confusing and silly plot to its triumphant conclusion.

ACADEMY

Buttoned, muffled and gloved, I am panting up a steep street at the foot of the Buda hills towards the Eötvös Academy, the venue for the reception where I am to deliver a short address as a token Australian Hungarian. The weather has turned wintry. A blast of cold air from the steppes has blown away the last remnants of the Indian summer that lingered for many weeks over the Danube basin. The sky is leaden, sheets of sleety rain are driven by swirling gusts. People are huddled at bus shelters, in the doorways of shops and blocks of flats, waiting for a momentary break in the downfall before dashing across the rainsoaked street, dodging between screeching and sliding cars rushing about at their customary breakneck speed. The academy turns out to be a handsome building halfway up a street that snakes its way to one of the lesser peaks of this steep terrain. The wind is screaming in my face. I am able to see next to nothing because my glasses have fogged up. Wheezing and spluttering, I struggle to shut my umbrella on the portico, exasperated, miserable and feeling very sorry for myself.

Almost as soon as Mozart's celebration of imperial clemency came to an end and I had said goodbye to the two ladies sitting beside me, I felt the telltale tickle at the back of the throat, the legacy of the person behind me who had sneezed her way through the performance, a sure harbinger of a streaming cold. My throat is on fire; my eyes are watering; I am probably running a temperature; and I have certainly all but lost my voice. It is in these circumstances that I must speak those few words to the gathering at the academy.

This institution occupies a curious place in the complicated and confusing network of Budapest's universities. It is one of those unexpected remnants of Kakania you come upon in odd corners of this large, noisy and decrepit city. The academy was established, I have been told, to produce a professional and bureaucratic élite, imbued with the supranational aspirations of the old Empire, to contain and to check excessively nationalistic sentiments, not at gunpoint but by the seduction of favour and privilege. Both the appearance and the location of the institution declare, with obvious symbolism, its otherness and privilege—a privilege that seems to have survived two wars, revolutions and dizzying changes of régime.

The large, crowded campuses of Budapest's universities and places of higher learning are concentrated in the flatlands of Pest. They grew as that city grew, and they mirrored its citizens' energetic determination to succeed, to exploit the new world of opportunity that came into being in the hectic birth of that crowded, often vulgar town from the sleepy villages and trading posts which had occupied that bank of the Danube for centuries. In those institutions people could learn to become engineers, or acquire the commercial skills which would enable them to better their lot and rise through the economic—if not the social—scale, and also to absorb a culture of sorts to complement their new-found wealth.

The Eötövs Academy stands, aloof from such vulgarity and ambition, at the foot of the Buda hills, in the heartland of the old Kakanian gentry, far away from the .bustling world on the other side of the river. It is housed in one of those palatial public buildings that have a subtle but unmistakably Viennese air—pilasters and niches, statues and medallions, crests and devices speaking of tradition, authority and stability. It is a palace rather than a temple of learning. Solidly cast and intricately decorated iron railings protect it from intruders. My cousin gave me a characteristically sour account of this academy when I told her that I would be staying on for a few days to attend the reception. Oh yes, she said, it was the breeding ground for Nazi intellectuals—or at least they called themselves intellectuals. Then it was reserved for the sons and daughters of Party bosses. Now, of course, the Nazis are back again. Whatever possessed me to agree to speak at a function in such a place?

I do not see swastikas or even the Hungarian variant of that infernal symbol displayed in the entrance foyer as I am asking the elderly gatekeeper to direct me to the reception room. Yet his surly unfriendliness, denying that any function is scheduled for this afternoon, insisting indeed that the place is about to close, does suggest something of the brutal secretiveness you associate with the headquarters of such organisations. But it is probably no more than the ingrained bloody-mindedness of totalitarian officialdom evident all over Budapest—in banks and railway stations, pharmacies and supermarkets, post offices and tourist bureaux. My task is made not a jot easier as I keep insisting that he must let me in, that I am one of the speakers without whom the function could not possibly proceed, while he continues doggedly to repeat that the building is about to be locked. I am saved by a middle-aged woman dressed in a severe blue suit, suggesting simultaneously a business executive and a prison warder, who has been attracted by the hubbub in the entrance hall. Oh yes, she says sneeringly, the salon has been booked for some sort of reception, and she will show me up.

She throws open a door on the ample first floor landing and stalks away. The panelled room is empty, though rows of chairs are set in a semicircle around a lectern placed on a small podium. There is no sign of life anywhere, except that I can hear laughter and clanking somewhere down the corridor beyond the open door. Making cautiously towards the source of that noise, I discover to my relief a small kitchen where Joe, the dispenser of curried prawns and rice, is supervising, with much hilarity, the preparation of supper by a group of enthusiastic helpers.

I offer to help, hoping to find something to occupy me to quell the anxiety and apprehensiveness I am experiencing at the prospect of having to say my piece as an Australian Hungarian. Joe has other ideas. He presses a glass of wine into my hand and tells me to go and sit near the heater. He says that I must look after myself because, mate, you don't want to get crook in this town—the doctors are the pits. And he goes on to tell me something that I've heard several times already, a part of a mythology of a kind that always springs up among exiles and expatriates. When the Embassy people need a doctor, he says, they choof off to Vienna; you can't trust the local buggers.

Seated in a comfortable armchair next to the central heating outlet, I find myself obliged, after all, to muse on my anxieties about engaging in the mixing or crossing of cultures on which I am about to embark. It's no use my telling myself that it is all my fault, that I should have declined the invitation and travelled to Vienna as planned. I am trapped now, called upon to do shortly what I least want to do. Even with my cousin, the only person who is at all important and valuable for me in this world, I have been reticent, unwilling to speak openly about the confusions, perplexities and ambivalences anyone like me who has been wrenched from one world to be planted in another must experience. I do not want to admit to the crossing patterns and mixed allegiances I have been aware of throughout these weeks. How Australian am I? someone asked me in Szeged. Ninety-nine percent, I replied with only slight exaggeration—I did not add, however, that the remaining one part in a hundred made all the difference.

Besides those constant preoccupations another much more immediate worry nags at me. This function is obviously intended to be diplomatic, ceremonial and anodyne. I know that I am expected to say something cheerful, optimistic and reassuring—to speak about co-operation, about the exchange of ideas, and how our two nations and cultures can learn from each other to the benefit of both. I have to admit that in an abstract, hypothetical sense I too believe in these aspirations, and (in my more optimistic moods) I convince myself that in the course of these weeks, as I have been talking about Australia to—admittedly mostly bored—students, I may have contributed a little to those aims. There are, however, private demons, personal nightmares that make it very difficult for me to approach this world with equanimity and without prejudice. I am ready to admit that many of the people alive in this city today, certainly those who will be coming to this reception, are far too young to bear any direct responsibility for what happened here almost half a century ago. I cannot escape, however, the sense, indeed the conviction, that a terrible and shameful past must not be swept under the carpet, that it is only too easy to say that it all happened a long time ago, that a line has been drawn under a shameful page of national history. There are too many spectral signs in this world—ones to which I may perhaps be more sensitive than others—to make it possible for me to forget or to ignore their threat.

That is the particular dilemma facing me today, one I shall have to resolve shortly, for at last people are beginning to arrive, peeling off their gloves, scarves and topcoats, smiling, shaking hands, effecting introductions. I recognise several familiar faces: people from the university and the Embassy, as well as the Transylvanian in the bow tie. The Ambassador arrives and walks around the room welcoming people, diplomatically expressing his pleasure at seeing them. We begin to say a few words to each other as the young Third Secretary mounts the podium, announces that the proceedings are about to start, and invites the Ambassador to speak. People crowd to find a place in the semicircle of chairs, though there are far more seats than people. The noises from the kitchen cease. Joe places himself just inside the open door—half-voyeur, half-bouncer—as the Ambassador takes a few sheets of paper from his pocket and begins his address.

His speech is matter-of-fact, efficient and diplomatic. He gives a brief outline of the scheme to send Hungarians to train in Australia. One of these people, who has recently returned to Budapest, will be speaking to us later on, he says. He stresses the importance his government places on this type of aid, and goes on to deliver a thumbnail sketch of Australia: size, population, climate, economy, political structure. He wishes the people about to depart every success; he is convinced that Australia—herself experiencing certain economic difficulties in these hard times—will be of some help to the Hungarian people's attempts to solve the many difficulties they are experiencing at this time of transition.

He is followed by a speaker representing a government agency, and then a youngish man in a well-cut dark suit with carefully groomed hair gets up to speak. In the curious monotone of the Americanised Hungarian-English spoken here nowadays, he identifies himself as an economist who recently spent three months in Melbourne acquiring financial and commercial skills. He speaks a few words describing how stimulating it was to learn from people who clearly possessed those skills that Hungarians must acquire if the nation is to survive in a competitive world. The bulk of his address is concerned, however, with the beauty of Melbourne. He didn't know what to expect: Hungarians know so little about Australia. Nothing had prepared him for his first sight of that stunning city: the wide, clean-swept boulevards, the shiny automobiles, the wonderful skyline of tall buildings glinting in the clear sunlight, and above all the sky, the quality of the light, penetrating, revealing but also exhilarating. He continues

in this vein for a minute or two and then comes to an end
by expressing his gratitude to all concerned for giving him the
privilege of those wonderful months in Australia. The Third
Secretary rises to his feet again, and introduces me as the next
speaker.

My head is throbbing; my mouth is dry; no sound, I am
convinced, will issue from my burning throat. I fiddle with
the sheet of folded paper on which I've jotted the odd phrase,
cough, and begin to speak. At first things go well enough.
Though my voice is like sandpaper, I am at least audible. I
say how much I've enjoyed my weeks in Hungary, how much
I appreciate the kindness and hospitality I've received, and how
valuable it was to get to know again the country of my birth.
So far, I think to myself, so good—I may have been gilding
the lily a bit, but I'd stand by most of what I've said. The
next part is also easy enough. I give a brief biographical sketch.
I mention how I was born in a clinic just around the corner
from the Australian Embassy; how I spent the first two years
of my life in an apartment also very near the Embassy, and
I give a brief description of my parents—entirely ordinary and
reasonably affluent middle-class inhabitants of Budapest. I say
something about their way of life, stressing all the time that
it was typical of the Budapest bourgeoisie between the two
wars. I recount a few anecdotes from my childhood—skating
on the frozen pond in the municipal park, waiting for the wave-
machine in the baths on St Margaret's Island to be switched
on, visits to Gerbeaud's and other scrumptious cafés. I reveal
that my mother, although technically an Austrian at the time
of her birth, loved to dance the *csardas*, the fiery Hungarian
national dance.

Listening to myself, all this sounds innocuous enough—
anecdotal, even perhaps inconsequential but (or so I hope)
diverting. I wonder though how many of my audience realise
the extent of my deviousness, that this meandering assemblage
of family history leaves out as much as it includes. That
exclusion is quite deliberate. I find, as I am building up this

picture of ordinariness, that the demons are returning, demons
that I intend to let loose in a moment or two on my relaxed
and comfortable audience. I am conscious of the dangers and
even of the potential impropriety of what I am about to do.
Yet these are compulsions I cannot resist, unwise and undi-
plomatic though it might be to give in to them.

I have deliberately omitted from my account of my parents'
very commonplace life any mention of race or religion, and
in truth those concepts played only a very small part in their
early married life. Yet that is precisely what I have to speak
about now—how that ordinary family came to be hounded
and persecuted just because some blood coursed through its
veins that offended the sensibilities of many true-blooded
Magyars. As I begin my account of the familiar story of the
persecution of Central European Jewry, which started as a series
of annoying prohibitions and ended in the gas chambers of
Auschwitz, the demons of my past—indeed of my early
childhood—flood back with noisy insistence. I remember not
merely the pleasant, public images of family life about which
I have spoken, but also those intangible, intimate relationships
that existed in a large and on the whole loving family. And
it comes home to me with a particularly searing pain once again
that most of these people were killed in 1944, amid God-
knows-what brutality and suffering, that they were not allowed to live their allotted span, to be born and to die within
the orderly rhythms of life.

As I speak about these things in an attempt to explain as
candidly as I can why I am no longer able to think of myself
as a Hungarian, why I can never think of this country as home,
something unexpected and shaming occurs. I have thought and
spoken often enough in the past about my family's fate,
indistinguishable from the fate of millions of others, I have
even on occasions written about it. However, I have never stood
before a group of people—especially a group including many
Hungarians—and remembered, publicly and ceremonially, the
dead, my own dead and by implication all those who were
tortured, humiliated and killed. This ceremony of remem-

brance proves more distressing than I could have imagined. Recalling the sufferings of people who would all be dead by now, even if they had been allowed to live their three score and ten, literally and embarrassingly brings tears to my eyes. It is no use pretending that I must stop to blow my nose or clear my burning throat. For the first and I hope the only time as a public speaker I dry up, unable to continue, only too conscious of what a ridiculous sight it must be to behold a squat, bald, middle-aged man with a streaming nose turning away from his audience as he is overcome by emotions.

The moment passes. I recover as much equilibrium as I can muster and continue on the next part of what I intend to say: my praise of Australia, a society which despite its occasional crassness, intolerance and narrow-mindedness is, nevertheless, basically healthy and just, a world where you could grow and develop with fewer restraints placed on you, and a world, above all, that gave you opportunity not only to grow but also— and this is something I want particularly to stress—to fail. And that, I go on to say with a little more self-control, is why I think of myself as ninety-nine percent Australian, why I appreciate the opportunity I have been given to return to Hungary, why I hope that the country of my birth and I may have achieved a reconciliation, but why I must speak tonight as the Australian I think I have become.

The Ambassador is looking at his boots. Is he annoyed, I ask myself, because I've broken the bland conventions of such gatherings? The Third Secretary seems somewhat rattled too as he rises to his feet to announce the next speaker. My own feelings are a curious mixture of fatigue, embarrassment and satisfaction at having spoken out. I am most conscious though of my fiery throat and congested chest.

The evening draws to a close. I say my farewells. The Ambassador and I exchange a few polite words. Joe tells me again to look after that cold. I tell the historian from Melbourne that she mustn't come near me because you don't want to get crook in this country. The Third Secretary says we ought to find something to eat somewhere, perhaps that recently opened Thai restaurant which, he's heard, is quite decent.

WINTER JOURNEY

The rain has stopped. A cold sun shines in a wintry sky. It has got even colder with the clearing weather. Snow is forecast for the weekend, heavy in places—but by then I should be far away from here, floating in the dark sky above Asia.

We are driving along a busy motorway, Budapest's western artery. My Szeged colleague's husband is a steady, sensible driver, refusing to join in the daredevil games of the other motorists—drivers of clapped-out Ladas and Trabants, the occasional golden youth of the new Hungary in a Porsche, helmetless motorcyclists. Grim towers of socialist flats line both sides of the road. I catch sight of a woman shaking out an eiderdown from a high window. Another young woman holding a small child by the hand waits patiently at a pedestrian crossing. A large advertising hoarding entices you to smoke a well-known brand of cigarettes.

As the city is left behind I notice that we are approaching a small town—by now no more than an outer suburb—where in 1944 my father was interned in a forced labour camp. Travelling past that dreary little town's mean houses, small factories, decrepit shops, I begin to wonder where the barracks might have been in which my father was confined. I realise that he must have walked along this road the night he escaped, picking his way in the darkness to the place in Budapest where my mother and I were hiding. And it must have been along this road, too, that he returned after four or five days to give himself up, when he could no longer bear being confined behind the wooden slats of the coal cellar where my mother had hidden him from the gaze of the curious.

On the other side of that perfectly ordinary little town, which may no longer remember that it had once been the site of a minor infamy, the countryside begins. We now have the road pretty much to ourselves. The golden youths have sped on into the distance, the spluttering Ladas and Trabants have been left far behind. We chat desultorily in the way that near-strangers who have been thrust into each other's company for a few hours seek some topic of conversation to fill in the silences. Over a cup of coffee in a small roadhouse beside a chicken-run my companion says that we should think of where to stop for lunch, and I suggest Sopron, the town where my mother grew up, a place I'd wanted to have a look at very much but could not find an opportunity to visit. He looks hesitant. I recall something my cousin had said—that when she last visited the place four years ago she was appalled by the high prices: the same as they charge in Austria, just down the road. I say to my companion that he must, of course, be my guest and he, smiling and obviously relieved, accepts the offer.

Half an hour later another roadsign. This leads us into a largish town, an important railway-junction called Györ, its grey ill-kept buildings hinting at former Kakanian splendours. The sun has disappeared behind slate-coloured clouds. Swirls of wind lift the autumn leaves lying in the gutters. Here is another site of my personal mythology, the town where my father's eccentric cousin, the religious maniac who forced her daughter to join a convent and whose son committed suicide in one of those brutal Kakanian military academies, ruled with an iron hand her mild-mannered, ineffectual husband, the Major. I recall the last time I saw that lady—just before she too, despite her fervent Catholicism, was swallowed by the madness and hatred of the time.

We visited my mother's Sopron relatives for Easter in 1943: we all knew that it would be our last visit. The war was closing in, menacing and terrible. My father's cousin came to the station to see us during the train's hour-long halt. As she was leaving, when shrill whistles warned of the train's departure, she pressed a brown paper parcel into my mother's hands—eggs, she said, she was sure we hadn't had any in Budapest for a long time. Ten minutes or so after the train drew out of the station into the dusk of early spring a huge explosion not very far away shook and jolted the carriage, hurling the eggs from my mother's lap. As we sat for many hours in that freezing carriage, waiting for the line ahead, which had received a direct hit, to be repaired, we watched the sticky mess of eggs on the patterned carpet first coagulate and then freeze over.

Soon we are clear of that town too. Indeed we shall soon be clear of Hungary, so short are the distances in this tiny country. The landscape becomes more undulating; there are now the odd vistas and prospects visible through the misty rain. We pass through several small towns or large villages. I have all but stopped looking at the scenery, or paying attention to the roadsigns, concentrating instead on my running nose and aching throat. I catch sight of the name of a dreary dun-coloured village etched on the façade of a crumbling town (or village) hall. The seemingly endless row of letters that makes up the name of the place attracts my attention. It is, I realise, Fertőszentmiklós, yet another stage on this unintended pilgrimage to my past.

This is the place where my mother was born, where her father taught in the village school until his untimely death in the third year of my mother's life. It was here that my great-grandfather supervised the transportation of milk from the estates of the Eszterházy family to the great capitals, nearby Vienna and much more distant Budapest. And it was here in 1919 that the Bolsheviks ransacked my great-grandfather's house, causing his family—my great-grandmother, my grandmother and my mother as well as my cousin's as yet unmarried mother—to seek shelter in a heavily barred cellar. It was from this place that they moved with their few remaining possessions to the nearby town, Sopron, which they knew by its Austrian name of Oedenburg, to be succoured by the contemptuous charity of relatives. Such a place should be charged with resonances. Yet it is no more than a dull, down-at-heel little town in the last stages of decay, except that a garish video shop beside a small unkempt park suggests that some life may, after all, remain here.

A few stretches of farmland and a couple of straggling hamlets bring us to a corrugated iron shed, beside which a faded and pockmarked metal sign announces that we have entered the town of Sopron.

THE WATCHTOWER

The outskirts of Sopron, as of most towns, are anything but inspiring. The rust-encrusted shed gives way to a series of mean single-storey dwellings, interspersed from time to time with red brick workshops and the mess and confusion of a car yard or scrap metal dump. A little farther along, the size and ambition of the buildings increase; there are occasional ornate decorations and pompous inscriptions to be seen. Soon, as always happens, the first institution slips past, turrets and porticoes behind a rusting iron railing—school, hospital or madhouse. There are groups of shops visible now, few distinguished by any sign—you get the feeling that in this part of the town people know where to go for goods without needing to be told. A small park, a church and then, with a slight rattle of wheels, we're off the bitumen, driving along a narrowing cobbled street.

We all carry in the secret recesses of our imagination a myth world—a place, a house, a landscape, a time—which often speaks to us most eloquently precisely because it is remote, perhaps forgotten, a very particular symbol of our longings and dreams. For me the name of this town, much more so than a handful of hazy, fifty-year-old memories, fleeting and unrelated images, stands at the centre of that network of nostalgia and yearning—and also of fears and demons—which have been following me in my rambles around the two countries that meet here, Austria and Hungary, the remnants of the fabled realm of Kakania. This little German-speaking town that became Hungarian as a consequence of a somewhat suspect referendum held after the Great War provided the focal point from which my mother surveyed the bitter early years of her life in Australia, and it was here that the many strands of her mythology—elaborated and embellished with the passage of time—converged. Now, as the cobblestones set up a curious shuddering, I am about to enter that world as a middle-aged Australian with a cold in the head.

That mythology had many centres, many points of departure from which the filaments of anecdote and story snaked out, tangling with other strands leading to other centres. One centre was formed by my mother's bitter memories of her cousins' icy charity, the cruelty that hid behind a loving smile, when they persisted in reminding their unfortunate relatives of their nobility and altruism when they helped them out in their great need after the disaster of 1919. That cycle of tales told of insults and humiliations, and also of my mother's revenge, years later, after her transformation into the metropolitan *grande dame*, when she was able at last, she said, to teach these provincial cousins a thing or two.

The other tales were much brighter than that saga of petty revenge. The most elaborate constellation circled around the Ursuline convent where she was educated. It presented her with images of the gracious and cultivated way of life led by those noble women who had retreated behind the walls of a luxuriously appointed institution, there to pursue a life of study, reading, polite conversation and other civilised amenities of the good life. She spoke of the handsome apartments the good nuns occupied, the delicacy of the dishes prepared for them by their servant sisters, the distinguished visitors they received in their handsome salon. She spoke of these with great fervency in our poky flat in an outer suburb of Sydney where the rising damp left intricate yellow patterns on the white-washed walls.

For me, as a young child in Hungary, and later as a pimply adolescent in Sydney, the most fascinating and momentous of these tales found its location in the hills that rise on the perimeter of the town. It was there in 1928 that my sixteen-year-old mother met my father, a mature adult of twenty-four.

That story, vaguely reminiscent of one of the episodes in those Kakanian romances that fill the bookshops of the Mariahilferstrasse, seems as if it occurred in a distant century, in a fabled time of myth and legend, rather than a mere, prosaic sixty-odd years ago—yesterday, or at most the day before.

It was wintertime. The Ursuline ladies had given their pupils a half holiday to celebrate some great event—a saint's feast-day, an important anniversary in the annals of the order, my mother couldn't remember which. With a friend she tramped through the drifting snow to the top of the hills ringing the town where, for a few pennies, you could hire rickety wooden sleds. They spent a delirious afternoon screaming down a winding track to the foot of the hill, laboriously dragging the sled uphill only to scream down once more, most of the time entirely out of control and ecstatically happy. Occasionally a wonderfully sleek two-seater toboggan slid past them, with two young men frantically waving them out of the way.

Towards the end of the day, in the failing light, my mother and her friend decided to go for one last slide. The runners of their usually slow and cumbersome sled had iced over by this time: it slithered down the hill with the speed of light. Now they found themselves wholly unable to control its career. As they approached the bottom, lurching out of the last curve, they saw themselves heading straight for the sleek toboggan. Its drivers, who were adjusting something on its complicated frame, had just enough time to jump out of the way before their contraption was smashed to smithereens by two silly schoolgirls, who were now tumbling head over heels in the soft snow.

A dreadful scene followed: recriminations, threats, insults—a slanging match that echoed through the hills and certainly reached the ears of the town's gossips and meddlers. The story spread around the town. The Neubauer girl ('You know the one, David Weiss's granddaughter, she lost her father in '14.') has to pay for a new toboggan, or one of those young men ('His name's Riemer, he comes from Budapest—yes you do know him, he is the manager of the weaving mill.') is going to go straight to the nuns to ask them to intervene. People took sides, as always happens, in this provincial tempest. One party—led by my mother's charitable cousins—insisted that this was merely proof of what they'd been saying all along: my mother would come to a bad end, and serves her right. The other side asserted that it was surely a little childish of a grown man to be so vindictive towards two foolish girls. Accidents do, after all, happen, and surely he must be earning enough money to be able to afford a new toboggan.

The controversy raged for some time. Then people noticed that my father kept on calling at my great-grandfather's flat almost every day—to discuss the terms of settlement, he insisted, but there were those who thought they knew better. Then one summer day a fresh scandal broke. The cousins hurried in deputation to my great-grandfather: they'd seen Elisabeth riding pillion on young Riemer's motorbike. Imagine, they went round and round the square in front of the watchtower for all to see, laughing, waving to friends! My mother was locked in her room for a week, allowed out only to use the bathroom. Because of the severity of the punishment she had already endured, the Ursuline ladies decided not to expel her. A year later, when she had finished school, she became engaged to my father.

My mother spent the next six years in an ecstasy of anticipation. They had to wait until my father had enough capital to establish his own business before they could marry. He took a well-paid job in Budapest. Every weekend he would zoom down to Sopron on his infamous bike to see his fiancée. Now and then she would go up to town to stay with his mother, who was at first suspicious of this provincial orphan but grew at length to like her. Occasionally during my father's visits to Sopron, the young couple would take the early train for Vienna—suitably chaperoned by my grandmother or some other responsible person—to spend the day strolling along the Graben or the Kärtnerstrasse, to marvel at the great cathedral, or eat delicious cakes in one of the elegant cafés, or (if the weather was particularly fine) to ride on the great wheel in the Prater, or to take the tram to Grinzing and stroll through the Vienna Woods.

My mother's happiness knew no bounds. The delicious thrill of anticipation with which she prepared her trousseau over those five or six years spread out to embrace her family, her friends and the little town itself, with its cobbled streets, beautiful buildings and the great watchtower looming over the rooftops. Her life was rich, and it was to become even richer on that day in 1935 when she left Sopron to travel to Budapest. It was to be her triumphant entry into a life of metropolitan sophistication, which was to last until it crumbled in the storm of hate unleashed in the beer halls of Munich by the little painter of Linz. I was born, exactly nine months and a week after her entry into the married state, on the bitterly cold leap-year day of 1936.

Retrospect and nostalgia cast a golden glow over her memories. They were transmitted to me, at various points of my life, and in various circumstances—when we sheltered in a damp cellar during the siege of Budapest and in the harsh light of an Australian suburb in the late forties—as a cycle of legends and myths of a lost world, a time of innocence and well-being before the corruption of experience set in. The more those days receded into the past, the more sentimental and embellished its images became. She forgot the pettiness, the provincial boredom, the poverty her family had endured. They were replaced by the glowing memories of Sopron's winding cobbled streets, the great watchtower standing as a comforting guardian or sentinel over its rooftops, the predictable rhythms of provincial life—the café, the little municipal theatre, outings to the wide shallow lake or the wooded hills where she first ran into my father. They set the standards of security, well-being and contentment which none of her later life—not even the five or six years of metropolitan affluence in Budapest—could equal.

For me, who possessed only fragmented memories of this place, that legacy is more emblematic than epic. Though I knew the sagas of the Ursuline convent and the wooded slopes, I have acquired and retained a predisposition towards the more abstract elements of this world. My own longings for Europe, which are most pronounced in Australia, where I try to compensate for them by private and professional activities and aspirations which would nowadays be sneeringly labelled by many as 'Eurocentric', find their fullest expression in social, aesthetic and emotional priorities which are probably embodied most clearly in places such as this town, or at least as it used to be.

I have learnt over many years of travel that the magic realm of Europe, which governs so much of my imagination, cannot be found in the present—or at least in those parts of modern Europe I have got to know on my professional and private travels. The excitement of Paris, the patina of Rome are both thrilling and enthralling. Yet experiencing them is somehow different from the promptings of that sentimental image that I carry around with me, which is labelled with the specific but highly abstract term 'Europe'. The longing for a world I barely knew, indeed one which I may not have experienced at all, but only received as carefully nurtured myth, appeals to aspirations essentially different from the life of contemporary Europe.

From time to time, nevertheless, unexpectedly and therefore with curious potency, I have caught a fleeting glimpse or impression of that private fantasy in various places, almost always in that geographic and spiritual realm identified as Central Europe. It came to me one summer day in the cobbled streets of Salzburg—except that the crowds of sightseers jamming those narrow thoroughfares, the advertisements for *Mozartkugeln* and the great fortress scowling over the town provided jarring, incompatible overtones. It also came to me several times in Vienna, not in its great monumental spaces, but in a sidestreet, an alley or a passage lined with old-fashioned gaslights, where the scale was smaller and more intimate. It is also evident sometimes in the social rituals of small, out-of-the-way cafés, in a particular type of gentility—urban but not necessarily urbane—as with the two elderly ladies with whom I fell into conversation on my last visit to the opera in Budapest. And it came most surprisingly and disconcertingly—surrounded, it is true, with sardonic ironies—in Szeged with its memories of imperial Vienna reduced and tamed to provincial cosiness.

I have come to understand in the course of these weeks, as I have been dipping into this world, that my private images of a time of innocence, perhaps of a paradise from which I had been expelled even before I was born, are concentrated in a distillation of that family myth world—as so often, preserved and transmitted through the maternal line—which took its inspiration from the rituals and aspirations of old Kakania's provincial bourgeois life. Despite my irony, close (it seems to me at times) to a deracinated cynicism, I am still devoted to that world, longing for the impossible, a quality of life and experience which had probably all but ceased to exist by the time of my true origins—that snowy day when my mother and her friend dragged a rickety sled up a winding path to the hills surrounding the little town of Sopron. The vision lodged in my imagination—the cobbled streets meeting at a sharp angle, the barred windows, the faintly glowing streetlight, the warm light of a shop or a café illuminating a square of cobblestones, the smell of vanilla and coffee I have encountered often enough in the cafés of this world—had their origins, I am convinced, not merely in this part of the world, but here, in this town.

Is that image a scrap, a remnant of an early experience, an all but forgotten memory of one of our visits to our Sopron relatives? Or is it, in a way even more contingent and remote, an assembly of bits of that mythology which have coalesced for me, its recipient, into this arbitrary, perhaps totally insignificant impression? I have no means of resolving that puzzle—my cousin knows even less about our family's life in this town than I do; her mother was clearly not a myth maker. Yet the source of the image, impression or sensation is less important than its effect or consequences. It provides a focus for the almost infinite, confusing and contradictory pressures and experiences of life. It becomes a still centre, something to which the emotions and the sensibility—though rarely the intellect—may return to find a point of reference or of departure.

Most people, it seems to me, have such a centre, focus or still point to which they instinctively return. For many it is, no doubt, more substantial, intellectually and even spiritually more respectable than this essentially gimcrack illusion. For some a religious sense or conviction might provide such a focus; for others patriotism or deeply-etched ethnic allegiances. It may be my personal misfortune that the centre of my imagination— something that persists like a steady beat or the unvaried pattern of a figured bass—should be located in something as insubstantial and trivial as these scraps of mythology. Yet as I have been approaching the site of that myth world—even without realising that it was to be reached—I have been anticipating (I realise now as my acquaintance's car is making for the centre of the town) the moment of integration. The discrete, fragmentary impressions, experiences, observations and emotions which began when SQ24 was screaming towards Vienna airport always carried that shadow or afterimage: the cobbled street leading to a modest café of the old Habsburg world.

I am all too aware of the risks inherent in coming face to face with a myth cherished for many years under different skies. A year ago, after that hectic winter visit to Budapest, I had tried to break my return journey to Vienna for a night's stay here in Sopron. It could not be done: the inns were full, there was no room for the sentimental pilgrim. I left Hungary with the knowledge that I had not penetrated to the deepest level of nostalgia—and also of hostility—that governed my redis- covery, after almost half a century, of the world that had bred me. Sopron was to remain a romantic memory, a hazy image of a fabled place guarded by its massive watchtower; it was not to be tarnished by the rust of experience.

The failure to achieve that goal left, nevertheless, a sense of dissatisfaction and even frustration. One part of my per- sonality urged me to lay those ghosts—no matter how kindly or seductive they might be. The other part, though, insisted that illusions should not be shattered: and for that reason I made no attempt, in the course of these last weeks, which had been taken up with all sorts of trivial or mundane pursuits, to do what it would have been entirely possible to do—to catch a train and spend a day in Sopron. And now, with the intervention of fate or chance, it is absolutely clear that my steps were guided, that everything seems to have conspired to bring me back, in this year of the palindrome, to this centre, focus or perhaps shrine of an eccentric mythology.

The centre of the town is obviously close. The buildings are more substantial, there are many more shops, and they are no longer anonymous. There is, besides, quite heavy traffic jamming the streets. Everything looks drab and commonplace. The buildings are mostly three storeys high, uniformly covered in grey stucco and dotted with small square windows. The people shuffling along the footpath are squat, dumpy and elderly. They are muffled in shapeless coats to keep out the biting wind. The women's heads are wrapped in scarves; the men wear little peaked caps, some with flaps turned down over the ears. One or two people are fidgeting with small collapsible umbrellas, for a light drizzle has begun to fall.

My companion seems to know his way around the town. We make a right-hand turn into a narrow passage, broad enough for his elderly Saab to pass through without scraping the walls rising on either side. The alley ends in a large irregularly shaped open space. Its centre is filled with angle-parked cars, nose to nose like snarling dogs. We find an empty space and, locking the car securely for it contains my luggage, we make for the footpath on the long side of this space. The pavement is crowded. Groups of people stand outside the line of shops inspecting the merchandise displayed on racks and in containers placed untidily on the footpath. Some of the shopkeepers are busily removing racks and containers to protect their goods from the steady, sleety drizzle. Most of the signs, I notice, are in German.

We stand on the footpath discussing what to do. It is too early for lunch, my companion says, though we shouldn't delay too long because eating places get very crowded in Sopron— it's all those Austrians coming over the border, he sneers, looking for what they reckon are bargains. I have reached the stage of mild disillusionment where I do not much care what we do. Sopron, as I had expected, is just another small Central European town looking drab under a steely sky. Then, turning towards the other side of this open space—probably an occasional market, it occurs to me—I glimpse, peeping over the roof tiles of the buildings opposite, the top of a charac- teristically Austrian steeple: not a church, it comes to me with a rush, but the watchtower, my one clear memory of this otherwise unfamiliar place.

That over there is the old town, my companion remarks as we begin to cross this large space, dodging puddles and the occasional manic car bearing down on us. We walk through a narrow alley and, suddenly, we are confronted by another world. Admittedly it looks just as drab and decrepit as the rest of this town, indeed as most of this sad country that has suffered so much neglect and destruction. Stucco peels from the walls of many buildings. The cobbled streets are a series of potholes. Some of the sturdy bars protecting ground-floor windows are bent, many have rusted away. Several of the wooden slats in the massive gate of one building are missing; they have been replaced by chicken wire. Nevertheless, I am able to impose on this image of decrepitude something of the memory pattern I have been nurturing (often without being aware of it) throughout much of my life.

As we wander through a network of cobbled streets and lanes, always skirting yet not coming upon the tower that dominates this part of the town, I begin to recognise, on crumbling façades, symbols and images of that dream world. A nearly illegible Latin inscription commemorates an eighteenth-century benefactor. A dirty marble plaque, yellow where water from a leaking gutter splashes on it, marks the house where a famous son of Sopron used to dwell. One house displays, more or less intact, a row of plaster medallions beneath its eaves, each depicting a smiling cherub. The sharp angle where two streets meet is occupied by the apse of an ancient church. No doubt it once stood detached in its own grounds; now, however, and probably since the seventeenth century, it is inextricably joined to the dwelling houses of those two streets.

Coming round a corner not far from that truncated church, we find a small square dominated by a tall, somewhat off-centre monument, a miniature version of the huge plague columns that rise in the ceremonial spaces of Austrian towns. One side of the square is occupied by a four-storey building painted in an unpleasant shade of blue-green. A sickly potted rubber-plant is visible on the sill of a first-floor window. A very clean, very white enamel plate beside the entrance announces, in bold black lettering, that this is the convent and school of the Ursuline order.

Walking past the convent, we turn another corner, and find ourselves in St George Street. Here, at Number 11 according to my cousin, was the poky flat where my mother and her family led a miserable life of destitution. The building is surprisingly large: its windows rise in four levels in strict classical order of size and decoration. The façade is freshly plastered and partly painted. A handsome arched gateway is secured by a well-polished slatted door. A notice fixed to one of its wings, and protected by a sheet of plastic, advises that the restoration of 11 St George Street will be completed by early 1992, when these self-contained luxury flats, each with its lock-up garage at the rear, will be offered for sale.

Two or three cobbled lanes cast into dark shadows, but illuminated by handsome converted gaslights which have been turned on in the early afternoon gloom, take us to another, quite large space lined with public buildings. And there in front of us is the tower, just as I remember it, at its base a squat, rough-hewn construction but rising to a graceful baroque steeple. A tunnel-like passage runs through its cumbersome base—the tower's Roman foundations, I remember being told by my mother half a century ago on the occasion of one of our visits to Sopron.

Here, therefore, is the moment of integration, the re-entry into mythology. This is the watchtower and this space, where groups of people are craning their necks to inspect the steeple, is no doubt where the town was scandalised by my mother's disgraceful antics on a motorbike. Beneath the present-day appearance of this drab and neglected town, more dreary-looking, in all probability, because of the lowering winter sky, I can feel—in a mild though by no means unpleasant way— a tenuous connection with the past. I experience an entirely irrational sense that somehow or other I belong here, in a way that I do not quite belong in Budapest, that city of terrible memories, or Vienna, despite its allure, or even Sydney, the familiar place I now fondly call my home. Looking around this open space in front of the massive tower, where the cobblestones once clattered under the wheels of my father's motorbike, I am able to understand how this little Habsburg town, which has managed to retain much of its essence despite the vicissitudes of time and history, somehow concentrates the symbols of a way of life that I can only identify by the mock-serious name of Kakania—symbols I have encountered, though dispersed and at times almost obliterated, in the cities and towns of this world.

There is no illumination, no sense of a peace passing all understanding as this goal is achieved. There is, however, a mildly pleasant sense of satisfaction—despite aching eyes, running nose and fiery throat—that the myth world which has coloured so much of my imagination in the course of my life does have at least some foundation, that it is not entirely the product of misplaced longings and dissatisfaction. I have not come upon those streets meeting under a burning gaslight, nor seen the rectangle of light illuminating a patch of cobblestones. I have not found the Habsburg café depicted on my private iconostasis. But I have found the elements of that vision scattered throughout the square kilometre of this little town that nestles so comfortably around its watchtower.

It is well after two, time to look for a meal, my acquaintance says—the restaurants should be emptying by now. Then, looking up at the tower, he suggest that perhaps we should climb to the top, there's bound to be a reasonable view, despite the cloud and drizzle. But we find the entrance heavily barred: a notice advises that the tower is closed for winter; it is open for inspection from April to October.

CROWN AND EAGLE

We leave the overheated cellar restaurant after an indigestible paprika-laden meal—my last exposure for a long time, I think with considerable satisfaction, to Hungarian cooking. As we climb the short flight of steps leading to the street I can still hear some elderly Austrians protesting loudly about the outrageous cost of their meal—which was probably as low as ours had been. My companion thanks me for my hospitality, and I, in turn, thank him for the lift, for his kindness in showing me around the town. It is time to get under way again. In a few minutes, he says, we'll be at the border. He hopes that there won't be a long delay, but you can't tell. This border crossing is quite good, he adds, because it has a separate lane for road transports. Elsewhere, especially on the road into Czechoslovakia, you can be kept waiting for ten or twelve hours if you are unlucky.

On our way back to the large parking lot, it strikes me that I should offer my companion some coffee before we start on our journey—for it is not good form in this world to take coffee in the restaurant where you've had your meal. Glancing at his watch, he says that that would be very nice, as long as we don't take too long, because he'd like to get me to the airport hotel before it gets dark: the roads around there are very busy and he finds them very confusing.

Around the next corner we come upon a sign placed in the gateway of one of the few freshly painted houses. We step inside a surprisingly spacious courtyard where, at its far end, another sign over a doorway identifies the location of a café. The place resembles—and once it probably was—a ground-floor apartment. The first room we come upon contains the obligatory glass-fronted and mirror-backed counter displaying a selection of homely cakes and pastries. One of the two doors in this hallway leads to the café itself—a series of interconnected small rooms, each with two or three marble-topped tables and plush chairs. The second door obviously leads to the kitchen.

All the tables in the first room are occupied. At one, a pair of elderly ladies are scraping the last bits of a creamy confection from shallow glass dishes. We find a table in the second room. The only other occupant is a middle-aged gentleman in a baggy suit. His briefcase has been placed on the chair opposite him. He is reading a newspaper while finishing a cup of coffee. An untouched glass of water stands on a small saucer on top of a paper doily.

The suspicion that this café had once been a dwelling is even stronger in this room. Two sash windows with lace curtains look onto the courtyard—an undesirable aspect according to the domestic hierarchies of this world. A large winged door on the opposite wall leads to another room, perhaps the owner's apartment. The walls are papered with a pattern known in English as Regency. A chandelier of Bohemian glass hangs from the moulded ceiling.

It would be easy to imagine this place as it would have looked when it housed some worthy citizen of Sopron. As we wait for our order to be taken, I begin to spin fantasies about this place. Who lived here in the 1920s, the years in which my mother was growing up in this tight little town? Since this was a courtyard flat on the edge of the old town, it is unlikely that its occupants were grandees. It is much more likely that they were relatively hard-up, like my mother's people, though no doubt able to aspire to some measure of bourgeois propriety and comfort. Did they know my mother? Were they parts of the rumour mill that spread the news of her scandalous conduct around the town? Did my mother visit friends or acquaintances here? Perhaps this was where the not-very-accomplished portrait painter executed a likeness of her on a large oval board—commissioned to commemorate her first ball—which she always detested and took some pleasure in chopping up to provide firewood in the bitter winter of 1945, as Budapest lay in ruins around us.

The atmosphere of the café is comfortably somnolent. The tiled stove in the corner sends out a mellow heat. We are silent, each lost in his thoughts. Perhaps my acquaintance is thinking about what he must do in his three or four days in Austria. I, for my part, looking around at the comfortable furnishings of this little café on the border of what used to be the two great nations of the Habsburg realm, am struck by a sense of curious appropriateness. It seems to me entirely fitting, indeed inevitable, that these months of wandering around the territories of what used to be Kakania, that world which gave the various members of my family many of their dreams and preoccupations, their fantasies and also their fears, should come to an end here, in a café, perhaps the most characteristic and poignant image of that world's communal dreams.

It also strikes me with particular force that the anomalies and paradoxes of this world are beyond resolution, just as my own confused and ambiguous responses to the tinsel pomp of Austria and the turmoil of contemporary Hungary must always remain balanced on a knife-edge between scorn and attachment, fear and indifference. Yet in this little town, rich with images of a mythic world, and in this unassuming café, there may remain a few echoes of a former life, of a lost world, capable of being cherished and recaptured, briefly and provisionally, in this fossil of the Dual Monarchy, the bitter-sweet, serio-comic dream of Kakania, which once, in the distant past, beguiled so many members of my family, seducing them with its siren-song of the good life.

As my eyes travel around this warm, comfortable, slightly dowdy place, I notice the faded etchings and lithographs decorating its walls. They show perspectives of this city, always dominated by its watchtower, some executed with great skill, others with a charmingly naïve ineptitude. In each of them, whether accomplished or amateurish, the engravers and draughtsmen have managed to include, somewhere in the elaborate designs framing these views of the town, a curiously-shaped crown, the emblem of the Kings of Hungary, and the proud double-headed eagle of the Habsburgs.

The waitress arrives to take our order. Only coffee? Nothing to eat? Could she perhaps recommend her *Sachertorte*, home-made, according to the original recipe, far superior to anything we'd find in Vienna?

SQ23

We rise into a leaden sky. Soon trees and fields, roads and houses are blotted out as we climb, shuddering and jolting, through a thick blanket of cloud. Later the turbulence ceases, the pilot extinguishes the seat-belt sign. Weak winter sunlight flows into the cabin. Nothing is visible through the porthole beside my seat except the thick cloud-cover from horizon to distant horizon. Below, the countries, provinces and districts that had once formed the world of Kakania—their towns and cities, their hopes and terrible hatreds, and those cafés that seem to stretch from one end of this realm to another—slip by unseen. Towards dusk the clouds begin to disperse. Just before sunset I catch sight of a snow-covered crag burning with the last glimmer of evening as we hurtle eastwards, into the night.

OTHER IMPRINT TITLES FROM ANGUS & ROBERTSON

Inside Outside

ANDREW RIEMER

O N A FREEZING NOVEMBER DAY IN 1946, ANDREW Riemer, then a ten-year-old with mumps, left a bomb-scarred Budapest on his way to Australia. A few days before Christmas in 1990 he returned to the city of his birth where, amid the decay of a world waking from totalitarian rule, he tried to reconstruct the past from shreds of memory and family myth.

In the years between, his career had taken him from being an expert in French-knitting, a skill acquired when, unable to speak English, he was put in a class for intellectually handicapped children, to Sydney University, where he now teaches English Literature.

'Andrew Riemer has written a classic. Witty, lucid, heartrending and wonderfully funny. No reader will ever forget his two worlds, or the profound questions he asks about them.'
JILL KER CONWAY